Transforming Reformation

Transforming Reformation

Reformation in Perspectives

Editor
Songram Basumatary

Gurukul Lutheran Theological College & Research Institute

United Evangelical Lutheran Churches in India

Christian World Imprints(TM)

First Published in 2017 by

Gurukul Publications
Gurukul Lutheran Theological College & Research Institute
in collaboration with and initiative of Rev. Dr. A. G. Augustine Jeyakumar, the Executive Secretary of
United Evangelical Lutheran Churches in India
94/95 Purasawalkam High Road, Kilpauk, Chennai-600010
gltc.principal@gmail.com
www.gltc.edu
Phone: +91 44 42651072

&

Christian World Imprints(TM)
Christian Publishing & Books from India
H-12 Bali Nagar, New Delhi-110015
info@christianworldimprints.com
www.ChristianWorldImprints.com
Phone: +91 11 25465925

ISBN 13: 978-93-5148-255-0 (HB) ISBN 13: 978-93-5148-256-7 (PB)

Cover Design: Designed by Sajo Thomas Joseph (BD IV). The emblem in the middle that signifies "unity and communion" is designed by Rev. Jeevaraj Anthony based on the conceptual idea given by Rev. Dr. A. G. Augustine Jeyakumar, the Executive Secretary of UELCI.

Cataloging in Publication Data--DK
Courtesy: D.K. Agencies (P) Ltd. <docinfo@dkagencies.com>

Transforming reformation : reformation in perspectives / editor, Songram Basumatary.
pages cm
ISBN 9789351482550 (HB)
ISBN 9789351482567 (PB)

1. Reformation. 2. Lutheran Church--Missions--India. 3. Church and social problems--India. 4. Church and social problems--Lutheran Church. I. Basumatary, Songram, editor. II. Gurukul Lutheran Theological College and Research Institute. III. United Evangelical Lutheran Churches in India.

LCC BX8063.I4T73 2017 | DDC 266.410954 23

Printed in India

Contents

Foreword

I am so delighted for this great opportunity to write few lines of prologue in this book which is published as part of commemorating the 500th Years of Reformation. Nailing of *95 Theses* by Martin Luther five hundred years ago at the door of Castle Church, Wittenberg had revolutionised the western world and led to transformation in various aspects. The Sixteenth Century Reformation inducted by Martin Luther brought immense changes in the life of the church, its theology, worship, music, social action, etc. The impact of reformation does not end there. Even after five long centuries, Luther's theology continues to make many strides and impact the life of the church and individuals.

Therefore, publishing this book "Transforming Reformation: Reformation in Perspectives" is a fitting piece of tribute to Martin Luther who dedicated his whole life in reforming the church and society towards realising the *Reign of God* on earth. But more than this, the book comes as a ground breaking piece for carrying out the reformation legacy in our times with new eyes and new vigour.

Needless to say, India stands as the oldest Lutheran Church communion outside Europe and Northern America. The contributions of the Lutheran Missionaries of Europe and Northern America played a significant role in establishing Lutheran congregations in India and the Indian Lutheran Church played a major role in the composition of Christianity in India. Today, the one third of the Lutheran Christians in Asia is from India. The composition of Lutheran communion in India is predominantly Dalits and Adivasis (tribals). Each member churches within the communion are from unique cultural backgrounds and from different mission agencies. However, in spite of various diversities, the Lutheran churches in India are unified by the theology and teachings of Luther and Lutheranism.

As the Lutheran World Federation initiated the celebration of the commemoration of 500th Anniversary of Reformation in 2012 with the main theme: "Liberated by God's Grace" with the sub themes "Salvation not for Sale", "Human beings not for Sale" and "Creation not for Sale", the United Evangelical Lutheran Churches in India (UELCI) also has taken up the challenge and started series of programmes and celebrations since 2012 in order to encourage and motivate the member churches to inculcate the core vision and values of reformation. At this juncture, I want to thank Rev. Dr. Martin Junge, the General Secretary of the Lutheran World Federation and his staff members who have conceived the idea for global celebration of this historic event along with the Lutheran communions around the globe.

All the programmes, activities and publications during the period from 2012-2017 by the various departments and institutions of the UELCI are centred around the reformation themes. For example, the theological wing of UELCI – the Gurukul Lutheran Theological College & Research Institute has been playing a major role in educating people on the theological core of reformation through various initiatives since, 2012. To mention few, the *solas* of Luther such as *Sola-Scriptura, Sola-Gratia* and *Sola-Fide* were used as theme of the year as well in the publications like Gurukul Daily Devotions and Gurukul Jyoti. The reformation days were celebrated every year with different activities based on those themes. One of the remarkable initiatives done on this regard is "*95 Contemporary Theses*" for Indian Church during 2016 Reformation Day Celebration written by UELCI/ Gurukul community members. This was in fact, an eye opener for the churches to evaluate their call and commitment in the light of Luther's basic fervour of what the Church is all about.

This prompted UELCI and Gurukul with the help of Christian World Imprints to come out with an idea of publishing this book so that the theological challenges of Luther in the Sixteenth Century and his vision of reforming the church may be carried out in our times. To this end, the book presents various perspectival readings and implications of reformation and Luther's theology to the present day contextual realities of Church and society. I can proudly say that by the guidance of the UELCI, the member churches has taken Luther and his teachings with great zeal and organised various programmes and celebrations to take the message of reformation to the grass root congregation members.

For we know that the common people during Sixteenth Century were struggling with various issues. But the Church was indifferent and filled with power abuse, corrupt and oppressive of common believers against which Martin Luther fought tirelessly. Similar to this, the people and the churches in India particularly, the Lutheran churches are facing various issues and challenges. What is the responsibility of the Church towards these issues? How does the church respond to these issues? Should the church at all challenge the unjust structures within and around?

These questions bring out alive the challenges and protest of Luther against all corruption and injustices going on both in theological notions as well as ecclesiological structures. For Luther, Church is a communion of justified sinners gathered around the Word and Sacrament, and as justified community, the church should consciously challenge the structures that are against the core of gospel – the *Reign of God* here and now. Therefore, the church being the body of Christ and communion of saints, it should be characterised and governed by the Biblical principles of Stewardship, Accountability and Transparency in all its mission and ministry in order that the churches in India become salt and light in bringing justice, peace and harmony.

With this note, I take this opportunity to thank the editor Rev. Dr. Songram Basumatary, the Head of the Department of Theology & Ethics, and Luther Studies, Gurukul Lutheran Theological College and Research Institute for shouldering great responsibility in bringing out this book. For he has done a great job in editing and compiling the seventeen essays within a short time. I also thank Dr. Walotemjen for extending help to the Editor in going through the manuscripts. Word of gratitude to Christian World Imprints as well for helping us to publish and release this book to mark the climax of 500th Years of Reformation Celebration on 31st October, 2017. I also express my thanks to all the contributors of this book who in a short time have reflected and written essays on reformation and reformation theologies in different perspectives.

I hope and pray that the essays in this book would enlighten, challenge, inspire many men and women, young and old, theologians and lay people, leaders and ordinary folks and commit themselves for transformation of present day Church and society.

May God bless all of us!

In God's Mission

Rev. Dr. A. G. Augustine Jeyakumar
Executive Secretary UELCI & LWF National Committee of India

22.09.2017

Introduction

The Sixteenth Century Reformation is considered by historians as next to the introduction of Christianity. In fact, it was like relaunching of Christianity itself and Luther not only was a reformer, but a Messiah of Christian faith and Christian theology. For Luther with his revolutionary transforming vision brought a Copernicus Revolution like turn around in the Christianity. He brought almost complete paradigm shift in Christian doctrine and theology. The Church was never the same as before, theology was never again static after Luther.

Beside religious realm, the Reformation movement also impacted upon the culture and civilization of western world and beyond. The Reformation in general and Luther in particular, directly or indirectly provided an immense impulse and a propelling force to every forward movement towards modern world and human civilization. Luther, a theologian, a pastor and a preacher managed to excite every sections of people in his time to look for better world. Even five hundred years after, he continues to challenge and inspire, theologians, pastors, preachers, revolutionaries, politicians, social scientists, economists, psychologists, playwrights, musicians, etc.

What made Reformation and Luther such influential and never dying inspiration to people generation after generation? Answer to this question perhaps lies neither in the greatness of reformation nor in the heroic work of Luther. Instead, it is solely on the ecclesiological and societal contexts and situations peoples face. It is the context and situation that demand and recall the spirit of reformation and the revolutionary theology of Luther. For the context and situation of Church and society time and again revolves back to the context and situation of Sixteenth Century. We could see the same context and situation in the Church and society of our times.

In fact, the Church of our times today is no better than that of Luther's time. In many aspects, the present Church is full of corruption, position/power/privilege politics. Often the unjust and corrupt leaders are enthroned, but the faithful and just are dethroned from the leadership of the Church. Similar to the Church of Luther's time, the human authority is above the divine authority. Instead of governed by the Gospel and the Word of God, the Church is governed by the wish, words and laws of human authorities. The self-righteousness overshadows the God's righteousness. The Bishops and pastors, the shepherds of the sheep are mostly busy with managing economy rather than Testimony. One can perhaps sum up the context and situation of our times in a rhetoric way that "the glory of the Rome is alive; the clergies of the Sixteenth Century are alive; work of the law is alive, purgatory and indulgences are alive, salvation currencies are alive….!" In fact, to a large extent, the times now are even worse than that of Luther. Salvation is on sale…Human beings are on sale…creation is on sale…!

Times such as these demands and recall the Sixteenth Century cry of Reformation for the transformation of Church and society. Reformation therefore is not a historical monument to be venerated and adored, nor is Luther a hero or a Saint to be celebrated and worshipped. They are the agents of living inspiration for transforming vision and reformation of Church and society.

What can we think and what can we take from the commemoration and celebration of 500th Years of Reformation then? Indeed, the year 2017 marks yet another historic milestone in the history of Christianity. The worldwide celebration, not only by the Lutheran Communions, but also by the Churches and Institutions across the denominational boundaries is something great and remarkable event the Church has ever witnessed. This suggests a sign of change and transformation towards a neo-ecclesiology – an inclusive and embracive Church, the Church of unity in diversity. However, one cannot think and take that it is celebration of the greatness of Reformation or Luther was a great reformer and theologian. If at all a celebration, it is just because of the fact that the Church got new life; that people got liberty, identity and dignity; that all need grace of God and all are righteous because of God's righteousness bestowed on sinners in and though Christ. It is perhaps the celebration of the grace of God and God of life Luther discovered.

Therefore, as we see commemorating the 500th Years of Reformation around the world among all denominational Church and across all sections of people, we could see really reformation alive because of people's cry for liberation and transformation in their lives. Setting this trend into consideration, here comes in this book the collection of 17 challenging essays in various perspectives written by the eminent scholars and teachers of the Word of God hailing from different denominational backgrounds.

The **first** essay - *An Age of Crisis: Relevance of Reformation Today* by Dr. *Walotemjen* is a kind of ground breaking one that sets the entire reformation movement into a context and presents challenges as to how it is relevant in an age of crisis, particularly in India today. The **second** essay – *Luther and Gutenberg's Print Technology* is in communication perspective where the author - Thomas Manoj Samuel presents how the movable type print technology developed by Johannes Gutenberg in 1440 brought an exponential revolution in Europe and how Luther effectively utilized this media to its optimum potential in communicating the reformation challenges and messages.

The **third** and **fourth** essays in series are from the Biblical perspectives. In *Celebration of Faith Towards Community-Solidarity*, the author Rev. Dr. K. Balakrishnan clearly brings out the true New Testament meaning of Faith emphasizing very strongly its praxiological nature that one need not bolster only the orthodoxy of faith but also the orthopraxis of faith in order to continue the legacy of Luther's vision and mission of renewal and transformation. With similar vein, Rev. Nagaiyasamy N.S. Samuel in his essay – *Justice and Unity as Faith Issues: Martin Luther's 500 Years Reformation Perspective* brings out another dimension of faith in relation to issues of justice and unity in the Church and society. The author here clearly expresses that the justice and unity are integral parts of the righteousness of God and the Church, the community of believers. The author challenges that the Luther's prophetic and transformative concept and understanding of Justice, Righteousness and Unity must be emulated by the present day Church to be a witnessing community in the pluralistic society like ours.

The **fifth** and **sixth** essays are from the mission or missiological perspectives. Rev. Dr. K. David Udayakumar, one of the eminent Indian missiologist, in his essay – *Missional Church: Tracing Roots in Martin Luther's Theology* brings out a challenge as to how the Indian Church can be a missional Church in the light of Reformation tradition. By surveying the paradigm shifts in the understanding of mission (missionary church to church in mission) and making clear what the missional church is all about (missionary nature of God, the *mission Dei*), the author juxtaposes with reformation and concludes that the missional ecclesiology is what the present the Church need in order to bring the reign of God in the world. From a similar perspective, *Rebecca Azariah* in her essay – *A Missiological Reading of the Women in Reformation* attempts to bring out the role played by women in the Reformation by highlighting few women from the Bible. The author claims that 'discerning the Will of God', 'relying on the Word of God the Bible' and 'proclaiming the Good Works of God' are some of the distinctive characteristics of women that plays important role in bringing transformation in the Church and society. Emphasizing on the "Priesthood of all believers", she is on the opinion that the reformers regarded men and women as spiritually equal.

The **seventh** essay is from the ministerial perspective where Mr. Livingstone Arputharaj in his essay – *Care against Commodification in the Context of Free Market Economy: Reflecting on Pastoral Care with the Spirit of Reformation* makes efforts to critique the principles of free market economy, which in many ways reduces God's creation as mere commodities. Considering the pastoral nature of Luther's challenges, and the Reformation as protest against "commodification of salvation, human being and creation" and the failure of providing pastoral care, the author challenges the Church of our times to move from "personal care to prophetic care", "comforting to compassionate resistance", and from "caring individual to caring communities."

The **eighth** essay in this book is reading *Sola–Fide* in Dalit perspective. In this essay, Rev. *Samuel Logan Ratnaraj* critically reflects on how the Lutheran doctrine of "Justification by faith alone" gives a message of hope and solace for the marginalized and oppressed communities like Dalit. By juxtaposing critically the notion of Divine rejection by the Dalits and Lutheran doctrine of *Sola Fide* he attempts to bring out helps them to overcome from the belief of suffering as natural based on Karma theory.

The **ninth, tenth** and **eleventh** essays in set are from religious perspectives. Rev. Jeevaraj Anthony in his article – *Re-vitalising Dalit Religious Tradition in the Light of the Impact of Luther's Reformation* schemes through the various features of Dalit religious traditions and their struggles for finding identity and dignity of life; and by juxtaposing with the reformation challenges and outcome, he seeks for a possibility of re-vitalize the Dalit Religious Traditions for their liberation. He strongly envisions that Luther's "Priesthood of all Believers" and "Communio Sanctorum" are great help to understand and challenge the contemporary caste ridden hierarchical Church of India.

Likewise, Rev. J.M.P. Thomas Birla, in his article – *The Teaching of 'Priesthood of all Believers' in Today's Pluralistic Context* makes an attempt to point out the false understanding of "priesthood" and re-envision for a proper meaning of 'priesthood' by exploring the Biblical understanding, role and responsibility of "priesthood". By doing so, the author affirms the reformer's view and challenge for 'Priesthood of all believers' and tries to draw relevance for the contemporary Church and for multi-religious context of India. The author is of the view that the "Priesthood of Believers" can not only bridge the gap between the clergy and laity in the church, but also can inspire to take this forward to unite and bridge the gulf between Christians and the people of other faiths.

In similar way, though it is not directly related to Luther or Reformation movement, Rev. Dr. S. Thomas Kennedy in his article – *Impact of Lutheran Reformation in India and Ziegenbalg's Mission in the field of Inter Religious Dialogue* challenges for the necessity of inter-religious dialogue by highlighting the contributions of Ziegenbalg, the first Protestant missionary to India. The author clearly tries to proof that the arrival of the Tranquebar mission initiated a transformation process and in certain decisive areas, and changed the religious, social and cultural patterns of Indian society. He strongly affirms that the model set by the Eighteenth Century German Lutheran missionaries for dialogue towards social integration and communal harmony continues to challenge the present day Church to live together, love each other, and break the wall of differences on the basis of colour, sex, caste, sex and religion.

The **twelfth** essay on the go is yet another piece on the contribution of first European Evangelical Lutheran mission in India. Tracing the history of first German Lutheran mission in India, the author, Rev. Dr. J. G. Jacob Sundarsingh in his article – *An Account of the re–formation of Tamil Society by European Lutherans and the Native Co-workers* brings out the fact that the transformation of Tamil society was just because of the work of the Lutheran mission. Following the reformation legacy of Sixteenth Century, Ziegenbalg the first protestant missionary to India was able to create, propose and execute a counter culture in Tamil society. The author strongly argues that the strong belief and the bold venture of both European Lutherans and their native co–workers brought an unimaginable transformation in the lives of natives particularly, among the Dalits and women.

The **thirteenth** essay – *The Foreclosed System of the Orthodox Church's Caste Identity: A Christian Ministry Perspective* by Fr. Dr. *George Varughese* comes as a tribute to Martin Luther and his legacy, in which the author tries to connect the life and ministries of two Orthodox practical theologian – Metropolitan Geevarghese Mar Gregorios of Parumala and Metropolitan Petros Mar Osthathios with reformation legacy. With thorough analysis of how theese theologians impacted the Church by radicalizing the pastoral theology and concretizing the pastoral engagement in the society, the author concludes that though they pioneered the church's mission among the Dalits, their "elitist strategy" did not help to fully integrate the converts into the mainstream of the church. The Dalit Christians remained as mere recipients and objects of care of high-caste Christians rather than as subjects of their own history. In practice the church continues to consider Dalit Christians as the "Other" and demonstrates a foreclosed system in spite of its self-perception to the contrary. Due to high-caste ideology still inherent in the practice of care, and a complete absence of Dalit traditions in the entire Tradition, the Orthodox Church is very exclusive in nature till today, which perhaps need reformation.

The **fourteenth** essay in this book is an attempt to connect the challenges of Reformation towards educating the common people with the Word of God and the ministry of theological education in the present day church, particularly the Church of South India. The author, Rev. N. Manova Santhosham in his article – *Understanding the Reformation and its Impact in the Protestant Churches with Special Reference to Lay Training in the CSI, Madras Diocese*, makes a strong claim about the Lay Training in the CSI, Madras Diocese, particularly the "Laity Institute for Transformation Education (LITE): Transformed to transform" which led to the realisation of the darkness of innocence and the slavery to superstition, and kindling a thirst for liberation, is nothing but a similar experience of the laity of the days of Martin Luther in the Sixteenth Century.

The last three essays, the **fifteenth, sixteenth** and **seventeenth** are reflective theological pieces. Acknowledging the contribution of Luther towards creating history and his teachings to look things differently, Florina and Gladston Xavier in their article – *Luther's Call to Examine the Conscience* critically examine the four articles of Luther's *95 Theses* from a socio-economic angle within the sphere of the church and its people especially the marginalized and vulnerable ones. By doing so, they try to connect the thoughts of Luther from yesteryears to the plight of the church even today and pose a challenge to look objectively the things where present day Church needs change and transformation. They ends with an inescapable necessity that there should be cleansing of the churches and true repentance; and the leaders and teachers who are more responsible are the ones who should take it upon themselves to bring about such change in order to bring transformation in Church and society.

Rev. Dr. habil. Roy Lazar A. in his article – *500 Years of Reformation: Reviewing from the Catholic Perspective* raises several critical question on reformation and review critically the very reformation of Sixteenth Century. He critically analyse whether Luther's Reformation was Reform or Rift, or was it consolidation of Division. However, notwithstanding the negative aspects of the reformation, the author presents number of 'blessings in disguise' for the future Church and the world. The author also critically discusses the developments towards reconciliation, unity and communion in order to heal the wounds caused by reformation. Reviewing the LWF initiative of "From Conflict to Communion" as well as "From Counter-Reformation to Co-Reformation" initiative, the author concludes with a remark that Luther's era was a period of *reform and renewal* of Christian witness. Therefore, the occasion of 500th Years of Reformation is an opportunity for all the believers to explore the possibility of living the *unity in diversity*. It is the *kairos* of new paths for *peace and harmony* for the entire universe, the common home for all humans and the entire creation.

The **last** essay in this book comes as a summary reflecting the title of the book where the author Rev. Dr. Songram Basumatary critically re-look at reformation, its theological challenges and their significance for contemporary Church. He concludes the articles with a strong affirmation that "there is hardly an issue confronting Church and society in our times today where reformation in general and Luther's theological insights in particular have no relevance." For the issues facing the Church and society in our times are not different from context of reformation times. There is certainly an undeniable significance of reformation both theologically and ecclesiologically. There is enormous theological significances for the transformation of present day Church and society. Contextually, what makes reformation more significant in our times is its very vibrant context oriented 'people centric theology' and its vision of gospel oriented 'community centric ecclesiology' which are unavoidable necessary fundamentals of transformative reformation.

Songram Basumatary
Editor

22.09.2017

1

An Age of Crisis
Relevance of Reformation Today

Walotemjen

1. Introduction

The period of the Reformation is one of the most interesting periods and also the most complex movement in the history of Christianity. The context of Europe before Reformation and during Luther's birth in the 1480s was enveloped with crises of several kinds. It was the time filled with plagues and wars, violence and sudden death. From Italy to England the Black Death of 1347-1351 had affected all aspects of life. In many pockets of Europe, a century later, were recovering from this deadly epidemic devastations. By the late 1400s, new crisis started to disrupt and threaten the continent. Businesses were at its lowest web, political violence was witnessed everywhere, and ancient traditional social system was at the edge of disintegration. Peasants were cruelly exploited by frustrated nobles. The church failed miserably to respond to such crises. This was an age crying out for prophet to reshape and reform the Biblical message. This situation paved the pivotal foundation for reformation.

When we juxtapose the context of Luther and our context today, we find a striking similarity. Our context is no better than that of Luther. Today the violence and atrocities against the Christians is rampant and increasing at an alarming rate. The political and legal system and religious institutions have failed miserably to stand and address the problem. Oppression, violence, discrimination, and dehumanization systematically and mechanically have become the routine of the day. This issues challenge the very core of gospel and our faith. Therefore, this paper is an attempt to analyse the Luther's context of Reformation and draw some relevances for our churches today.

2. Context in Europe: An Overview

The Reformation of the Sixteenth Century is, next to the introduction of Christianity, the greatest event in history. It marks the end of the Middle Ages and the beginning of modern times. Starting from religion, it gave, directly or indirectly, a mighty impulse to every forward movement, and made Protestantism the chief propelling force in the history of modern civilization.[1] The Sixteenth Century is the age of renaissance in religion, literature and art. The air was stirred by the spirit of progress and freedom. The world seemed to be renewing its youth; old things were passing away, all things were becoming new. Pessimists and timid conservatives took alarm at the threatened overthrow of cherished notions and institutions, and were complaining, fault-finding and desponding. Intelligent observers of the signs of the times looked hopefully and cheerfully to the future.[2] Intelligent observers felt that new things are bound to happen.

The political violence and economic disaster of Luther's age is too notorious to detail. Economic unrest was boiling within political chaos. Large merchant companies were experimenting with early forms of capitalism. Capitalism begun to break down the ancient social vision of a Christian Europe organized into priests who prayed, knights who fought, and serf who worked the land for rest.[3] The Capitalist yearned to get rich, and riches could carry him from the barn to a bought title of nobility. Aristocrats who founded their pretensions on land and blood discovered to their consternation that they were being thrust aside by merchants and bankers who clawed their way up in the world on talent and profit. Bankers lend money at interest in contradiction to the familiar prohibition against usury in the Christian Church. Interest were seen by Christians as vicious way of taking advantage. The Capitalist was well hated, and probably not until the Nineteenth Century did he begin to feel truly secure in Western society.[4] At the same time, rulers were trying to reduce the power of the nobles, their "lieutenants" in local areas. Peasants were trying to take power away from those same nobles, their rural landlords. As the authority of these rural nobles diminished, townspeople were gaining political powers. Within the towns, collisions of old wealth and new wealth produced social unrest; against all the wealthy stood the urban poor.[5] It was very pathetic context that needed drastic change.

Martin Luther was to grow up amidst the grumblings of peasants for freedom from their old feudal obligations to greedy lords; amidst the furious complaints of the German business classes against the extravagance of the Pope at Rome. The Germans at the time believed they were being handed the bill for high living, and extravagance by the Pope and his cardinals, and they deeply resented every glittering coin that fell out of German hands into the Roman coffers. The more gold and silver left the German lands, the less German Bankers and German merchants were going to have to stack in German counting houses. So they

1 Philip Schaff, *History of the Christian Church: Modern Christianity A.D. 1517-1530*, vol. 6, Reprint in India (New Delhi: Christian World Imprints, 2016), 1.

2 Ibid., 2.

3 Richard Marius, *Luther* (Philadelphia & New York: J.B. Lippincott Company, 1974), 21.

4 Richard Marius, *Luther* ..., 21.

5 Robert Kolb, *Luther's Way of Thinking* (Trivandrum: Luther Academy India, 2006), 5.

complained; but in fact these monies classes were more prosperous than they had ever been before.[6] So everywhere in the German lands there were a pent-up desire for something more, and there was a terrific anxiety lest those who already had something might lose what they had. It was a tense and disorderly situation swept by fear and desperate hopes, and in such confusion and change a passionate man might raise a standard and passionate souls would rally around if from far and near, seeking a ground on which to stand, a foundation that would not be moved in the wind or tumbled by earthquake. It would have to be religious standard, for it was a religious age, and only religion offered the vocabulary, the rhetoric, and the moral authority that would sanctify greed and anoint violence, comfort hearts afraid of change and yet changing, and set the engines of revolution in motion.[7] A time that needed change in all walks of life.

In such a world, order and hope seemed possible only through the church. For a thousand years and more, Europe had looked to Christianity to provide meaning for life and security for the next. But by the end of the Fifteenth Century, the actions of church leaders had called its moral leadership into question. The church was trying to exhibit earthy power in the same manner as kings. The papal court became a hotbed of plots and corruption, its luxurious lifestyle a bad example for everyone.[8] At the local level it was perhaps even worse. As people strove to fulfill the growing demands of the spiritual, satisfaction fell. A crisis of pastoral care developed; the poorly trained priests were unable to bring the message of Christ to hurting people. This was an age crying out for prophet to reshape the Biblical message for its day.[9] The Sixteenth Century reformation carried out by Martin Luther was basically a challenge for ordering the theologically disordered ecclesiology.[10] Equally it discerned the oppressive socio-economic and political life of Christians and necessitated the involvement of the Church for the emancipation and empowerment.[11] This was the world that Martin Luther forsook when in 1505 he entered the orderly tranquility of the monastery to dedicate his life in seeking salvation. He was like those who seek the solitude of their own way in our present wild century, a quiet refugee from the tumult of desperate and confusing times.[12] It needed only a leader capable of organizing the people into revolt against the status-quo. In a nutshell, looking at the situation of Europe, it appears that it only needed a dynamic leader to lead a reformation.

6 Richard Marius, *Luther* ..., 23.

7 Richard Marius, *Luther* ..., 23.

8 Robert Kolb, *Luther's Way of Thinking* ..., 5-6.

9 Robert Kolb, *Luther's Way of Thinking* ..., 6.

10 Songram Basumatary, "Reformation and the Indigenous Communities," *Religion & Society* 62/1&2 (March-June, 2017): 72.

11 Vincent Manoharan, "Reformation and the Subaltern Communities: A Dalit Perspective," *Religion & Society* 62/1&2 (March-June, 2017): 56.

12 Richard Marius, *Luther* ..., 23.

Germany probably provided the most conducive social climate for any kind of revolution.

3. Challenges and Issues Confronting Christians in India

Let us examine some of the challenges and issues that confront the Christians in India today that have direct bearings and consequences to the religion of Christians.

3.1. Politicization of Religions

In the history of India, religion and politics were interwoven and closely related. But due to the rise of communalism it has crossed the demarcation and thereby go against the very spirit of religion. Historically, one finds the pattern of interaction between religion and politics in varied forms and with varied social consequences. Religion always served politics and vice versa. Religion has never been able to fully extricate itself from politics. Thus, politicization of religion has taken place in some form at all stages of its history and as a result gave impetus to the rise of communalism or communal politics in India. The British rulers knowing the cultural diversities of India took advantage and encouraged among Indian people political divisions based on their religions. Indians were defined on the basis of their religion. This was culminated in the division between India and Pakistan.[13] British rulers introduced and encouraged communal divisions and politics among Indians. The close affinity between religion and politics continued after 1947. In fact, this interplay has been further strengthened by some factors and thus gave rise to the formation of religion-based political parties. Such parties freely make use of religion for political ends. Looking at the past, more precisely after the assassination of Indira Gandhi (1984) accelerated the communal attitude, feelings, and hostility in the minds of people. This perhaps is a clear indication of the politicization of religions. The effects of politicization of religion is that it hinders the process of national integration, gives rise to anxiety, fear, tension, and conflicts in society. This also has global implications because the major religions of India are outspread beyond the frontiers of the country.[14] At this point the minority religions like Christianity and Islam are at the worse receiving end. The religion based political parties in India do not give space to minorities thereby minimizing their existence in a secular set-up. This is a real threat that confronts the Christians today. On the eve of India's Independence celebration 2017 there was an issue of the link between religion and nationalism which had become a national debate.

---

13 James Massey, "Inter-Play of Religion, Politics and Communalism in India," in *Inter-Play of Religion, Politics and Communalism*, edited by Samson Prabhakar (Bangalore: BTESSC/SATHRI, 2004), 2-3.

14 S. J. Samartha, *One Christ-Many Religions* (Bangalore: SATHRI, 1992), 59.

3.2. Religious Fundamentalism

India is beautifully defined as a secular state but over against this, religious fundamentalism plays a pivotal role against the secular set-up of state. However, it is debatable whether all religious fundamentalisms emerge out of reaction to closed secularism. In our milieu, fundamentalism refers to religious intransigence, intolerance, fanaticism and extremism[15] Fundamentalism that is found in all religions stands for emotional rather than rational, undermining rather than appreciating, inflexibility on the understanding of one's own religion and disregard or unwilling to acknowledge other points of view. Fundamentalism has emerged in a violent form in different parts of India. Vincent Kundukulam opined that the fundamentalist are always certain of what they say and their value-system is non-negotiable.[16] According to K.P. Aleaz, the rise of Hindu fundamentalism of the Sangh Parivar[17] is affecting the security of minorities and the secular structure of India in terms of their suggested "Positive Secularism", change in the constitution of India,[18] denial of minority rights, change in History and change in education.[19] It came as a revival in the form of *Hindutva*[20] in the modern Indian history. Golwalker[21] one of the foremost ideologue of RSS himself surfaced opposition

---

15 Paulos Mar Gregorios, *Religion and Dialogue* (Delhi: ISPCK/Mar Gregorios Foundation, 2000), 45. The word 'fundamentalism' may simply mean "the adherence to fundamentals" or in the Christian context, "the maintenance of traditional orthodox beliefs," see also Honey Cabral, "Secularism in the Context of Religious Plurality," *Religion & Society* 48/1 (March, 2003): 71.

16 Vincent Kundukulam, "Unitive Pluralism: An Answer to Religious Extremism," *Eastern Journal of Dialogue and Culture* 1/1 (January-June, 2008): 42.

17 This is the combination of Rashtriya Swayamsevak Sangh (RSS), Bharatiya Janata Party (BJP), Viswa Hindu Parishad (VHP), Bajrang Dal (BD).

18 Their complaint is that the Constitution gives fewer rights and virtually no privileges to the majority community Hindus while it provides ample privileges for the minorities. Therefore according to them articles such as 25, which guarantees religious freedom, 30 which guarantees minorities the right to establish and run institutions in accordance with their own culture, 51 which describes the Indian culture as a composite culture, 317 which gives special privilege to the state of Kashmir, 371A which gives special privilege for Nagaland and 371G which accepts Mizoram with a special status should be scrapped. See K.P. Aleaz, "The Challenge of the Sangh Parivar in Doing Theology in India," *JTCA* 3 (2004): 59-60.

19 K.P. Aleaz, *The Challenge* ..., 57. The most important minority right namely religious freedom, the freedom of worship and the freedom to manage educational institutions according to the faith and culture of the minorities is in question. They are determined to write history to suit their ends, The teaching of history in the schools without recognizing the Muslim or British period of history is used by them to brainwash the children and finally wanted to make Sanskrit a compulsory language. See K.P. Aleaz, *The Challenge* ..., 60.

20 Hindutva is neither a Hindu religion nor Hindu spirituality nor a Hindu cultural renaissance. It is a narrow, nationalist ideology and adheres to the ethics of expediency, militancy, violence, communalism, fundamentalism, sectarianism, intolerance and the maxim end justifies the means.

21 He described Muslims as the first and the Christians the second threat to India.

against the minorities and his teachings are uncritically followed by the stalwarts and the affiliates of the Sangh Parivar till date.[22] Today the inevitable trend is the rise of Hindu fundamentalism in different forms. Their ideology is to use religion as a means to counter their needs that have raised several unanswered questions leading to obstruction to religious freedom. This dangerous phenomenon points towards the complete communalization and criminalization of the *Hindutva* regime and politics. Consequently, the attacks on Christians are escalating and it has become a matter of great concern. The Sangh Parivar looks down the religious minorities as non-nationals. The fundamentalist Hindu movement is diluting the religion and politics today. This is very evident when L.K. Advani said *Hindutva* is pure form of secularism.[23]

3.3. Communalism

The historical origin of communalism in India precisely goes back to the pre-Independence period. However, this section will not discuss on its historical origin and development up to the present state, but shall focus on its term and the consequences of Communalism in India. The term Communalism in its varied expressions, ranging from stereotypes and suspicions to manifest hostility and violence, is a telling indicator, constitutional ideals notwithstanding, of how far a society has progressed toward the goal of secularism.[24] It is a form of ethnocentrism.[25] Paulos Mar Gregorios is of the opinion that Bipin Chandra defined communalism as a political device adopted for purposes of exploitation of human credulity and religious sentiments. The object of this exploitation is seen to be some political or economic gain to the exploiter. In this line Paulos Mar Gregorios comments "Communalism is apparently a basic feature of what is known as 'fundamentalism.'"[26] In short, religious communalism in India has taken the shape of narrow and blind devotion to one's own religious community for acquiring political and economic benefits. In that sense, communalism is opposed to secularism and nationalism.[27]

---

22 M.T. Cherian, "Impact of Hindu Fundamentalism on Minority Rights: A Christian Response," *Doon Theological Journal* 1/1 (January, 2004): 30.

23 Manas Dasgupta, "Hindutva is Pure Form of Secularism, says Advani," *The Hindu*, 31 March 2004, 11.

24 Emil D'Cruz, *Indian Secularism: A Fragile Myth* (New Delhi: Indian Social Institute, 1988), 14.

25 Sumner used the term "ethnocentrism" to refer to "that view of things in which one's own group is the center of everything and all others are scaled and rated with reference to it." It is a group phenomenon in the sense that it is the tendency of all social groups to exaggerate their own importance and minimize that of others. Communalism may be understood as a form of ethnocentrism characteristic of a community. See Emil D'Cruz, *Indian Secularism* ..., 14.

26 Paulos Mar Gregorios, *The Secular Ideology: An Impotent Remedy for India's Communal Problem* (Delhi: ISPCK/Mar Gregorios Foundation, 1998), 68.

27 R. Khan, "South Asia Potents," in *India Nation-State and Communalism*, edited by G.S. Balla (New Delhi: Patriot Publishers, 1989), 40-42, quoted in Vincent Kundukulam, *Unitive*

The problem of communalism is so complex that not only does it impinge on several areas of individual and collective behavior, but also raises questions about our understanding of democracy, socialism and secularism which have to be answered if the ideals of the state as set forth in the constitution are to have any meaning at all. Today religious riots are the most violent expression of communalism. Ideological assumptions, economic and political factors play a larger role in communal riots.[28] Many have argued that the Hindu militant communalism of the RSS-VHP-Bajrang Dal matrix is bent on destroying the fundamental secular character of India, and political parties like B.J.P and Shiv Sena politicize religion in the name of *Hindutva.*[29] The minority community specially the Christians are under threat by these forces. The Hindu militant communalism is questioning the existence of Christian community in India. They claim that India is the land of the Hindus. They accuse that Christianity is the product of the West and so no place for the Christians in the land of Hindus. This perception culminates in persecutions of Christians.

3.4. Religious Conversion and Intolerance

The debate on religious conversion has been going on for more than a century. In the political context of India, this issue has become important for Christians as well as Hindu organizations. Conversion is indeed a sensitive issue in a country like India in its present context. The religious fanatics are very intolerant when it comes to the issue of conversion. Hindu revivalist like Rajaram Mohan Roy, Dayananda Saraswathi, Swami Vivekananda and Mahatma Gandhi and others wrote against the missionary policy of conversion and their attitude of denunciation of Indian society and culture. Today Hindu fundamentalists are randomly attacking the Christian missionaries alleging that they are engaging in proselytizing and thereby spoiling the very nature of Indian culture. All shades of the Sangh Parivar – from the expediently mellowed ministers in Delhi to their gun wielding terrorists in the field say one thing in unison – they are all opposed to "*Conversion* by force or fraud." To check conversion, Freedom of Religion Acts has been passed in some of the states prohibiting conversions by use of force, fraud or inducement.[30]

These Acts have abrogated the Right to freedom of Religion in the Constitution. The enactment of these Acts raise several fundamental questions.

Pluralism ..., 43.

28 A. Haque, *Mission and Dialogue in the New Millennium* (Delhi: ISPCK, 1999), 58. See also Roger Gaikwad, "Forces of Communalism in India," in *Inter-Playof Religion, Politics and Communalism*, edited by Samson Prabhakar (Bangalore: BTESSC/SATHRI, 2004), 31-41.

29 Somen Das, "Towards a Theological – Ideological Basis for an Inter-religious Community: A Dialogical Thought and Life," in *Dialogue in India: Multi-Religious Perspective and Practice*, K.P. Aleaz, ed., quoted in A. Haque, *Mission and Dialogue* ..., 58.

30 Anti-Conversion laws are now in force in six states: Gujarat, Orissa, Madhya Pradesh, Chhattisgarh, and Jharkhand.

The fundamental rights has been abrogated indirectly by these Acts. It is to be noted that conversion is not only confined to religion or to Christianity among religions. Conversion in religious sense is a spiritual experience, which involves a new vision and a rearrangement of one's value into a new value system. In conversion, human beings choose their ultimate ends. So freedom for conversion is the most important of freedoms.[31] It is worth noting that without conversion there would have been no Buddhism or Jainism, and later on, Sikhism in India, and no Christianity emerging out of Judaism in the first century.[32] In all religious life conversion is a legitimate term. However, in secular India this term is hard to digest that ultimately lead to confusions and persecutions. India has recorded a spike in violence related to religious intolerance in 2016. The U.S. State Department noted in its annual International Religious Freedom Report that the spread of laws and campaigns for cow protection and against religious conversion are among reasons for increase in violence. According to the Evangelical Fellowship of India (EFI), there were more than 300 incidents targeting Christians during the year compared with 177 in 2015. Incidents included assaults on missionaries, forced conversions of non-Hindus, and attacks on churches, schools, and private property.[33] India rises to 15 on the list of places where those practicing faith most likely to be persecuted.[34] There is a clear pattern of rising religious intolerance across Indian sub-continent which affects millions of Christians.

3.5. *Hindutva* and Secularism

The *Hindutva* ideologue claim that they are for 'positive secularism,' but in reality this claim does not reflect any of the established discernment of secularism. It is based on the view that majority alone should be the protector and dominator, whereas the minorities should be subservient to it. Though their slogan is "Justice for all, appeasement for none," in reality no justice is done to the minorities.[35] Instead, they insist that the word 'minority' be removed from the constitution. Hence, the security of the minorities (like Christians) guaranteed by the Constitution lies threatened. The *Hindutva* forces alleged that the Constitution is Anti-Hindu and demanding rewriting of the constitution. They claim that, "Indian Constitution is anti-Hindu, so it should be done away with and be substituted by one based on the Hindu holy books."[36] It is evident that the concept of 'positive

31 Mathai Zachariah, ed., *Freedom of Religion in India* (Nagpur: National Christian Council of India, 1979), 5.

32 Samartha, *One Christ* ..., 168.

33 Varghese K. George, "India did not act against cow vigilantes, says U.S," *The Hindu*, August 16, 2017, 10.

34 *The Guardian*, 11 January 2017.

35 K.P. Aleaz, *The Challenge* ..., 59.

36 Ram Puniyani, "Threats to the Constitution," *Indian Currents* (3-9 January 2000), quoted in Sarto Esteves, *Freedom to Built, Not Destroy* (Delhi: Media House, 2002), 187.

secularism' of *Hindutva* is decisive not according to the real concept of secularism enshrined in the Constitution. It is self destructive, disintegrating, high caste Hindu communalism that tries to wipe out the entire multi-cultural society and history of India existing since past thousands of years in order to make room for *Hindutva and* make it the spring and source of all national activity. Their demand for re-writing of the constitution has no significant whatsoever if their intention is to treat Hindus alone as citizens of India and others as second-class citizens. This kind of radical attitude of *Hindutva* has implanted great danger to Christians.

3.6. Conundrum of *Ghar Vapsi*

Today the state, under the BJP regime, is slowly progressing towards more pervasive involvement in matters of religion. The attitude of new regime towards minorities have emboldened the Hindu religious organizations like *Viswa Hindu Parishad* (VHP), *Rashtriya Swayamsevak Sangh* (RSS), *Sangh Parivar* etc. to carry out *Hindutva* agenda. For example, immediately after BJP came into power at the center, the RSS Chief Mohan Bhagwat made a statement that "Cultural identities of all Indian is Hindutva."[37] The salvo involved the organized programme of *Ghar Vapsi* (Home Return or reconversion to Hinduism) of Muslims and Christians to Hinduism.

The *Dharam Jagaran Samiti* (DJS) – an offshoot of the RSS and the *Bajrang Dal* – in the recent past announced that it aims to meet a target of converting one lakh Muslims and Christians into Hinduism every year. With the help of state's connivance, the *Ghar Vapsi* programmes organized by the *Sangh Parivar* are not only inciting violence and hatred between communities, but negating the very constitutional rights to freedom of conscious and religion. Christians at this point, particularly the Dalits are at the receiving end of such religious intolerance.

3.7. Indiscriminate Violence against Dalits

The rampant violence and atrocities against the Dalits is increasing at an alarming proportion. Discrimination against Dalits is widespread and fixed in the psyche across India, especially in rural areas. In some places it takes the form of oppression, in others it is disguised yet omnipresent. Close to seven decades after independence, in many villages of India the nature of certain social equations has not changed from what they have been for centuries. Such villages continue to remain what Dr. B.R. Ambedkar called "sinks of localism, dens of ignorance and narrow-mindedness."

The National Crime Records Bureau (NCB) reports a 44 per cent increase in violence against Dalits.[38] In Gujarat, *Gau Rakshaks* attacked Dalit youths with rods and knives on July 11, 2016. They were stripped and beaten for almost two hours for their crime that *they were skinning a dead cow*. The heinous nature of

---

37 *The Hindu*, 11 August, 2014.

38 32, 712 in 2010 to 47, 064 in 2014 (*July 23, 2016 Report*)).

such crime is beyond imagination. Despite protests from various angles, such atrocities against Dalits have not stopped since then. Not just violence, but other means of atrocities are also employed to trample the rights of the Dalits. Dalit scholar Rohit Vemula was driven to suicide by harassing him over non-payment of college fees.[39] While the government and political parties paid rich tribute to Balasaheb on his 125 birth anniversary, his office in Dadar was razed without permission from his grandson.[40]

This shows that the growing violence against Dalits follows a clear pattern. These incidents are directed towards reminding Dalits about their status in the caste-based social structure, and ensure that they remain there. These atrocities are committed to ensure that Dalits live a life of indignity, humiliation and exclusion from the mainstream society; that they continue to provide the caste-based services 'so essential for society' and remain at the bottom-rung without access to higher education and entrepreneurship. What can explain the continuing practice of manual scavenging and bonded labour despite legislation against them?[41] The dominant civil society and even the Church have always arrogated itself the right to decide the fate of the Dalit community through its caste sanctions. The larger civil society and the Church do not consider it necessary to intervene when Dalits are murdered in broad daylight, publicly beaten, paraded naked and raped.

3.8. Hindu *Rashtra*

The RSS ideologues state that this country is Hindustan, all people living in India are Hindus. India that is 'Bharat' to be more precise! That is what our Constitution says we are. So what is our Nationality, is it Indian or Hindus?[42] It is lately that RSS after gaining political strength wants to assimilate the religious minorities and wants to impose Hindu norms on these minority communities, so the assertion that they may be so and so but their nationality is Hindu. As per the Indian Constitution our nationality is Indian.[43] Hindu *Rashtra* is the goal of Hindu nationalist politics – a politics based on Brahmanical values of caste and gender hierarchy.[44] When BJP led NDA came to power it opened the path of restoring blind faith by introducing courses like *Paurohitya* (priesthood) and *Karmakand* (ritualism). Since the NDA came to power in 2014, the identity issues have been contested. Attempts have been made to undermine and bypass the issues related to Rights for food, education and health. A series of emotive issues such as Ram

39 Recent report (August, 2017) gave a contradictory statement saying that Rohit was not a Dalit and was neither driven to suicide by the institution.

40 *The Indian Express Online Media Pvt. Ltd* (July 23, 2016).

41 *The Indian Express Online Media Pvt. Ltd* (July 23, 2016).

42 Ram Puniyani, "What is our Nationality: Indian or Hindu?" *Christian Missiology* (16 June, 2017).

43 Ram Puniyani, *What is Our Nationality.*

44 Ram Puniyani, "Hindu Rashtra: Is it good for Hindus?" *Christian Missiology* (16 June, 2017).

Temple, Bharat mata ki jai, Vande mataram, Cow protection, Love Jihad and *Ghar Vapasi* dominated the social scene. The vigilante culture is getting promoted more and more due to Hindu nationalist agenda.[45] The religious nationalists with the help of majoritarian politics are attempting to forcibly reconvert people to the dominant faith imposing their religious belief, often through violence and vandalism. The Indian nation is appearing to be a Mob Lynching nation. The citizens of the nation are dictated what to eat, what to consume, what to wear, what to belief and what to practice. And it is no surprise that 24 out of the 29 States in India have imposed complete or a partial restrictions and penalties on the slaughter of cows.[46] Instead of promoting patriotism, such "cultural nationalism" according to Hamid Ansari, the outgone Vice President of India, "promotes intolerance, arrogant patriotism."[47]

4. Analysis and Conclusion

India has been credited as land of religious tolerance and secularism because of the presence of all major religions of the world. However, the very basic religion and structure of secularism stands threatened in recent times. Despite its beautifully framed constitution in secular nature, the minority communities threatened of their existence due to abrogation of religious freedom. Time and again the *Hindutva* forces are raising the question of conversion and propagation of religion. Today the violence and atrocities against minority communities is rampant and increasing day by day. The political and legal system and religious institutions have miserably failed to stand and address the problem. The systemic discrimination, oppression, violence and dehumanization have become the language of the day. In this age of crisis, what is the response of the Church and more so, what is the relevance of reformation? As stated, our context is no better than the Luther's context. The church needs to wake up from its deep slumber. We need courageous and bold leaders in the church.

This analysis is just a rudimentary view. In the age of crisis, the Church need to critically discern the status of Christians and respond to the pertinent issues with a prophetic voice. The Late Archbishop Oscar Romero who was outspoken about violations of human rights and social injustice said, "*A Church that doesn't provoke any crisis, a gospel that doesn't unsettle, a word of God that doesn't get under anyone's skin, a word of God that doesn't touch the real sin of the society in which it is proclaimed – what gospel is that*"? The church is not a place for power and prestige for the privileged few but it is a place where everyone is welcome to meet and commune with God and one another. The church is not a place for the patronage of power at the expense of the voiceless. Instead, it is a place where men and women can serve God and one another faithfully and transform the lives of

45 Ram Puniyani, *Hindu Rashtra.*

46 *The Hindu*, August 16, 2017, 10.

47 *The Citizen*, 10 August, 2017.

people. The Church and every individual Christian needs to take the cue from the reformation movement and bring transformation within the Church and society at large.

Considering the challenges of Reformation, we need to check how far the life and ministries of the church of our times is context oriented. In fact, it is sad to note that the sermons/preachings in our churches are too theoretical and abstract that there are no connections with contextual realities. The gospel we preach often does not reflect the present day realities our Church and society confront. Church Mission are more like projects and mere programmes. We practice a form of spirituality detached from ethics and morality. We talk about faith that is too personal and privatized which do not fulfill the need and aspiration of our society. We need to ask once again how faith and theology should inform our contextual thinking and engagement. Miroslav Volf[48] who has co-authored a book on "*Public Faith in Action: How to Think Carefully, Engage Wisely, and Vote with Integrity*" states that Christian Faith is a "Public Faith." The Christian faith is one single faith that we encounter in myriad of forms. By "Public faith" we do not mean some special kind of faith, but we refer to the public dimension of that one faith. It is faith as it concerns common goods like roads, water, electricity, educational institutions, monetary policy and inter-state relations etc. Since Christians believe in the God who created and is redeeming all things, Christian faith is concerned with all these common goods. We should not forget that there is no clear demarcating line between common goods and personal good, between public faith and private faith. We must also understand that God needs human beings to transform society and human beings need God's power. The question is - Is our church becoming irrelevant today? This question on the one hand challenges us to re-define and re-form the church as well as individuals, and on the other hand, to raise prophetic voice against the evils in the Church and society and engage prophetically like Sixteenth Century reformers.

48 Excerpt from an interview by Jonathan Merritt to Miroslav Volf (October 5, 2016 in religionnews.com)

2

Luther and Gutenberg's Print Technology

Thomas Manoj Samuel

Johannes Gutenberg developed the movable type print technology at Strasbourg by 1440. Being a goldsmith, he had the adequate skills needed for making movable type through casting and tooling lead metal. Utilising the existing materials like – paper, ink, the screw press, and imaging techniques, he improved the print technique to its optimum potential by printing lengthy texts possible.

Ample accessibility of paper in Europe gave remarkable thrust to Gutenberg's print technology in the middle of Fourteenth Century. The production of the paper begins by pounding either wood or linen fibres in a vat to form a pulpy liquid. A craftsman then dips a mould into the liquid and shakes it, thus fusing the fibres together to form a sheet of paper. The sheet is then placed on a piece of felt and layered with other sheets until dry.[1] These papers survived through the centuries, due to non-acidic high quality of durable linen fabric used in the paper making process.

Inks used for printing were made from "linseed or walnut oil, with powdered, calcined bone and pulverised glass be cooked for several hours at a high temperature. In this way, one obtains a very thick oil, perfect to mix with colours."[2] These inks were able to stick onto a metal surface. Printers often mixed their own ink and in some cases had secret ingredients to make their ink look unique. It seems possible that litharge (lead monoxide) was also added to accelerate the drying process. Gutenberg surely learnt that formula which improved its own typographic system.[3]

During Gutenberg's period, *xylography*, the art of printing from wood carving that originated from China, existed in Europe during the early Fourteenth

1 Lucien Febvre and Henri-Jean Martin, *The Coming of the Book: The Impact of Printing, 1450-1800*, translated by David Gerard (London and New York: Verso, 1997), 33.

2 Jacques Maroger, *The Secret Formulas and Techniques of the Masters*, translated by Eleanor Beckham (New York and London: Studio Publications, 1948), 31.

3 Ibid.

Century. This technique was common in printing the religious pictures and later accompanied by brief texts. The wood engravers became so skilful that the texts became more prominent than the illustration. The results were so encouraging that it validated the idea of typographic composition. However, during type setting, it encountered the problem related to the carving wood blocks as it is a delicate operation, since the roman alphabets were smaller than Chinese ideograms. Further, letters carved were not identically related on the wood block.[4]

Engraving imaging through the woodcutting technology was developed and the reproduction of images were accomplished during the Fifteenth Century. As the name denotes, the woodcutting printing methods form the image one wanted to print. It is carved such a way that it makes carvings into the image so that the peaks of wood remain after it holds the ink for printing the lines of the image onto the paper. Tessa Watt notes that a quality wood block could yield several thousand copies and that one particular woodcut block made of pear wood survived for ninety years and was used to produce large number of copies.[5] On the other hand, the engraving that involved cutting of images from copper sheets with sharp tools, costs higher than the woodcutting due to the prices of the metal and greater skills that required for tooling images. The metal engraved image printing produced limited copies, since the image qualities deteriorated after few hundred copies.[6] Hence, throughout the Reformation period, the images were printed by the way of woodcutting techniques, since metal engraving would not become cost effective until the late Seventeenth Century.

Gutenberg adapted the screw printing press from the wine press and used an oil-based ink spread on movable types put together to print a page of text. He used a simple technology of the one-pull design, where the single pull press required a series of steps to print one-half of one side of a sheet of paper per press cycle. This print process initiated with inking the form, aligning and setting the paper, using the screw pressure to force the platen to the paper to the form, and raising the platen removing the paper from the form. Thus, repeating the process. Gutenberg's printing methods had to do four complete single pull press operations to print both halves of both sides of a sheet.[7] For instance, similar techniques had been adopted to print the much-celebrated Gutenberg 42-line Bible.

Several significant improvements were made from the Gutenberg's printing technology until late Sixteenth Century. About 1550, Leonhard Danner replaced the wooden screws with iron. It greatly reduced friction and eased the pressperson's

---

4 Robert Lechêne, "Printing", *Encyclopaedia Britannica*, Encyclopaedia Britannica, Inc., (26 Dec 2016), https://www.britannica.com/topic/printing-publishing (Accessed on 2 Sep 2017).

5 Tessa Watt, *Cheap Print and Popular Piety, 1550-1640* (Cambridge: Cambridge University Press, 1991), 140-148.

6 Ibid., 142.

7 James Moran, *Printing Presses: History and Development from the Fifteenth Century to Modern Times* (Berkeley and Los Angeles: University of California Press), 20.

operation of the press. Innovators also added a double-hinged chase consisting of a *frisket*, a piece of parchment cut out to expose only the actual text and so to prevent ink spotting the nonprinted areas of the paper, and a *tympan*, a layer of a soft, thick fabric to improve the regularity of the pressure despite irregularities in the height of the type. By 1620, Willem Janszoon Blaeu introduced counterweight to the pressure bar in order to make the platen rise automatically. Finally, in about 1790, William Nicholson devised the method of inking using a cylinder covered with leather, which was the first introductory of rotary movement into the printing process.[8]

One of the notable effects of Gutenberg's movable type printing process is the speed at which multiple copies were reproduced at any printed work. As the printing technology improved, the rate of printing improved considerably. Considering the printing speed, it is to be noted that several factors had contributed into the equation including the skill of the operator, the quality of the print, the features of the press, the number of workers in the press, the paper and ink, the weather, and the number of breaks taken by the workers. According to Michael Pollak,[9] each wooden press could produce as many as 1,500 sides per day and that higher quality work reduced the rate considerably. A reasonable rate of production for normal printing was between 1,250 to 1,500 sides per day. A simple one-sided publication might have a run of 1,500 sheets in a single day. If the document was a portion of a full sheet, even greater quantities could be produced.

One can generally state that there were two types of printed materials published during Gutenberg's period, each targeted different sections of the society. The first type focused on simple publications designed as the illustrated printed material targeting those who could not read, while the second type of publication attended to the text dense books and pamphlets for the literate individuals.[10]

The illustrated publication was known as a broadsheet. It was a single sheet publication similar to the present-day poster. The early broadsheet had substantial graphics elements with minimal textual content. It is observed that during the period of middle age iconography, the church used pictures and paintings printed in the broadsheets to teach the people, since the majority of the population could not read and were prevented from learning to read. Hence, before the inception of Gutenberg's movable type, these publications were produced using woodcuttings, and thereafter movable type came into use. Broadsheets were made

8 Robert Lechêne, "Printing", *Encyclopaedia Britannica*...

9 Michael Pollak, "The Performance of the Wooden Printing Press," *The Library Quarterly 42* (April 1972): 262.

10 Richard G. Cole, "The Dynamics of Printing in the Sixteenth Century," in *The Social History of the Reformation*, ed. L. P. Buck and J. W. Zophy (Columbus: Ohio State University Press, 1972), 95.

using a combination of type and woodcuttings. Broadsheets were published for the obvious purpose of catechizing and teaching scripture lessons. Due to the high cost of Bibles, the broadsheets became a poor people's Bible.[11]

During this period, the books were quite expensive, not as high as the old manuscript editions. One of the factors that contributed to the high pricing of books was the cost of paper, which constituted as much as three-quarters of the material costs of the book.[12] Perhaps the cost factor could have been the reasons for many early books did not include blank papers during the binding processes. Since the papers were expensive, books remained affordable only to the wealthy individuals in the society.[13] Although Gutenberg's movable type had considerably improved the efficiency of book printing technology, yet books were still a rare product. Gawthrop and Strauss notes that the ordinary artisan living in 1522 would have to work for one-week to pay for a New Testament in German. To purchase a complete German Bible, one was required a month's labour.[14]

The pamphlets were a brief unbound booklet dealing with topics pertaining to sensitive subject matter. The German publications were involved in the printing of pamphlets, which Luther used skilfully.[15] He responded quickly to his opponents, since pamphlets could be produced quickly. Before 1518 there were minimal pamphlet production in Europe. However, by 1524, there were indication that the production of pamphlets had increased considerably and much of the increase was due to Luther's writings.[16] Pamphlets were effective publications, since it efficiently utilises the paper.

By late fifteenth century, movable type books were distributed throughout Europe. The new movable type books were sold through the same channels as the manuscript editions. As book sales grew, it became necessary to establish distribution outlets in the major cities of Europe.[17] Printers did their own advertising and distribution, since "as self-serving publicists, early printers issued book lists, circulars, and broadsides. They put their firm's name, emblem, and shop

---

11 G. H. Putnam, *Books and their Makers During the Middle Ages, vol. 1, 476-1600*, 2nd ed. (New York: The Knickerbocker Press, 1898), 350. Calaméo, http://en.calameo.com/read/0001070441b4bf85e1ea2 (Accessed on 2 Sep 2017).

12 Watt, *Cheap Print and Popular Piety*..., 262.

13 R. A. Houston, *Literacy in Early Modern Europe: Culture and Education, 1500-1800* (New York: Longman, 1988), 185.

14 Gawthrop and Strauss, "Protestantism and Literacy in Early Modern Germany," *Past and Present* 104 (1984): 31-55.

15 Richard G. Cole, ed. H. Koehler, "Reformation Pamphlets and the Communication Processes," *Flugschriften als Massenmedium* (1981): 150-51.

16 Cole, "Reformation Pamphlets...," 149.

17 Elizabeth Eisenstein, *The Printing Press as an Agent of Change: Communications and Cultural Transformations in Early Modern Europe* (Cambridge, England: Cambridge University Press, 1979), 57-58.

address on the front page of their books."[18] The bookshops were uncommon until late Sixteenth Century, except for in state capitals and large cities. Gutenberg's press had given rise to a growth industry in Europe.[19]

It is appropriate to note that during Fourteenth Century and Fifteenth Century, the European intellectual and cultural re-birth known as the *Renaissance* had begun to influence the people's values, their views of the world and the knowledge they sought. The innovation of print technology increased the number of books in circulation and helped to gratify the demand for access to information from an increasingly curious and inquisitive population. As the number of books in circulation grew, the way in which people read changed, and there was a move away from an individual reading a book aloud to a group, to private and silent reading. The activity of reading and gaining knowledge gradually broke down the monopoly that the literate elite had on learning and education. New ideas and novel thinking started to challenge the teachings and authority of religious and political leaders.[20]

At this moment, the Roman Catholic Church was a powerful organisation whose role was far-reaching. Being immensely wealthy, it was much more than a religious institution. It influenced the entire gamut of peoples' lives. In early Sixteenth Century, number of individuals began speaking out against some of the practices of the Church including the issuing of indulgences. Most famous among these early reformers was Martin Luther, an Augustinian monk in Wittenberg, Germany.[21]

Martin Luther nailed his *Ninety-Five Theses* to the door of the Wittenberg Church on October 31, 1517, calling for a disputation concerning indulgences. He did not act as defiant vandalism, since the church door was the church bulletin board of the day. However, Luther's request went unanswered during his day, and that the nailing of *Ninety-Five Theses* caused such controversy that today it is being credited with birth of the Reformation. Luther's handwritten document was later printed in Wittenberg in Latin. In 1518, the German translation was published and during the course of the next two years an additional twenty-two German editions were printed.[22] It is to be noted that if it had not been for the efficiency of Gutenberg's movable type printing for duplicating the document, Luther's reformation work and its influence on other reformers would have seen differently.

The expansion of the print industry in Germany has been a concern for the reformers. Luther and the other German reformers required adequate printing equipment for substantial distribution of their publications. The duration

18 Ibid., 59.

19 Houston, *Literacy in Early Modern Europe...*, 169.

20 Putnam, *Books and their Makers During the Middle Ages...*, 320-321.

21 Ibid., 176-177.

22 Ibid., 222.

between Gutenberg's first press and Luther's use of the technology in the 1520s has brought a significant increase in the number of printing businesses. Focusing on the print industries in Germany, Richard Cole concludes his analyses on the publication of the works by Martin Luther and other Protestants, states,

> There are almost fifty identifiable printers of Luther›s works in the 1520s printing in twelve separate locations in the Freytag data alone. There are another seventy printers in various locations printing mostly Reformation tracts. Overall for the sixteenth century, there are three hundred and ninety-one printers, eight hundred and ninety-four authors and one hundred and twenty-five cities noted in the Freytag data. Forty-two of the locations that surface in the Freytag data are mentioned by Schottenloher in his great bibliography of the sixteenth century as the object of significant historical research based on the historical records of printing. Eighty-two of the smaller locations where printers lived and worked have not been the subject of specific print research. The odds are overwhelmingly in favour of the contention that if a German printer published pamphlets especially in the 1520s, he published Protestant materials. What is often thought of as a war of pamphlets between the followers of Luther and pope in Rome may be seen as a lopsided one.[23]

Since Gutenberg's movable type printing technology originated in Germany, it would assume that the print industry could realise its greatest growth in the land of its invention. Presumably, in all regions of Germany, any purchaser could buy more books at lower prices and bring them into their study or library.[24] For Luther, Germany was an ideal location for publishing, since the country had enough printers to enable the largest distribution of his writings.

Gutenberg shifted his press to Wittenberg from Erfurt in 1508 upon the invitation from Wittenberg University. He was skilled and competent printer, who published the work of Andreas Bodenstein von Karlstadt's *Distinctiones Thomistarum*, as the first publication in Wittenberg where Hebrew type was set.[25] Like any writer selecting their printer for publishing the work, Luther chose Johannes Gutenberg as his first printer in Wittenberg. Gutenberg published Luther's translation and commentary on Psalms 6, 32, 38, 51, 102, 130, and 143, titled, *The Seven Penitential Psalms*. A popular publication, *The Seven Penitential Psalms* was republished in Leipzig, Strasbourg, and Erfurt.[26] Using Gutenberg for

23 R. G. Cole, "Reformation Printers: Unsung Heroes," *Sixteenth Century Journal* 15 (Fall 1984): 337.

24 Eisenstein, *The Printing Press as an Agent of Change...*, 72.

25 Maria Grossman, "Wittenberg Printing, Early Sixteenth Century," *Sixteenth Century Essays and Studies* 1 (1970): 65-69.

26 Ibid., 73.

his printer was convenient for Luther, since he could observe the printing process while he taught at the university.[27]

Luther brought one of the experienced printer Melchior Lotther to Wittenberg from Leipzig to establish a printing press, since he was dissatisfied with Gutenberg's work.[28] Lotther set-up the press in Wittenberg and later gave the management of the facility to his sons, Michael and Melchior the Younger.[29] It seems that Luther had a good relationship with the Lotther because Michael married one of Luther's first cousins.[30] Luther found the Lotther's printing business an efficient operation for publishing his writings and spreading the Reformation.

In his letter to John Lang written from Wittenberg in 1520, Luther mentions his work on *Second Lectures on the Psalms* for publication. In order to reduce the possibilities of a financial crisis, as was the case with one of his publications, Luther and the printer decided to print and sell the first section of the book. The number of sections sold was apparent indication of how many copies of each additional sections would be required. Gottfried G. Krodel, the editor of volume forty-eight of the American edition of Luther's *Works*, views that the publication of *Second Lectures on the Psalms* was the first time such a publishing technique was attempted.[31]

Two of Luther's classical contributions to the Reformation were his *German New Testament*, which was published in 1522, and the *German Bible* completed in 1534. For Luther, it was important to communicate the Word of God in the common language of the people. Nevertheless, the widely acceptance of his German translation was complicated by the lack of a common dialect in Germany. During the period when Luther translated the Bible, there were several dialects in the German language. However, Luther's translation of the New Testament not only provided a German vernacular version of the Bible, but was also used to teach and reading to the illiterate, thus promoting a unified German language. Along with several other publications by Luther, the New Testament and then the German Bible were well received masterpiece. Another prominent printer in Wittenberg was Hans Lufft, who produced thousands of Luther's Bibles between 1534 and 1574. Lufft even claimed to have obtained the copyrights to Luther's German Bible when the reformer died in 1546, but Luther had not granted the rights to anyone.[32]

---

27 Gottfried G. Krodel, *The Works of Martin Luther*, vol. 48 (Philadelphia: Fortress Press, 1967), 19.

28 W. G. Tillmanns, "The Lotthers: Forgotten Printers of the Reformation," *Concordia Theological Monthly* 22/2 (Feb. 1951): 261.

29 Putnam, *Books and their Makers During the Middle Age,* vol. 2, 230.

30 Ian Siggins, *Luther and His Mother* (Philadelphia: Fortress Press, 1981), 30, as quoted in Cole, "Reformation Printers," 333.

31 *The Works of Martin Luther*, vol. 48, 148-151.

32 Putnam, *Books and their Makers During the Middle Ages,* vol. 2, 223-224.

Alongside with Gutenberg, Lotther, and Lufft, there were several other printers who established commercial printing press in Wittenberg. Nickel Schirlentz operated a press in his home. Hans Weiss worked for the Lotthers until 1525, and later ventured his own printing establishment. Artist Lucas Cranach partnered with the goldsmith Christian Döring to establish a printing press. Due to this partnership, several dozens of Luther's pamphlets were produced between 1522 and 1525. One of Cranach and Döring's former employees, Joseph Klug, published Luther's "A Mighty Fortress" in his own press in 1529.[33] As Luther's popularity spread, he continued to write, while the printers took advantage of the boon – some honourably, while others dishonourably.

Unauthorized printing of Luther's work had been a perennial problem. Contemplating the potential profitability of Luther's popular work, publishers often print their own editions of his works, with very little concern for the quality of the finished product. In September 1525, Luther's unfinished books were stolen from his printers in Wittenberg. Luther lodged the complaint to the magistrates in Nuremberg that several pages of a book of his sermons were stolen from his local printer and were being used by a printer in their city to produce a pirated volume.[34] In a later edition of Luther's German New Testament he included in his preface a sarcastic comment, "I beg all my friends and foes, my masters, printers, and readers, let this New Testament be mine. If you lack one, then make one for yourselves.... But this Testament is Luther's German Testament."[35] Luther's successful use of the publication industry and his considerable labour of translating the Bible into German were seen by fraudulent printers as a means to exploit his credentials by all means for their commercial gains.

In addition to being frustrated by pirating his works, Luther was angry about the erroneous work produced by his printers as well. In his letter to George Spalatin in 1521, Luther expressed his discontent with careless typesetters who created errors in his writings and continued the compromised publications through successive editions of his works. Later on, in another letter Luther decided to go ahead printing the German homilies, since he had already started the project. Luther's problems with printers were not isolated one, because Andreas Karlstadt complained that whole columns of print were discarded and sentences disorganize by the printers of his works as well.[36] As Barry Waugh observes rightly that although the quality of the publications improved along with the print

33 Cole, "Reformation Printers," 335.

34 Putnam, *Books and their Makers During the Middle Ages,* vol. 2, 236.

35 M. H. Black, "The Printed Bible," in *The Cambridge History of the Bible: The West from the Reformation to the Present Day*, edited by S. L. Greenslade (Cambridge: Cambridge University Press, 1963), 433.

36 Gordon Rupp, *Patterns of Reformation* (Philadelphia: Fortress Press, 1969), 121.

technology, yet unfortunately technology could not improve the quality of the printers themselves.[37]

In conclusion, its noted that the development of Gutenberg's movable type printing technology had brought about exponential revolution in Europe. Luther utilised the print technology to its optimum potential that are evident through his publications of books, pamphlets, hymns and translation of the Bible into German language so that all could read the Word of God. However, the inception of new print technology encountered several challenges as well. Distribution of publications with varying literacy levels posed its concern in Germany. Since books were expensive to own, lower cost publications like pamphlets being used to limit number of pages with less satisfactory content. Scribes depending on old manuscript technology for their livelihood ridiculed Gutenberg's technology. Several authors were frustrated with careless compositions and editing from their printers and further worsened through the problems of manuscript thefts and piracy issues. In spite of these problems, the movable type printing technology sustained through centuries of use and became the way that texts were preserved and communicated.

37 Barry Waugh, "The Importance of the Printing Press for the Protestant Reformation, Part Two," *Reformation 21* (October 2013), http://www.reformation21.org/articles/the-importance-of-the-printing-press-for-the-protestant-reformation-part-two.php (Accessed on 31 Aug, 2017).

3

Celebration of Faith Towards Community-Solidarity

K. Balakrishnan

Introduction

Faith occupies a pivotal place in our lives. The writer of Hebrews affirms the core Christian truth that it is impossible to please God without faith. However, there is a dearth of clarity as to the notion of faith. We make a distinction between three kinds of "faith": a) credulity: which is the willingness to believe anything, even that which we know to be impossible or untrue, just because someone has told us it is true.; b.) Faith is also used to designate belief. "Different faiths" refers, in fact, to different belief systems. Theology uses the Latin term *fides quae* (literally, faith which) to refer to that which is believed (The historic creeds of the church); and c) Faith is also used to designate "belief in action." The Latin term *fides qua* (literally, *fides as*) to refer to the act of believing. Keeping these insights in mind, I would like to delineate faith in relation to salvation, praxis and community.

I. Faith and Salvation

Prior to understanding faith and salvation, it is important to ascertain the meaning of faith. The New Testament noun "faith" (*pistis*) or verb "believe" (*pisteo*) seem to give an understanding of faith. While the noun form faith denotes conviction of truth, confidence, reliance, and knowledge the verbal form to "to believe" suggests the progressive and personal involvement to God or Christ. Hence, faith is not used in generic terms. It is interesting to note that the verbal form, "*pisteo*" is predominantly used in the Gospel. In particular, the fourth Gospel uses the verbal form to denote the action of believing. In other words, the believing of a person or recipient to the message of salvation is termed as faith. The proclamation of the kingdom of God by Jesus called forth action on the part of the hearers. This action could be called as a human response to salvation. Jesus' praxis of the kingdom of God through acts of miracles necessitated faith on the part of his recipients to respond to Jesus' message. The teaching of the parables illuminate faith as a response to the kingdom of God. The message of the parables outside the faith response remains enigmatic to the outsiders. Although, salvation is the free gift of God, it takes a personal trust to respond to the gospel.

Among the NT writers, Paul makes profound contributions to the notion of faith. His letter to the Romans 1:17 Paul makes the pivotal truth affirmation that "the just live by faith." In this verse, Paul brings to the fore the truth that God justifies the sinners through faith. This faith is termed as faith-righteousness. God accepts the sinners on the ground of what God has done through Christ on the cross. Faith both in the gospels and Romans faith is active not stagnant. Although faith denotes the perception of reality, faith entails a commitment to God and his work on the cross. It is through this personal commitment that salvation is made accessible to us. In this aspect, Paul's argument in 16: "whoever believes" is an important pointer to personal referent to salvation. As far as salvation is concerned, one's personal commitment and responsibility to the gospel takes precedence over other things. This gives credence to the core acknowledged truth of the gospel that is Justification by faith. It is through this act that God declares his righteousness over the life of a sinner. Hence, justification by faith is an instantaneous act wrought by Christ work. This brings a change from the status of a sinner to the status of a child of God. In this act, one's personal faith or trust plays an integral part in internalizing the meaning of Jesus' death on the cross.

II. Faith and Praxis

While the gospels and the Pauline Epistles draw attention to the subjective experience of faith, James attests to the objective side of faith. In particular, James 2:14-17 locate and identify some arguments over the falsity of faith: "What does it profit, my brethren, if a man says he has faith, but has not works? Can his faith save him?" Jamess contention is further confirmed in 17: So also faith if it does not have works, is dead by itself. These questions indicate that certain conflicts in the community were related to some misconceived notions of faith among the members. The fallacious notion could be perceived from the use of the Greek pronouns "you" (*sou*) and "I" (*ego*) in v. 18 (you have faith; I have deeds). This refers not only to the writer but to the situation of the readers.[1] The idea that "even demons can believe" appears to preserve the position of those who does not evidence actions.[2] It is obvious that the idea of faith is addressed in two ways. On the one hand, faith is used positively in the sense of true faith in 1:3, 6; 2:1, 5; 5:15. On the other hand, it is used negatively in the sense of false faith in 2:14-26. It is important to note that there are no two kinds of faith. James does not demarcate a line between correct faith and false faith. For James, there are not two kinds of faith which are qualitatively distinguishable but only one. That is to say, the author does not recommend to his readers one type of faith

1 R.P. Martin, *James: Word Biblical Commentary, Volume 48* (Waco, Texas: Word Books, 1998), 78.

2 Martin, *James...*, 99.

which is empirically recognizable by its deeds over against another sort. Hence, James's rebuttal begins with a mocking challenge to the man of faith without works (18b): "show me your faith apart from the deeds, and I will show you my faith by what I do."

Scholars such as J.H. Ropes and M. Dibelius have understood James's retort to insinuate that the addressee cannot fulfil the demand since the faith that has no works is no faith at all and therefore cannot be demonstrated.[3] Thus, the demand "to show me your faith" is central to mocking the humiliating impotence of the opponent's piety in contrast to James's own. In the face of this challenge the faith of James's interlocutor reveals itself to be unfit to achieve the mercy of God and more than that of demons. At the same time, the deeds of the author manifest his superior religious service.[4] According to R. P. Martin, faith becomes authentically genuine only if it is evidenced by orthodoxy. He terms this dimension of faith as "saving" faith, which is replete with action induced by love.[5] In the light of the aforementioned perspectives, one can understand that the distinction between faith and works in James chapter 2 is not between an inner quality and its outward manifestations, but between the individual's vertical relationship to God and his horizontal behaviour among men.

In this framework, the author insists that one's God-ward service cannot be divorced from righteous deeds, for obedience is the most holy form of faith. Viewed in this light, it becomes evident that James is not seeking to denigrate the importance of faith in 2:14-26. Faith without works is not profitable on two accounts: It has no efficacy for the person claiming this kind of faith, for such delusion can end in eschatological disorder. On the contrary, faith retains its role as the primary distinguishing feature of the community. James reiterates his commitment to the community which is enriched by sharing faith through actions in the community. This makes the point clear that one's faith cannot be practised in isolation, but in participation in life with others. This indicates that faith ought to be praxiological in relation to the other members in the community. This is vividly seen in James's definition of religion: "religion that is pure and undefiled before God and the father is this: to visit the orphans and widows in their afflictions and to keep oneself unstained from the world." (James 1:27). This verse articulates advocacy in favour of the poor which suggests a plethora of social action and justice towards the reconstruction of the society. Moreover, in spelling out his social concerns, he depicts God as the champion of the poor, one

---

3 J.H. Ropes, James, 110; Martin Dibelius, *A Commentary on the Epistle of James*. Translated by M.A. Williams (Philadelphia: Fortress Press, 1976), 160.

4 D.J. Verseput, "Reworking the Puzzle of Faith and Deeds in James 2:14-26." *New Testament Studies 43* (1997): 110.

5 Martin, *James...*, 99-110.

who secures the right of those who suffer distress and oppression.[6] In particular, the portrayal of God as creator of all the humans in His image (1:26, 27) and father of all orphans and widows in their affliction and suffering is an interesting thought in the defence of the poor. Hence, James evinces a preferential solidarity with the poor. For this intention, the notion of God in James that God is the widows, orphans and the poor (1.27) and the faith of Jesus serves as the model for action-oriented faith (2.1). In particular, the concept of the royal law serves as an incentive for social action in the community. It is the love that creates a neighbourhood which creates a space for others in the community.

James' contention that one's faith needs to be shared with the needs of the community was based on the grave the situation that encountered the poor members in the community. The poor suffered from their wages being withheld (5:4); legal exploitation (2:6); social humiliation (2:1-4); and hunger and lack of adequate clothes (2:15).[7] This illuminates the awful situation of the poor who were oppressed, discriminated and dragged into the law courts. Moreover, the concentration of the land was also part of Palestinian economic life, causing grave economic problems to the population.[8] The rich farmers paid a paltry amount of payment to the workers. As a result, there were pressures which eventually led many to high way robbery. Josephus reports that the Zealots looted the houses of the wealthy and murdered their owners and set the villages on fire (War 2.13.60). It is in this context that James deplores violence, anger and killing.[9] In James 5:4-6, the writer castigates the attitude of the rich as murder. The strong word may suggest that the rich were engaged in certain hostile activities such as physical violence and economic exploitation. In the castigation of the rich, James clearly undertakes a social justice stance.[10] In this framework of faith and work, the author insists that one's God-ward service cannot be divorced from righteous deeds. Rather, one's faith needs to be compatible with their action. This action for the community, means sharing goods with the poor (James 1:27). Hence, James's notion of faith takes social ethics and justice into serious consideration. This necessitates that we bolster not only the orthodoxy of faith but also the orthopraxis of faith.

---

6 P.H. Davids, *The Epistle of James: New International Greek Testament Commentary* (Grand Rapids: Eerdmans, 1982), 159.

7 W.J. Webb, "Suffering." Pages 1135-1141 in *Dictionary of the Later New Testament and Its Development*. Edited by R.P. Martin & P.H. Davids (Leicester: InterVarsity Press, 1997), 1139.

8 F.C. Grant, *The Economic Background of the Gospels* (Oxford: Oxford University Press, H. Milford (1926), 66.

9 Martin, *Life Setting* ..., 97-103.

10 P.U. Maynard-Reid, *Poverty and Wealth in James* (Maryknoll, NY: Orbis Books, 1987), 96-97.

III. Faith and Community Solidarity

Having identified the significance of faith in relation to actions, it is important to perceive as to how the praxis of faith contributes to the formation and solidification of the community in some other Epistles which include: ***Hebrews*** incorporates faith in the context of the community growing weary (Heb. 2:1-4; 5:11-6:8; 10:35ff; 12:12ff) and its deviation from its responsibility. These developments were seen as symptomatic of serious erosion of faith and hope. In the context of countering deviation, the author employs the pilgrim motif in order to help the members to move forward, to forge ahead, to preserve, and to look ahead in the march towards the goal of their journey (Heb. 4:11,16; 10:22-25; 12:1-2). For deSilva, the list of the exemplars of faith in Heb. 11 embodies the central value for the minority group, namely, faith. Faith is that virtue to which the addressees are called upon to preserve in midst of persecutions and conflicts.[11] Since faith sustains pilgrims, the qualities of firmness, reliability and steadfastness, celebrated in 11:1-40, should be evident in the lives of the pilgrims. Faith also implies confession; confession in the form of action is indispensable exhibiting the quality of life needed within the confessing community. For Attridge, faith functions as a stimulus and sustaining power to provide basic motivation to the community.[12] It is faith that sustains the pilgrim community to live as vibrant members through the vicissitudes of its wanderings existence on earth.

In ***Johannine Epistles,*** the discourse on faith assumes importance in the context of the community being entangled with the onset of false teaching. The author points out that the false teaching threatened not only the Christians' understanding of the nature of Jesus Christ, but their understanding of the nature of God himself.[13] It is in this line that the writer reiterates that one's right belief should refer to the historical dimension of faith: the incarnation of Jesus Christ. Not only should one's faith refer to the historical dimension of faith, it should also relate to right action of love. Hence, the writer called for a different kind of love in action and reality. That love is understood in terms of showing compassion for the brother who is in need by sharing the material good things of life with him (3:17). On the basis of this action and example, the readers are exhorted to love one another (4:11).[14] Love becomes the measuring yard whereby one's sonship in the divine love is tested. For the Elder, the confession of Jesus as the Christ and Son of God, coupled with the commandment of love for one another becomes

---

11 D.A. de Silva, *Despising Shame: Honour Discourse and Community maintenance in the Epistle to the Hebrews. Society of Biblical Literature Dissertations Series*, 152 (Atlanta: Scholars Press, 1995), 145.

12 H.W. Attridge, *The Epistle to the Hebrews: A Commentary on the Epistle to the Hebrews*. Edited by H. Koester (Hermeneia / Philadelphia: Fortress Press, 1989), 308.

13 Kee, H.C., and F.W. Young. *The Living World of the New Testament* (London; Darton, Longman & Todd, 1960), 344-45.

14 Painter, J. "The Opponents in I John," *New Testament Studies* 32 (1986): 63-64.

indispensable to the notion of faith (1 Jn. 2:22-24; 2:7; 3:11 and 2 Jn. 5-6). In this conception, love is not law but gospel. For John, the death of Jesus Christ is both model of perfect love and the atoning sacrifice (2:1-2; 4:10). It is the praxis of love that creates a community of kinship, equality and solidarity.

In the ***Pastoral Epistles***, Paul urges to emphasize sound doctrine and sound faith (1Tim. 1:6-14; 2:1-13; 3:10-4:5, 2 Tim 1:13, 14). To be sound faith (Tit. 1:13) is to think in accordance with right teaching. In this sense, there is a "common faith" (Tit 1:4), a body of truth that Christians share in common. Hence, it is essential to understand that emphasis on faith as a sound doctrine includes not only right teaching about God but also right teaching about the ethical conduct of Christians. To hold faith is to maintain a good conscience (1 Tim. 1:19, 6:3). Though the church leaders lacked the intellectual competence to deal with the deeper aspects of the problems, but they realized the fundamental truths of *Kergyma* and sought to organize the community into a semblance of unity in belief and ethical conduct against those who would rather change the gospel and subvert the common fellowship.[15] It is evident to note that the teaching of faith in these epistles contributed towards the solidification of the community. In all these epistles, the authors demanded faith that will have extension in the world we live.

IV. Celebration of the Life of Martin Luther and the Reformation Day

Having perceived the notion of faith in relation to salvation and praxis and the community solidarity. It is important to note the significant contributions that Martin Luther, the Reformer over to the church at all ages. His contribution to the protestant movement is pivotal for it served to uphold the authority of the scripture and faith. As part of celebrating his life and the 500 years of Reformation, I would like to highlight salient features that signified the Protestant movement.

1. Centrality of God's Word

Luther's significant contribution to the church and Christian life is found in his emphasis on the centrality of God's word. For him, the word of God takes precedence over all other things. In this connection, the key word for his fulmination against the heresies of the Medieval church is drawn from Rom 1.17: "The Just live by Faith." It is from this verse, he formulated his main message, Justification by Faith. Luther regarded this to be as the central article of faith. This justification by faith becomes a doctrine, profoundly connected to personal experience. For Luther, it is the scripture alone which plays a pivotal role in determining one's right standing with God. Luther has thus placed the word of God over the nefarious practices of the church. Luther's emphasis on Justification by Faith purely connects to the personal experience of the individual. Although Luther has been criticized for his overemphasis on one's personal experience, his

15 Kee & Young, *Living World…*, 348-49.

insistence on the personal experience is significant in relation to God's word. It attaches importance to the inner voice of the Individual. This line of thinking is useful to what I construe it as "the personal voice Biblical Interpretation." This means that the word of God is being read in the light of human experience. In vice versa, human experience is read in the light of God's voice. In this process, the word of God assumes a central place in life. We have multivariate interpretations and approaches, through which, the scripture is interpreted. At times, these multiple interpretations seem to impede us from letting the scripture to speak to us. Instead of letting the text, we speak to the text. Listening to the text creates in us conviction, receptivity and ethical responsibility. This gives us an ethically responsible interpretation.

2. Resistance to Commodification of the Gospel

The Medieval church was engaged in traditions and corruptions which were contraveneous to the basic tenets of the scripture. The leaders of the church needed money in order to build ST. Peter's Basilica. As part of raising money towards this project, the leaders of various ranks authorized the sale, known as indulgences. The purchase of the sale guaranteed one's entry into heaven from purgatory, a place of 'spiritual discipline.' For this purpose Tetzel was authorized by the church to preach thus: "As soon as pennies in the money chest ring, the souls out of their Purgatory do spring." This provoked Martin Luther to nail *95 Theses* at Wittenberg to castigate the malevolent practices of the Bishops, clergy, leaders and people. Luther, thus challenged the church against the sale of forgiveness. Today, the church is around the globe is grateful to Luther for his bold conviction and daringness to witness to the truth of gospel. However, it is appalling to note that the politics of power and the abuse of money proliferate the Indian church today. Ascendency to a hierarchy of leadership is done at the expense of trivializing and jeopardizing the gospel. This causes a huge damage to the spirit of unity in the church in India. We live at a time in which we increasingly witness to the 'prosperity doctrine' which negates suffering. The pagan teaching which aims at enriching oneself creates a 'market economy' in which attractive testimonies are marketed to allure the people. This practice is not compatible with the teaching of the Bible. The Life of Martin Luther sounds a caveat to those who promote the prosperity gospel. The history of the Reformation movement reminds us that we resist the temptation to sell the gospel.

3. Community - Affirmation

Martin Luther's contribution to the church is his teaching about the community. Although there is a connection between community and society, the notion of community seems to differ from the understanding of the society. A community is a sociological construct which entails a set of instructions, human behaviours that have meaning and expectations between its members. It has actions based on shared expectations, values, beliefs and meaning between individuals.[16] The word "society" refers to all classes of people or people at large. In other words, the community refers to all people living in a special locality whereas the society refers to the totality of human condition. The society refers to the customs and practices of men and women.[17] Keeping this line of demarcation, we need to look at Martin Luther's notion of community. Luther's vision for community derives from his conception, *communio sanctorum*. This word denotes communion which speaks about the act of participation with someone. The members in the community were called to share their possession with all others. Luther aptly remarks: "All things are common, that the good of each one belongs to the other, and that no one possesses anything that is in his own. As a result of all prayers and all goods works of the entire community help me and every believer; they stand by and strengthen each other in every time of life and of death so that each one bears the other's burden, as St. Paul teaches."[18] This indicates that Luther attached greater significance to the community life. Since Luther advocated the priesthood of all believers and the laity, he was averse to the secular structure of the church which is based on the hierarchy of leadership. In Luther's time, the ecclesiastical positions were traded as economic and the political interest was infused into the life of the church.[19] By countering the hierarchical model of the church, Luther gave us possibility to envision church as egalitarian community. Although Luther referred to the community of all believers, his community vision thus, provides an optic vision towards the construction of an inclusive community which is characterised by equality, mutuality and relationality.

V. Faith in Indian Context

India is a land of multi-religious and pluralistic faiths and practices. In Indian context, the Bhagavat Gita teaches three ways of attaining liberation or moksha. These three *margas* are known as *Jnana Marga*, *Bhakti Marga* and *Karma Marga*. The *Jnana marga* teaches that knowledge and meditation as the path way to attain *moksha* (liberation); the followers should devote a great deal of time to learning and knowledge. The *Bhakti Marga* necessitates devotion or bhakti as the path way to gain salvation.[20] The last *marga*, the *Karma Marga* attaches priority to deeds as the path way to gaining salvation. These *margas* make attainment of knowledge, devotion and performance of deeds as conditional to salvation. These

16 Phil Bartle, "What is Community? A Sociological Perspective," cev.vcn.bc.ca/cmp/whal com. htm

17 www. difference between.com/ difference between- society- and vs- community/

18 WA 7, 219, WA 10, 394.

19 Walter Altman, *Luther and Liberation: A Liberation Perspective* (Minneapolis: Fortress Press, 1992), 6.

20 Sarvepally Radhakrishnan, *Recovery of Faith* (New York: Harper & Brothers Publishers, 1955), 160.

margas can be complementary because they focus on knowledge, devotion and deeds. However, these *margas* do find significance only in the aftermath of one's salvation. For Christians, these *margas* should not be deemed as a condition to salvation but as a response to salvation. In this context, perspectives conveyed through this write-up, should make our faith to meaningfully relate to others. It has reminded us that faith should not remain in the head, but it should result in a loving relationship. When James says that faith without works is dead he is really saying that beliefs which remain ideas in one's head rather than ways of being in the world are dead. The Christian theologian must be careful not to insist on beliefs that have no extension in the real world. Too often in the past the test of faith has been consigned to intellectual beliefs that have no correspondence to the world we live in and consequently have no outward sign. The Christian is not concerned with beliefs (*fides quae*) which have no corresponding consequence in the world. Freedom of Conscience is fundamental: so, John Wesley said, "If your heart is the same as mine give me your hand."

Conclusion

The Bible affirms the duality of orthodoxy and praxis of faith. In order for faith to be authentic and meaningful, it ought to be oriented to action. It is the action-injected faith that contributes towards the construction of the community thereby solidifying the coherence of the community. The faith that does contribute towards building up a wider community becomes inauthentic. This accentuates that faith is not a private affair; it is related to the community-life. In sum, I would like to reiterate that spirituality is not attained in isolation, but it is in participation with life. This gives imperative that faith ought to have extension to the others. It is this faith that relates to others, thereby lending a helping hand to the indigent, the vulnerable and disadvantaged. Martin Luther left behind a great legacy for the church to participate in the life-affirming values of the gospel and to resist in the life- negating forces. Hence, we need to imbibe the values he inseminated in giving birth to the reformation movement. The Indian church ought to emulate the life and mission of Martin Luther for the task of undertaking the mission of renewal and transformation.

4

Justice and Unity as Faith Issues
Martin Luther's 500 Years Reformation Perspective

Nagaiyasamy N.S. Samuel

Introduction

The concept of Justice, Righteousness and Unity have been the issues of faith down through the centuries. The reason behind these issues wrestle even beyond the centuries is the powerlessness of the poor who experience social, economic, political, cultural, and moral subjugated and oppression. The poor people's personal experiences and struggles for the liberation compelled them to encounter injustice, inequality, exploitation, corruption, dehumanization, disunity, etc. Justice, the integral value and essential message of the Christian Gospel[1] for ages has been not totally addressed by the Churches in India, for several reasons. The Indian Church faces challenges from outside such as religious pluralism, religious fundamentalism, caste oppression, violence, etc., and also faces challenges within the church such as Denominational divisions, caste divisions, gender divisions, class divisions, urban-rural divide, ethnic divisions, generational divide, etc., which leads to *faith* crisis on the basis of the teachings of Jesus Christ. Psalmist says that righteousness and justice are the foundation of your throne; steadfast love and faithfulness go before you (Ps. 89:14). The Lord God demands only justice and righteousness from his people (Dt. 16:19, 20; Mic. 6:8). The justice (and righteousness) should be practiced with the poor who is in lawsuit (Ex. 23:6).[2] Justice should not be perverted to the poor and the needy.[3]

The people of Israel were instructed and taught to practice justice and righteousness in their own context. The unjust exploitative conditions demand the prophets of the Old Testament, particularly Eight Century BCE prophets to

1 Mt. 23:23.

2 "Cursed be anyone who deprives the alien, the orphan, and the widow of justice." All the people shall say, "Amen!" Dt. 27:19 (NRSV).

3 Amos 5:24.

raise their voice against oppressive system that was against the poor and the needy. Insights from the Old Testament and its prophets could contribute for the present day context of the Church[4] and Society. In this pursuit one may have to address questions like: How justice and unity was understood and perceived? What is the theological position of the present day Church in relation with justice and unity? How the justice and unity incorporated in the liturgical and homiletical context of the Church? How the Church can contribute to establish justice and unity within the Church and outside? What are some of the challenges that Church faces in practicing justice and unity? These are some of the questions which need to be addressed in discussion with the justice and unity as a faith issues. When Martin Luther said about the righteous shall live by faith, he meant that the justice is the faith issues than doctrinal. This paper also would deal the justice and righteousness is an integral issue of the church and its unity with the churches and draw insights for the better understanding of justice, righteousness and unity within the Church(es) and among the Church(es) and a faith communities as Martin Luther envisaged.

1. The Concept of Justice

The Hebrew word מִשְׁפָּט (*misphat* = Justice) occurs 422 times in Old Testament,[5] in which 144 times it occurs in the prophetic literature.[6] Although מִשְׁפָּט encompasses a variety of meanings, it has decided judicial connotations.[7] It may mean as follows: 'judgment; a matter under judgement; what is determined by judges and lawgivers, what is right, Justice.' What is most often the topic of concern is the process governing the settling of some dispute, whether between human parties or between God and the Israelites, or the actual verdict itself.[8] The justice and righteousness always go hand in hand. The Hebrew word for righteousness/rightness is צְדָקָה. (*Ṣ^edāqā*) is the righteous that belongs to those who fulfill the responsibilities which their relationships to others involve. The righteousness always has the connotation 'right with God,' 'what God thinks right,' and therefore the Lord desires that the outflow of religion should be Justice and Righteousness.[9] Justice and Righteousness must roll down like the floods after the winter rains, and persist like those few wadis whose streams do not fail in the summer drought (Dt. 21:4; Ps. 74:15; Amos 5:24; Mic. 6:8).[10] Broadly,

4 Church here in this paper means the Universal Christian Church.

5 G.J., Botterweck, H. Ringgren, H.J. Fabry, (Ed.), *Theological Dictionary of the Old Testament,* מִשְׁפָּט, vol. IX (Michigan: Wm. B. Eerdmans Publishing Company, UK, 1998), 87.

6 W.A. VanGemeren, (Gen. Ed.), *New International Dictionary of Old Testament Theology & Exegesis,* מִשְׁפָּט, vol. 2 (UK: Paternoster Press, 1996), 1142.

7 W.A. VanGemeren ..., p. 1142.

8 G.J., Botterweck, H. Ringgren and H.J. Fabry, מִשְׁפָּט ..., 87.

9 Ibid., p. 132.

10 J.L. Mays, *Amos, A Commentary* (Philadelphia: Westminster Press, 1969), 108-109.

therefore, Justice is correct moral practice in daily personal and social life, and righteousness is the cultivation of correct moral principle (both for self and for society); Justice is mainly outward, righteousness inward.[11]

1.1. The Use of Justice in the Biblical Texts

The God of the Old Testament is the God of Justice and Righteousness. The Lord is faithful to the Lord's covenant and reveals to people how the people have failed in their relationship with God and with one another in the society. The focus is often a breach of Justice suffered by Israelites at the hands of their corrupt leaders (Is. 1:17, 21; 5:7; 10:2; 59:8-9; Hab. 1:4). B.S. Childs argued that there is no justice, no righteousness and no truth. Indeed, those who seek to depart from such evil become the targets for persecution.[12] As a result, the Lord himself enters into judgement with his own people. The Lord's judgement is not only directed against corrupt leaders but also people for their sin (Is. 4:4; Jer. 5:1; 7:5; Eze. 5:6-7; 20:11, 13, 16, 21, 24; Hos. 5:1, 11; Mal. 3:5). Like the Psalmist and Job, the prophet also calls on God's Justice for his own sake (Ps. 7:8-9; 82:3; 112:9; 89:14; 119:121; Job 8:9; Jer. 10:24; Mic. 7:9).

The Prophet Amos consistently uses righteousness and justice as terms for the qualities which ought to be present in the social order (Amos 5:24; Is. 6:12; 5:7, 15), and this movement from rejection of sacrifice to a call for a kind of life described in these or similar terms is found in Is. 1:10-17; Mic. 6:6-8; Hos. 6:6. In Amos מִשְׁפָּט (*misphat* = justice) is specifically associated with the court in the gates and means the judicial process and its decisions by which right order is maintained in social unity, especially the protection of weak and poor through the help of the court.[13] God has told human what God seeks from human. God seeks from human what is good: '*to practice Justice*'; '*to love kindness*'; and '*to walk humbly*' (Mic. 6:8).

Isaiah 56:1-8 makes the imminent salvation and righteousness of Yahweh (v. 1b) the basis for exhorting Yahweh's community to do justice and righteousness (v. 1a). It directs the exhortation universally in v. 2 and specifically to the Eunuchs and foreigners in vv. 3-7, prompting them to righteous action. It assures them that they will be included in Yahweh's community, the Zion Community (3-7). It then ends with the announcement of further inclusion/gathering of 'yet others' (v. 8).[14]

---

11 J.A. Motyer, *The Message of Amos* (1974), 132.

12 B.S. Childs, *Isaiah* (Louisville: Westminster John Knox Press, 2001), 488-489.

13 J.L. Mays, *Amos* ..., 108-109.

14 E. Mohol, "The Confessional Community of Isaiah 56 – 66: A New Paradigm for Mission," in *Missiology for the Twenty First Century, South Asian Perspectives*, edited by R.E. Hedlund & P.J. Bhakiaraj (Delhi: ISPCK/MIIS, 2004), 30.

Relations with the Divine indicate relations among human beings and coincide with social Justice; this is the whole spirit of the Old Testament.[15] Justice, therefore, is right behaviour in relation to others, whereby they 'taste' or 'experience' what is good and pleasant.[16] Justice is both gift and demand. It is a gift when God accepts them as God's own and it is a demand by which God wants the people to accept one another with equality and self-respect. To do Justice is to know, that is to love God (I Jn. 2:29). When Justice does not exist among human beings, God is ignored. The Justice is demanded from the humans and has right relationship with God and with the fellow human beings.

1.2. Justice and Worship (Liturgy)

The absence of justice and righteousness is the issue. Prophet Amos condemned Israel's worship[17] because they emphasized more on the cultic practices that was not implied by the Levitical and Deuteronomistic Codes. The Biblical text clearly states that the relationship with God and with the fellow human being should be exercised with justice and righteousness. To belittle one's neighbour through the means of exploitation, oppress the slave and the poor persons is equivalent to offend God. The Old Testament demands the right relationship with the neighbour and with God to love and know the Lord. To Love the Lord requires the establishment of just relationships among the neighbours. Thus, to know God is to practice Justice (Jer. 22:16). When Justice does not exist, God is not known.

The prophets in the Old Testament were highly critical of the liturgical feasts, the practice of fasting and pilgrimages and even construction of temples and alter. When the Israelites started to worship the idols, molten images, the prophets were bold enough to point out the idolatry of the people against their God. They criticised the domesticated religion of monarchy and its service to the royal powers rather than divine power. The prophets strongly condemned the practice of piety, sacrifice and cultic practices without justice as worthless and hypocritical. God expects justice rather than sacrifice from the people who do not practice justice in the everyday affairs. In knowing God and inter-human relationship (justice), prophet Hosea states: '*For I desire steadfast love and not sacrifice, the knowledge of God, rather than burnt offerings.*' (Hos. 6:6).[18] Consequently, knowing and worshiping God demands the observance of justice

15 L. Stanislaus, *The Liberation Mission of the Church among Dalit Christians* (Delhi: ISPCK, 1999), 214-215.

16 J.A. Motyer, *The Message of Amos* ...,132.

17 How can a human worship God? One answer is: with sacrifice, things, good work. The other answer is reflected in Mic. 6:8. God requires not some external gifts from human worshiper, but a humble communicant who loves to serve God and practice Justice toward his fellow human. R.L. Smith, *Micah – Malachi, Word Biblical Commentary*, vol. 32 (Texas: Word Books, 1984), 51.

18 The questions about sacrifice are comprehensive. Burnt offerings represented total dedication. Calves a year old represented the most desirable kind of sacrificial animal. Thousands of rams

in both the religious as well as societal contexts. 'God requires not some external gifts from human worshiper, but a humble communicant who loves to serve God and practice Justice toward one's fellow human.'[19]

1.3. Justice as a Norm for Christian Church(es): Theological Positioning

The Church ought to be a mirror of Justice and must have the thirst for Justice and yearning for humanity. The Church is called to participate in the death and resurrection of Christ and Justice demands her to specify the terms and demands of that participation. The Church can contribute to this philosophical and cultural revolution to uproot the system where the Justice is not practiced in its literal sense.[20] The need to commit for the cause of peace, justice, human values and human well-being should be the prime concern of the Church to promote the holistic development of the just society with human values extended to God's creation.

Justice leads to the affirmation of concrete and right relationships with God and with fellow human being. Therefore, there should not be demarcation on the basis on caste in the church who is a member in the body of Christ. The Church as the body of Christ should not practice high or low or outcaste; pure or impure; and no discrimination and exploitation on the basis of caste or sex. The equality of the members of the Church should be convergent point and no space for the practice of untouchability in the Church and in Society.

Stanislaus says that the God of Justice demands the abolishment of the customary tradition of the oppressive caste system and the restoration of the normative tradition of the rules of true righteousness. True faith in God, and the God of history and Justice, demands that the Church affirms human dignity and rights of the Dalits and be with them to restore the lost human values. True love of God demands that the church not only articulate Justice for the Dalit Christians, but also commits herself totally to abolishing the caste system, to eradicating injustice in the Church and Society and to creating a community ('*contrast community*') where equality and human dignity and rights prevail.[21]

1.4. Church the Prophetic Voice

The prophets did not just talk about justice on the theoretical formulation, but took effort to actualise the justice into the social practice at the city gate for the rights of human individuals whose rights were denied. In this pursuit, Amos proclaimed: '*Let Justice roll down like water, and righteousness like an ever-flowing stream*' (Amos 5:24). The God of the pre-exilic prophets was a morally infuriated

and ten thousand rivers of oil represented lavish sacrifice. One's first-born represents one's most valuable possession. R.L. Smith, *Micah-Malachi...*, 51.

19 R.L. Smith, *Micah – Malachi ...*, 51.

20 L. Stanislaus, *The Liberation Mission ...*, 322.

21 Ibid., 218-219.

God who hear the cries of the oppressed (Ex. 3:7-9; 22:23-27), who roars like a lion against the oppressors (Amos 3:8), rends like a wild beast (Hos. 13:7-8), slays and blasts like dynamite (Hos. 6:5; Is. 9:8). The prophets also speak of God as directly coming to judge the oppressors (Is. 3:12-15; Mic. 6:1-2; Hos. 5:1).

The prophets attack the unjust behaviour of rich people, legislators or judges, leaders. But the problem in Israel is beyond unjust conduct; there is also the development of a social order and an economic system that are structurally corrupted. The simple social order of a nomadic people gives way to one which is much more socially stratified. When the prophets condemn injustice, they are protesting against the whole socio-economic structure and not just against the individuals alone.[22] In the Old Testament, there is the presentation of two fundamental demands of the Covenant - worship[23] and Justice as inseparably united. Loyalty to the Lord must find concrete exercise in monotheistic worship and confession. Relation to the Lord must find actualization in just relationship with others. Both demands have the same roots: the love of the Lord for his chosen Israelites who he frees.[24]

The Church ought to be a '*cause of transformation*' of the liberative Gospel beyond the world clutches to realise the Kingdom values in its full sense here on earth. In the Old Testament God reveals Godself to human as the liberator of the oppressed and the defender of the poor, demanding from human faith in God and Justice towards human's neighbour. It is only in the observance of the duties of Justice that God is truly recognized as the liberator of the oppressed. M. Azariah states that unless there is deliberate focus on the most oppressed and worst of victims and vulnerable sections of Indian society, all our efforts for Justice and development of the least and the lowest sections of people would be totally diffused and become diversionary and ineffective like watering the Sahara desert.[25] This kind of holistic development/ enrichment cannot be achieved at once. It is an ongoing process to abolish the evil practice of the present condition of oppression and exploitation of the Dalits, Tribals, Adivasis, Women, Children and other groups.

---

22 Ibid., 214.

23 Worship is necessary for human, because it is the outward expression of true humility before God, of that humble trust which is essential. It is when worship ceases to be this that it is a hindrance and not a help; so long as it is the outcome of true and humble conscious devotion to God, it can and does strengthen those bonds which bind God and human together through Christ. Worship is also necessary because a human should be full of praise and thankfulness to God; but as soon as the aim of hymns and sons and music generally becomes aesthetic, it is the time to beware. R. L. Smith, *Micah – Malachi* ..., 51.

24 L. Stanislaus, *The Liberation Mission* ..., 214.

25 M. Azariah, *Mission in Christ's Way in India Today* (Madras: CLS, 1989), 73.

2. Unity of the Church(es)

The Justice and Unity go hand in hand in the biblical passages. When the justice is practised, the unity, oneness is maintained. If justice is not practiced then the whole concept of justice dichotomized, and disunity prevails. The Greek word for unity is ἑνότης (*henotes*), primarily mentioned in the Ephesians 4:3, *maintain the unity of the Spirit;* and in 4:13 *unity in the faith.*[26] The Greek root word εἷς, for unity means one, oneness, togetherness, one accord unity, etc. This kind of oneness goes back to the Old Testament concept that God as one and the only one. The monotheistic emphasis drawn from the Deuronomistic teachings could be seen very much in the Decalogue. The formula εἷς φεός "God is one" is the teaching of the *sh^ema* in Dt. 6:4 : יהוה אחד. There is no God beside him (Mk. 12:29, 32). In one God the origin and goal of the world, and in the one Christ history and Soteriological history, is unity.

This conception of εἷς (One), however, has significance in early Christianity. It resists all dualism and eliminates any either/or relationship between God and anti-god. Human can serve only one Lord (Mt. 6:24). It denotes the elemental and inviolable union, the ἑνοσις (*henosis* = unity) of married couples, and also points to a higher union with the Lord.[27] This thought is particularly pursued and worked out in Ephesians. The Unity of Church(es) is attained again only in Christ. The Church(es) is to bring unity to human, its own unity is a paramount consideration and it must remember the central guarantees of unity set in Christ.

2.1. Plurality of Unity (of Church/es)

The unity of the body of Christ, of course, leaves room for a multiplicity of local congregations that may, in accordance with New Testament usage, be called 'Churches,' but it excludes a plurality of rival and conflicting denominations that reject one another's doctrines, ministries, or sacraments. Almost since the beginnings, however, this dividedness has been the actual condition of Christianity. What is in theory abnormal has become in practice normal, and this anomaly calls for theological explanation. All major Christian traditions have had to grapple with the dilemma posed by the theological necessity of oneness and the factual context of division. This unity demands the wider oneness of the whole creation and with the pluralistic religious communities.

26 W.F. Arndt and F.W. Gingrich, *A Greek-English Lexicon of the New Testament and other Early Christian Literature* (Chicago: The University of Chicago Press, 1957), 267.

27 G. Kittel, (Ed.), *Theological Dictionary of the New Testament*, vol. II (Michigan: Wm. B. Eerdmans Publishing Company, 1976), 434-435.

2.2. Internal and External Pluralism

Pluralism[28] is already very great, perhaps too great in some of the Protestant Churches. The challenge of the Church is pluralistic in nature. It has the dimensions both within and outside. The pluralistic nature of the Church within is injustice, violation of human rights, corruption, discrimination on the basis of the caste, sex, wealth, social status, and power struggles etc. The pluralistic nature of a particular Church outside is regionalism, denominationalism, doctrinalism, traditionalism, egocentrism, authoritarianism, etc.[29] The early Christian church did not heed to these kinds of '*isms*' in its literal sense as the body of Christ.

2.3. A Possible Cause for the Disunity among Churches: A Study

2.3.1. Comity Principle[30]

This concept derived from the general principle that mission groups ought not to compete with one another. The method used to promote this concept was to make one organisation responsible for evangelism in a particular territory or among a particular people. Double occupancy of a region, with the exception of big cities, was to be avoided. Historically the term owes its origin to the late-nineteenth-century missionary conferences (for and by missionaries, with some nationals participating as guests) that took place first in Asia, and then in a less extensive fashion in parts of Africa and Latin America. The first such conference, the '*General Conference of Bengal Protestant Missionaries*,' took place in Calcutta in 1855, and was followed by numerous regional and national conferences over the next half century, leading up to the great World Missionary Conference in Edinburgh (1910). The establishment of the principle of comity in mission was one of the most outstanding results of these early conferences.

The need for *Comity* arose because missions entered many territories in a rather haphazard fashion, with frequent chaos and overlap. The resulting waste of limited resources was widely abhorred, as was the confusion caused to those newly receiving the gospel. Because the good stewardship of personnel and money was a universal ideal among the various societies, the principle of *Comity* quickly gained board acceptance. Verbal and personal agreements among missionaries became the order of the day, with missions agreeing not to open up work in areas where another mission was already established. This approach led mission historian R. Pierce Beaver called *'denominationalism by geography.'*

28 Pluralism here is not religious pluralism, but pluralism within the Church and among/between the Churches. It also means struggles and challenges both within and outside the Church for various reasons.

29 I Cor. 3:1-9.

30 A.S., Moreau, ed., *Evangelical Dictionary of World Missions* (Michigan: Baker Books, 2000), 212.

On the whole, the system worked well as long as people stayed where they were. However, as greater mobility for purposes of work and education became the norm, the system increasingly showed its limitations. Its chief legacy in evangelical missions' circles is in the courtesy and cooperation shown among agencies in discussing future plan and in not duplicating existing efforts.

2.3.2. The Consequence of the Comity Principle

The intention behind the comity principle was great on the basis of saving time, resources, energy and mutual understanding between the missionaries and mission boards both within the Country (India) and outside for the easy and faster proclamation of the gospel of Christ. When this principle reached at the post Independence era, the mobility of the people from one place to another and the emergence of the new Independent Indian Church which was trying to do mission work independently, the vulnerability of comity principle revealed in the form of the sectarianism, denominationalism, regionalism, etc., which resulted on the divisions among the Indian Christian Churches. This has become like fighting for territorial region in the colonial India. Probably this would have paved the way for the regionalism and the territorialism, etc., among/between the Churches. The original intention of the comity principle lost its essence in the long run when the Church underwent different stages and challenges. This kind of division widened in the minds of the Church rather than acceptance and unitarianism as the body of Christ.

2.4. The Church and The Churches

New Testament thinking of Church is neither individual nor collective, but organic.[31] The existence and reality of the Church derive only from the historical fact of Jesus. The Church is a fellowship with a common destiny standing under the νόμος Χριστοῦ (law of Christ). Each must intercede for and suffer with the others. (I Cor. 12:26; cf. Gal. 6:2; I Cor. 4:6). This unity of the Church does not imply uniformity. It is organic unity. Within it there are variations of the parts of the body of Christ rather than the differences on the basis of the rich and the poor, freemen and slaves, caste people and casteless people, etc. Indeed, the pneuma (*pneuma* = Spirit) in whom the Church has its unity manifests itself in a rich plurality of charismata (I Cor. 12:11ff.). This means that early Christianity knows only one saving event, the cross, and only one Church. But this is neither a national Church nor a universal Church; it is the Church of the nations.

3. Justice and Unity: Faith Issues and Theological Positioning

3.1. Practice of Justice in the Church(es)

The prophets of the Old Testament affirmed the faith in Yahweh that Yahweh is righteous demanding the people to practice justice in their every activities and

31 G. Kittel, *Theological Dictionary* ..., 435.

endeavours. Prophet Amos is known for calling the people to practice justice both in the religious life and social life. He vehemently opposed the offence of persecution, cruelty and exploitation through unjust ways of making money and living in splendour at the expense of others. He forcefully taught, '*seek good and not evil*; ... *hate evil and love good ... let justice roll down like waters, and righteousness like an ever-flowing stream.*' (Amos 5:14, 24).[32]

Justice needs to be applied with Gospel to any structures, systems and institutions of the society, where in all the human relationships are united together. Unfortunately, the Church the body of Christ also stained with inhuman, oppressive, exploitative system called caste which is totally against the Bible and its teachings. The injustice and violation of human dignity and human rights are evident in the life of the Dalits. The Dalit Christian too undergo double fold oppression, inhuman treatment, the society undermined their status as a human and being a Dalit Christian were neglected their right status in the Church.

3.2. The Task of the Church

The Church realizes her task and calls all people to discern and make a conscious effort to transform society from within. In each local community, social discriminatory practices, like unjust separation of places in the Church, separation according to caste in burial grounds, not allowing equal participation in pastoral councils, excluding Dalits in village feast celebrations, etc., have to be eliminated.[33] In the liberative process among Dalits, the Church needs to discern the community's needs, priorities, goals, world - view and offer the Gospel to its collective psyche. The role of the Church is to work out possible ways and means that the Gospel message becomes leaven in the community towards a social change towards liberation from every form of oppression.[34] The statement continues, we will become builders of peace by raising our voice against all forms of injustice and discrimination. This calls for the unity within the Church and among the Churches to meet the challenges ahead. To this reason the Churches ought to be United together to liberate the people with the liberative Gospel of Christ.

The oneness of God is foundational to humanity's (Church/es) oneness. The unity of humanity is in fact the goal of the whole redemptive process of the Gospel of Christ Jesus. '*Sin*' for Ignatius of Antioch was basically *division*. It was that lack of unity which made humanity so vulnerable to the forces of evil. The Churches are divided on the basis of denominationalism, regionalism, doctrinalism, sectarianism, authoritarianism, casteism and sexism etc. This even went up to brand Jesus Christ as a denominationalist, casteist, sexiest, etc. The Church(es) named their Church as: the name of the Church and then Christ the

32 J.R. Chandran, "Justice in Old Testament," in *Bible Speaks Today: Essays in Honour of Gnana Robinson* (Delhi: ISPCK, 2000), 34.

33 L. Stanislaus, *The Liberation Mission ...*, 326.

34 Ibid., 326.

Redeemer Church[35] This widens the gap between/among the Churches rather than uniting the Churches in the One of Christ Jesus.

The Comity principle was initiated with good intension to propagate the Gospel of Christ with limited resources and time. On the other hand this itself turned as a basis for the division among/between the Churches with denominationalistic and regionalistic differences. The Comity principle is an organic unity and not the justice based unity. The need of the hour calls the Church/es to join together as the members of the body of Christ, to come to a common platform where differences can be sort out with the spirit of Christ to build the Kingdom values here on earth with Justice, Unity, Peace prevails for the generations to come. Unity then, was the supreme gift of Christ Jesus each one's own limitations and acceptance. The goal and the responsibility of the Church should be therefore the unity of humanity with humbleness and servitude to the Church at large.

Conclusion

Church(es) as Servant: An Inclusive Community

The word שָׁרַת (*sharath*, vb. Pi.) in Hebrew means *'minister, serve.'* When the same word is used in Is. 61:6; and 56:6, it denotes 'of foreigners admitted to priesthood. So probably Samuel conceived as Priest in I Sam. 2:11; 3:1;[36] variant in 2:18 indicates Samuel's twofold function: on the one hand, he is consecrated to Yahweh (1:11); on the other, during his minority he is subordinate to the priest Eli (1:25-28).[37]

The theology of Trito - Isaiah includes the universal expectation that God will integrate all the people of the earth into his kingdom "and even chooses 'priests and Levites' from among them without the legitimation of priestly descent." Therefore Trito - Isaiah includes foreigners (Is. 56:6; 66:10) among God's future שָׁרַת servants. If they join themselves[38] (*nilwu*) to Yahweh to be his שָׁרַת servants, to love his name, to be his servants, to keep the Sabbaths and hold fast to the covenant, not only can they-like the eunuchs (Is. 56:3-5) become fully recognized members (proselytes) of the congregation of Israel, they can even become priests of the congregation (Is. vv. 6-8). This latter possibility is clear from the language of v. 6, which implies the usual marks of priest service.[39] But in the practical

35 For Example, TELC Holy Redeemer's Church, which indicates that the TELC has its own Redeemer and the other Churches have their own Redeemer.

36 F. Brown, S.R. Driver, C.A. Briggs, *A Hebrew and English Lexicon of the Old Testament* (Oxford: The Clarendon Press, 1968), 1058.

37 G.J. Botterweck, H. Ringgren, H.J. Fabry, ed., *Theological Dictionary of the Old Testament*, שָׁרַת, vol. XV (Michigan: Wm.B. Eerdmans Publishing Company), 507.

38 The root word is נִלְווּ, join, be joined (This word in Niphael verbal conjugation functions as a reflective, so, it can be translated as join themselves).

39 G.J. Botterweck, H. Ringgren and H.J. Fabry, שָׁרַת ..., 507.

Christian life still there is a discrimination on the basis of caste, gender, social status etc. which needs to be uprooted from the Church and social structure to liberate the church from the clutches of the caste oppression. God calls the people to serve irrespective of caste, gender and foreigners even to be the priest in the temple. It clearly indicates that God does not discriminate people on any basis. The instruction in Is. 56:1, '*keep justice and do righteousness*' implies conduct of ethical holiness. The Yahweh adhering foreigners did the right, and were therefore holy and righteous before God (Is. 5:16; 1:27). Yahweh redeems his people by his righteousness but expects them, as those who have joined him through the covenant, to show themselves to be holy through righteousness.[40]

The model of the Church(es) as a Servant, serves humankind precisely by looking to Jesus who revealed in the form Servant in the gospels. Only by acknowledging the sovereignty of God's word can the Church avoid an uncritical and unhealthy complacency. Only becoming a faithful servant of the Servant Lord can the Church effectively proclaim the good news of the Christian revelation. The term διακονια (*diakonia* = servant) is certainly one of the most important New Testament terms applied to the Church. The term applies to all types of ministry - including the ministry of the word, of sacraments, and of temporal help. All offices in the Church are forms of διακονια. The '*multi-faceted methodology*' which is pluralistic in its nature is relevant to the context of the Churches in India and the '*methodology of inclusio*' with the spirit of Christ must be found to overcome these inherited divisions, so that committed Christians in different denominational traditions may find each other once again in the same community of faith, dialogue and worship. Short of full reunion there may be many possibilities of mutual recognition, doctrinal accord, joint worship and practical co-operations. Thereby build the Kingdom of God here on earth which leads to the nation building.

J.R. Chandran once said that the Church is the presymbol of the miniature form of the Kingdom of God where we can practice all ethical/kingdom values. The Church, as servant of the Kingdom, would have a certain unity, holiness, catholicity, and apostolicity of its own. Its unity would be that of a team collaborating for the realization of the Kingdom. It would be holy insofar as it effectively dedicates itself to the realization of the Kingdom. Rather than the place where holiness is found, the Church would be seen as a catalyst of holiness in the larger human community. The servant Church would seek to break down estrangement and alienation, to reconcile human with themselves, with their brothers - sisters and with God. The servant role of the Church consists in its dedication to transformation of the world into the Kingdom.

In this transformative process, one can learn from the biblical example to live in co-existence with mutual understanding and appreciation of others (brothers and sisters) with Spirit of Christ. For example, one can take the quarrel narration

40 E. Mohol, E., *The Confessional Community of Isaiah 56-66* ..., 34.

in the Bible that is in Gen. 13:1ff. In this passage, there was a quarrel between Abram's herdsmen and Lot's herdsmen. Abram propose to settle the quarrel and says '... *for we are kindred (brothers)*' (Gen. 13:8). This kind of proposal for the settlement is not nobility or generosity of Abram, rather he takes this as his responsibility to settle the issue as a family. This model calls the Church(es) to take the responsibility to settle the quarrel of caste, gender and/or any form of discrimination within the Church and outside as a family issue, which will bring the Church(es) to come to a common platform to chart out any form of their differences with the Spirit of Christ and be a witnessing community here on this world. Then one can say courageously as Psalmist in 133:1 *"How very good and pleasant it is when kindred* (sisters and brothers) *dwell in unity!"* Thereby the Christian Church can partake in the nation building as P.D. Devanandhan once said: 'my faith constrains me to get involved in the activities of the nation building', as Proverbs states that Righteousness exalts a nation, but sin is a reproach to any people (Pro. 14:34). Martin Luther envisaged that the Justice and Righteousness must be emulated in the Church to have *faith* unity in the midst of the plurality of the Churches and in the pluralistic society to live as a witnessing community.

5

Missional Church
Tracing Roots in Martin Luther's Theology

K. David Udayakumar

'Missional Church' or 'Missional Ecclesiology' has been subject to extensive research and articulation in the last two decades. In his article "As the Father has sent me, I am sending you: Lesslie Newbigin's Missionary Ecclesiology" Michael W. Goheen[1] outlines important aspects of the missional ecclesiology of Lesslie Newbigin. And in another corresponding article[2] "The Missional Church: Ecclesiological discussion in the Gospel and Our Culture Network in North America" he outlines key aspects of the missional ecclesiology belonging to the heirs of Newbigin: the Gospel and Our Culture Network (GOCN). The focus of these two articles is on missional ecclesiology of Lesslie Newbigin whose missiology was largely formed by the mission theology that took shape within the International Missionary Council (IMC) conferences during 1950s and 1970s, the most significant of these conferences was Willingen, Germany in 1952. At Willingen, the conference recognized that the church could be neither the starting point nor the goal of mission. Central to Newbigin's understanding of mission is the work of the Triune God in calling and sending the church, empowered by the Spirit, into the world to participate fully in God's mission.

In this article an attempt is made to understand "missional ecclesiology" in the light of current discourses and see whether its origins can be traced in Reformation tradition. It is done in three parts – understanding the terminology "missional ecclesiology', then development of missional ecclesiology and finally tracing its origins in Reformation tradition.

---

1 Michael W. Goheen, "As the Father has sent me, I am sending you: Lesslie Newbigin's Missionary Ecclesiology," *International Review of Mission* 91 (2002): 345-369.

2 Michael W. Goheen, "The Missional Church: Ecclesiological discussion in the Gospel and Our Culture Network in North America," *Missiology: An International Review* 30/4 (2002), 479-490.

I. Understanding "Missional Church"

The concept of a "missional church" covers different aspect of a church's self-understanding and practices. In this section, which is divided into two sections; firstly let us try to understand the term "Missional" and secondly relate this term to "Missional Church".

Firstly, the root of the word 'missional' is the word mission. Mission is derived from the Latin word *missio,* which has the central meaning of 'being sent'. Mission scholars observe that 'missional' and '*missio Dei*' ('the mission of God') are intrinsically related. 'Missional' is an adjective. As an adjective, 'missional' is paired with and describes nouns. When the word 'missional' is used in an adjectival form then its meaning would be, of or relating to the Mission of the Triune God (*mission Dei*). It is God who is calling all His people and inviting them to participate in His mission.

In ordinary terminology 'missional' means that it is not assigned vocation of pastors and missionaries who are chosen to serve people on behalf of all God's people but it is the call of all Christians to actively live out a lifestyle through service to all people with a conscious decision to proclaim the Gospel through their lifestyle.

Secondly, all theological articulations contain a discussion about the nature of the Church. It is the discussion of what the Church is called to be and to do – its nature, its purpose, its hopes, its structure and practices.

It is Guder (1998) and his team who first attempted to club the word 'missional' to the word 'church' in a book – *Missional Church: A vision of sending of the church in North America* published in 1998· The writers of "Missional Church" were working as part of a project under the auspices of *The Gospel and Our Culture Network* (GOCN) in North America, an organisation set up to further the ideas of British missiologist Lesslie Newbigin, in particular his suggestion that the biggest challenge facing the church in the West was not the extension of Christianity around the world but the conversion of our own late modem, secularised, post-Christendom culture. For more than 150 years the church in the West had seen itself as a *sending* church; it now needed to see itself as a *sent* church. The word *missionary* is a portmanteau adjective applying to the many and various aspects of the entire mission endeavour of the church, whereas the word *missional* seeks to put the emphasis squarely on the *sentness* of the church. He himself puts it like this: "With the term missional we emphasise the essential nature and vocation of the church as God's called and sent people."[3]

According to those involved in the GOCN the term "missional" points to a paradigm shift: "The church of Jesus Christ is not the purpose or goal of the gospel, but rather its instrument and witness. Thus, our challenge today is to

---

3 G. Hill, *Salt, Light and a City: Introducing Missional Ecclesiology* (Eugene, OR: Wipf and Stock, 2012),171.; Darrell Guder, *Missional Church: A Vision for the Sending of the Church in North America* (Grand Rapids, MI: Eerdmans, 1998), 11.

move from church with mission to missional church."[4] For this Lois Barrett gives the following definition of a "missional church" when she states:

> *A missional church is a church that is shaped by participating in God's mission, which is to set things right in a broken, sinful world, to redeem it, and to restore it to what God has always intended for the world. Missional churches see themselves not so much sending, as being sent. A missional congregation lets God's mission permeate everything that the congregation does – from worship to witness to training members for discipleship. It bridges the gap between outreach and congregational life, since, in its life together, the church is to embody God's mission.*[5]

From the above mentioned observations we notice that missional church refers to basically calling of all believers to engage in God's mission.

II. Development of Missional Church

A. Roots of the Missional Church

Knud Jorgense[6] in his article "The Emergence and Challenge of the Missional Church Concept in the West" says the following regarding discussions that ultimately prompted for the development of "Missional Church-Concept:"

1. The Catholic Church in Latin America following the Second Vatican Council (1962-65), put much emphasis on the *base congregations* as the carriers of God's mission.
2. Within the World Council of Churches during the sixties in its study program on *The Missionary Structure of the Congregation* aired several interesting ideas were with regard to the identity of the church as missional and a need for new forms (e.g. house fellowships).
3. Within the evangelical context there was an increasing focus on *the local church* due to the influence from the church growth movement.

B. Beginning of Discussion on *Missional Church*

1. But the idea of *missional church*, itself came out of *The Gospel and Our Culture network,* inspired by Leslie Newbigin, which was initially established in England in 1989, and was soon exported to North America.
2. It was the American *Gospel and Our Culture Network* that created and popularised the term *missional church*. This is particularly evident in the *book Missional Church. A Vision for the Sending of the Church in North*

---

4 Guder, *Missional Church…*, 5f.

5 Lois Y. Barrett ed., *Treasure in Clay Jars: Patterns in Missional Faithfulness* (Grand Rapids: Eerdmans, 2004), x.

6 Jorgense Knud, "The Emergence and Challenge of the Missional Church Concept in the West," *Swedish Missiological Themes,* 92/4 (2004): 53-55.

America. This book was the result of a three-year study project aiming at analyzing the situation of the American church and at defining its challenges within a mission context. Here, *missional* is defined in order to underline "the essential nature and vocation of the church as God's called and sent people."[7] With the neologism "missional church" a paradigm shift is named, which breaks with the traditional understanding of mission as an church enterprise among others and focuses on mission as the *esse* not only *beneesse* of church.

3. Guder, raises the issue of the conversion of the church in another book, *The Continuing Conversion of the Church.* This conversion is related to re-thinking theology, evangelization, worship, leadership and structures. Most importantly, it demands undertaking measures against the *gospel reductionism* within the church: The early church went from movement to becoming an institution, Constantine's church replaced the understanding of the gospel as an event with the formulation of a defined faith system consisting of truths; the Kingdom of God was conceived as the eternity that awaits a Christian after death; salvation was given to the individual by the church, in particular through the sacraments. On the basis of these gospel reductions, the organizational structure of the church was transformed into state religion and the administrator of religious meaning in the society.[8] Likewise, according to Guder, the reformation and pietism have reduced the gospel to a matter of salvation for the individual: "The benefits of salvation are separated from the reason for which we receive God's grace in Christ: to empower us as God's people to become Christ's witnesses. This fundamental dichotomy between the benefits of the gospel and the mission of the gospel constitutes the most profound reductionism of the gospel."[9] Salvation is not for our own benefit, but to make us witnesses.
4. Another central network, also inspired by Newbigin, is an international research project *A Missiology of Western Culture,* established in 1992. Out of this research project came a number of small books from 1995 and onwards. The aim of these was to investigate the challenges and developments of the Western culture, in order to raise the awareness within the church of its missional obligations in a bewildered culture.
5. Also within the World Council of Churches there has been an interest in issues related to *Gospel and Culture.* A study process within the member churches was initiated, and *Gospel and Cultures* was the topic for mission conference in Brazil in 1996.
6. Within the evangelical context the issue has appeared increasingly often, especially within the World Evangelical Alliance, where the theme has been

7 Guder, *Missional Church...*, 11.

8 Darrell Guder, *Continuing Conversion of the Church* (Grand Rapids, 2000), 103ff.

9 Ibid., 120.

made the topic for a study project, which was discussed at a consultation in Singapore in 2004.

7. Continental Europe has been more reluctant with regard to Newbigin's ideas; his pessimism about the Enlightenment and Western culture might account for this. It has been argued that it is not constructive to wish that the Enlightenment had never taken place. The contrast between modernity and post modernity may sometimes have been painted in terms that are too dualistic in the Anglo-Saxon world. Still, the issue has also been taken seriously in Europe, but the point of departure on the Continent has been *missio dei* rather than *missional church.*

C. Four Distinctive Marks of *Missional Church*

In his book *The Missional Church in Perspective: Mapping Trends and Shaping the Conversation*, Craig Van Gelder (2010) suggests the following four theological distinctives that mark missional churches

1. God is a missionary God who sends the church into the world. This sending is rooted in the sending by the Father of the Son and the sending by the Father and the Son of the Spirit. The church should not be seen as having a missions program or component. Instead, God's mission has a church. The church in its core identity is simultaneously sent and sending.
2. God's mission in the world is related to the reign (kingdom) of God. This reign encompasses all that God has planned since the beginning for extending his rule through human beings to the entire earth.
3. The missional church is an incarnational (versus attractional) ministry sent to engage a postmodern, post-Christendom, globalized context. In its many global and glocal expressions, the church engages its context incarnationally and contextually.
4. The internal life of the missional church focuses on every believer living as a disciple engaging in mission. The church is not only the gathered church but is also the scattered church, infiltrating every sphere of society, every geographic and economic location in a community, and every node and network in an interconnected world.

D. Missional Church in the Mission Document of the Lutheran World Federation

From a Lutheran perspective in the mission document of the Lutheran World Federation "*Mission in Context: Transformation, Reconciliation, Empowerment. An LWF contribution to the understanding and practice of mission*", the term 'missional' is used "to denote mission as pertaining to the *being* of the church, while 'missionary' is reserved to describe mission as the *action* of the church." It also states that "for a missional church, participating in God's mission is at the core of its nature as a church."[10]

This comprehensive Lutheran understanding of the missional church results from a history of different paradigms. Péri Rasolondraibe, former director of the LWF Department for Mission and Development, has distinguished the following ones:[11]

i. *The church without mission.* The Lutheran church of the sixteenth and seventeenth centuries not only saw mission as a function of the state but also was so preoccupied with self-justification that it was unable to carry out mission.

ii. *Mission without the church.* In the eighteenth and nineteenth centuries, mission took place through revival movements, apart from the institutionalized mainline churches.

iii. *From Missionary church to the church in mission.* In the second half of the twentieth century, ecclesiology and mission were brought together, and the church began to understand itself as "God's people, created and empowered by the word, fed at the Lord's table, and sent and led by the Holy Spirit to participate in God's mission in the world.

E. A Clarity in Understanding Missional Church

Roxburgh and Boren laid out the following eight trends[12] in the missional conversation that creates confusion in trying to illustrate what missional church is.

1. Missional church is not a label to describe churches that emphasises cross-cultural missions. While cross-cultural missions are important, the missional church conversation is not about missions as traditionally understood.
2. Missional church is not a label used to describe churches that are using outreach programs to be focused externally. Because the term missional means "being sent," people assume that the missional church is focused on outreach. The church has long used this language of inside/outside that divides its life into internally and externally focused segments. The assumption is that the way insiders' minister to outsiders is by doing something for the outsiders through programs or mission.
3. Missional church is not a label for church growth and church effectiveness. Being missional is not about getting people to a building.

10 Geneva, LWF 2004.

11 Peri Rasolondraibe, "Eccsiology and Mission: A Lutheran Perspective," in *International Review of Missions*, XC/358 (2001):331-333.

12 A.J. Roxburg, *Introducing the missional church: What it is, why it matters, how to become one* (Grand Rapids, MI: Baker Publishing House, 2009), 31-34.

4. Missional church is not a label for churches that are effective at evangelism. While missional church does not want to diminish the importance of individuals choosing to trust Jesus as Lord, the common perspective of evangelism can lead people to misapply what it means to be missional.
5. Missional church is not a label to describe churches that have developed a clear mission statement with a vision and purpose for their existence.
6. Missional church move beyond relevance and concern themselves with how they are engaging and relating to the surrounding culture in everyday life.
7. Missional church is not a label that points to a primitive or ancient way of being a church.
8. Missional church is not a label describing new formats of church that reach people who have no interest in traditional churches. Being missional is more than being postmodern attractional.

III. Missional Paradigm of the Protestant Reformation

David J Bosch (1991) identifies Romans 1:16-17 "For I am not ashamed of the gospel; it is the power of God for salvation to everyone who has faith, to the Jew first and also to the Greek. For in it the righteousness of God is revealed through faith for faith; as it is written, "The one who is righteous will live by faith." as the paradigmatic text that embodies the Protestant Reformation.

Martin Luther's rediscovery of this truth was a guiding light of light in the obscure *soteriology* of the time. It's not that justification by faith was completely absent from Roman Catholic theology, but it was obscured by auxiliary stipulations-charity, self-mortification, good works.

The main emphasis on justification by faith points towards an urgent motive for involvement in mission.

A. Ecclesiology in Lutheran Tradition

For an understanding on ecclesiology Lutherans refer to the Augsburg Confession (AC) (Augsburg Confession 1530). Article VII of the AC presents a peculiar understanding of the church: "*The Church is the congregation of saints, in which the Gospel is rightly taught and the Sacraments are rightly administered.*"

Given the historical context of the Augsburg Confession, the emphasis is placed on *what God does* rather than on *what the church does*. What guarantees the being of the church in time is God's gracious self-giving action in word and sacraments, which creates and sustains a living faith; the faith that bears fruits, viz. good works (AC VI, XX).[13]

13 The emphasis on what God does is congruent with the main concern of the AC, namely, justification of the sinner by grace through faith in Jesus Christ. The perdurable question, however, has been the relation of that justification to the life and work of the church in society.

Luther's doctrine of the church, in its concise formulation, is shaped by two formative elements, the Word and the sacraments. These form the marks of the church as expressed in the Augsburg Confession of 1530, article VII of which reads as follows: "*The Church is the congregation of saints, in which the Gospel is rightly taught and the Sacraments are rightly administered.*"

Mission, as churches came to speak of it later, is not explicit in the entire Confession. It has been argued that the Lutheran reformers did not speak of mission as a function of the church. Thus, the move from a church without mission to mission without the (established) church took place. Granted, in that period, mission was understood mainly as foreign mission aimed at the conversion of pagans into Christians.

B. Martin Luther a Mission Theologian?

Historically, ever since Gustav Warneck's (the founding father of modern missiology) stinging critique of Martin Luther for lacking a theology and awareness of mission, scholars came to the conclusion that Lutheran theology provides no real resources for a contemporary, relevant Christian missiology and engagement with the world religions and religious pluralism. David Bosch agreed with the main thrust of Warneck's critique of Luther, claiming: "We miss in the Reformation not only missionary action 'but even the idea of missions, in the sense in which we understand them today."[14]

In contrast to Warneck's pessimistic assessment of Luther's theology as James Scherer contends "For Luther, mission is always pre-eminently the work of the triune God – Missio Dei – and its goal and outcome is the coming of the kingdom of God.... [T]he rich but untested potential of Luther and the Reformation for mission practice comes down to the present, not as definitive guidance, but certainly as inspiration and challenge for missiology today."

Mission scholars state that Luther saw Sixteenth Century Europe as a mission field, God's mission field. With his reformation came the realization that a mission field is any place where people trust 'other' gospels, that is, gospels clearly different from the gospel of Jesus Christ as found in the New Testament.

Primarily, Luther's theological thinking is 'Trinitarian' and at the same time "Christ-centred'. In his theological structure, God the Creator is the important starting point. The world and all people are His creatures. The Creator's hand, power, and care extend to the evil and the good, Gentiles, Jews, and Christians as well.

The use of terms like sanctification has robbed mission of its depth (the focus is on individuals performing their tasks at their stations) and its width (with a concentration on individual vocation and not on the calling of the congregation of saints to witness in the world).

14 David Bosch, *Transforming Mission: Paradigm Shifts in the Theology of Mission* (Maryknoll, NY: Orbis Books, 1991), 216.

Luther's missiology has to be seen in the context mentioned above. God's plan of salvation and mission belong firmly together. The activities of churches and missions are important, but what God has done occupies a central place. God does not reject any individual, but gives her/him his righteousness and salvation.

In light of the *missio Dei* (mission of God), the Church's mission needs to be properly understood, in terms of its distinctive shape, content, and emphases? While constructing a confessional Lutheran missiology we need to look into following resources from the Luther's theology:

- *the gospel as promise*
- *the law/gospel distinction*
- *a theology of grace as promise of mercy fulfilled*
- *a theology of the cross utilizing the hiddenness of God*
- *eschatological phenomenon*

The law of God as accusing, yet connecting humanity to its Creator; the gospel as the comforting promise of vulnerable, loving mercy, and the hiddenness of God as elusively mystifying form the overarching framework within which a contemporary Lutheran missiology seeks to engage the religious other by dialectically relating gospel proclamation and dialogue. Finally the Reign of God, should be seen as a present reality, but from an eschatological perspective.

C. Some Important Features of Missional Church as it Appear in Lutheran Mission Theology?

1. Missional Church is about Actively Participating in the *missio Dei.*

Many times we wrongly assume that the primary activity of God is in the church, rather than recognizing that God's primary activity is in the world, and the church is God's instrument sent into the world to participate in His redemptive mission. This was the thrust of Martin Luther's theology.

This key distinction clarifies the difference between a church with a missions programme and a missional church. A church with a missions programme usually sees missions as one activity alongside many other equally important programmes of the church. A missional church, on the other hand, focuses all of its activities around its participation in God's agenda for the world. God's mission must form and inform everything we do. All activities of the church must be catalyzed by and organized around the *missio Dei.*

As a sent the missional church understands its fundamental purpose as being rooted in God's mission to restore and heal creation and to call people into a reconciled relationship with Himself. It is God's mission that calls the church into existence. In other words, we can no longer see the church as the starting point when thinking about mission. Instead, the church must be seen as the result of God's mission. In the words of David Bosch (1993): "It is not the church which undertakes mission; it is the *missio Dei* which constitutes the church." Or stated in a slightly different manner; "it is not so much that God has a mission for his church in the world, but that God has a church for his mission in the world."[15]

2. Missional Church is about the Missionary Nature of God and His Church.

Martin Luther's theology focussed on missionary nature of the church and the Church. He recognized that both God and the church are intrinsically and principally 'missionary' in nature. God is a missionary God who sends a missionary church. In fact, a survey of the term 'sending' in its various forms in Scripture reveals the missionary nature of the Triune God, as well as the very essence of the church. The redemptive activity of God, his relationship to the world, and his dealing with humankind is described in Scripture by the word 'sending'.

3. Missional Church is about Incarnational Ministry in a Post-Christendom Context.

Missional churches see their primary function as one of actively moving into a community to embody and enflesh the word, deed, and life of Jesus into every corner and area. Alan Hirsch speaks of the 'missional-incarnational impulse', where the word 'missional' expresses the sending nature of the church, while 'incarnational' represents the 'embedding' of the gospel into a local context. In other words, 'missional' speaks to our direction – we are sent; while being 'incarnational' is more about *how* we go, and *what* we do as we go.

The *priesthood of the believers* has been central to Lutheran tradition since the reformation has profound implications for the missional church. Darrel Guder writes, "... we have forgotten how to read the New Testament as it was intended to be read, as equipping of God's people for mission."[16]

Those with a missional perspective no longer see the church service as the primary connecting point for those outside the church. While there is nothing wrong with attracting people to participate in various meetings of the church, the missional church is more concerned about sending the people of the church out among the people of the world, rather than getting the people of the world in among the people of the church. Some have described this missional-attractional distinction as a challenge to "go and be" as opposed to "come and see."[17]

15 Christopher J. H. Wright, *Mission of God*: Unlocking the Bible's Grand Narrative (Downers Grove, IL: IVP Academic, 2006), 62.

16 Guder, *Continuing Conversion...*, 118.

17 Centripetal and Centrifugal aspect of mission.

4. The Missional Functioning of the Priesthood of all Believers

The missional mandate considers how to strengthen the missional aspects of the training and formation of every member of the church.[18] The priesthood of believers are by their baptism commissioned 'to proclaim God's marvellous acts' to the world.[19] The 'gifts' and the laity both function within a community to build up the body of Christ. In the missional model, the function of the 'gifts' is to equip the laity so that they can fulfil their calling both within and outside of the church. The biblical image of the body of Christ is an image of the missional ecclesia which has a networking nature (Eph 4:12).[20] Wright writes about the gifts that 'he may well be referring to the wider apostolic (missionary) role, especially in planting and nurturing churches in the first place,'[21] but this view identifies the gifts exclusively with missions. In the missional church, the emphasis is not upon missions but being an incarnated missional presence.

Conclusion

Though the concept '*Missional Church*' is relatively new, we could find its salient features in the theology of Martin Luther, though not clearly articulated. The '*missional Church*' development could also be found in the Roman Catholic Church, after the Vatican II Council. It was predominantly discussed by the ecumenicals and evangelicals. Though the European continent had reservations about the concept, but they were not opposed to *mission Dei.*

In his book Guder writes:

> Therefore, the Church's own mission must take its cues from the way God's mission unfolded in the sending of Jesus into the world for its salvation. In Jesus' way of carrying out God's mission, we discover that the church is to represent God's reign as its community, its servant, and its messenger.[22]

This understanding of the church as representing the reign of God is helpful in that it sees mission in a holistic way. With regard to the church representing the reign of God as its servant, the team writes:

> Our responses of compassion and service, like our actions for peace and justice are deeds of authority and therefore signs that the reign of God is present now in our world and is on the way as its future... Whatever our responses may be, they bring wholeness and dignity to

---

18 D. Balia and K. Kim, *Witnessing to Christ Today.* Regnum Edinburgh Centenary Series, vol. 11 (Oxford: Regnum Books International, 2010), 266.

19 Cf. Balia and Kim, *Witnessing to Christ Today*..., 26.

20 Cf. Balia & Kim, *Witnessing to Christ Today*..., 30.

21 Balia and Kim, *Witnessing to Christ Today*..., 216.

22 Guder, *Missional Church*..., 102.

the world and thereby provide a taste of a future in the reign of God under the rule and authority of Christ's lordship. These are signs that invite people to "enter and taste more, to eat and be full.[23]

Final remarks on Missional Church

- ❖ A missional church is a church that is shaped by participating in God's mission, which is to set things right in a broken, sinful world, to redeem it, and to restore it to what God has always intended for the world.
- ❖ A missional congregation lets God's mission permeate everything that the congregation does – from worship to witness to training members for discipleship.
- ❖ Missional churches see themselves not so much sending, as being sent.
- ❖ With the neologism "missional church" a paradigm shift is named, which breaks with the traditional understanding of mission as an church enterprise among others and focuses on mission as the *esse* not only *beneesse* of church.
- ❖ Conversion of the church: it demands undertaking measures against the *gospel reductionism* within the church.
- ❖ God's mission in the world is related to the reign (kingdom) of God
- ❖ The missional church is an incarnational ministry sent to engage a postmodern, post-Christendom, globalized context.
- ❖ The church is not only the gathered church but is also the scattered church, infiltrating every sphere of society, every geographic and economic location in a community, and every corner and place in an interconnected world for a missional church, participating in God's mission is at the core of its nature as a church
- ❖ To talk about the priesthood of all believers was to reintroduce the idea of every Christian having a calling and a responsibility to serve God, to be actively involved in God's work in the world, and thus to break with the concept of "ordinary" believers being mere 'minors' and immature 'objects' of the church's ministry.
- ❖ With Martin Luther's reformation came the realization that a mission field is any place where people are trusting "other" gospels, that is, gospels clearly different from the Christ-gospel proclaimed in the New Testament scriptures.

Key Concepts that Influenced Missional Church had its Roots in Luther's Theology:

1. *Trinitarian missiology:* We must start with the Trinity in order to understand mission, for Trinity introduces us to a sending God who is a missionary God.

---

23 Guder, *Missional Church…*, 106.

2. *Missio Dei:* The emergence of this conception of the mission of God reframes our understanding of mission from being church-centric to becoming theocentric, a view articulated especially by Newbigin.
3. *Reign (kingdom) of God:* The message of Jesus is cantered on the reign of God, which must be understood as both already and not yet.
4. Church's missionary nature: God is a missionary God, and God's mission involves a church sent into the world to represent the reign (kingdom) of God. Thus the church is missionary by nature.
5. *Missional hermeneutic:* It is necessary to use a missional hermeneutic to read Scripture in order to understand the full intent of God's mission.

6

A Missiological Reading of the Women in Reformation in Light of the Women in the Bible

Rebecca Azariah

Introduction

The Reformation involved not only influential people like Martin Luther, John Calvin and Zwingli but also involved women who through their commitment, faithfulness and courage played important roles in the Reformation. The women were called by God to various vocations in which they were able to serve the home, society and church[1] through the Christian virtues of love, tenderness, sharing of goods, self-effacement, humility, reconciliation, compassion and bearing of one another's burdens[2] carried on their mission of expressing their faith through varied paradigms.

This Paper attempts to highlight the role of women and the varied mission paradigms involved by these women in fulfilling their priesthood in the Missio Dei.

Priesthood of All Believers

This was one of the cardinal principles of the Reformation.[3] Martin Luther argued that all who belong to Christ through faith, baptism and the Gospel[4] shared in the priesthood of Jesus Christ and truly belonged to the spiritual estate.[5] It is a call to ministry and service; to be a witness in the world, the world for which

1 http://lutheranReformation.org/history/faithful-women-Reformation

2 Roland H. Bainton, *Women of the Reformation: In Germany and Italy* (Minneapolis: Augsburg Publishing House, 1971), 9.

3 Walter Altmann, *Luther and Liberation* (Minneapolis: Fortress Press, 1992), 47.

4 I Corinthians 12:12-13, Paul says that we are all one body, yet every member has its own work by which it serves the others. This is because we all have one baptism, one gospel, one faith and is all Christians alike.

5 It is an invention that Pope, Bishop, priests and Monks are called the Spiritual Estate.

Christ died.[6] Luther emphasizes the Christian's authority to come before God on behalf of the brethren and the world. In a community of saints, God has so tempered the body that we are all priests[7] to each other. We stand before God and intercede for one another, we proclaim God's Word to one another and we celebrate His presence among us in worship, praise and fellowship.[8] This included the women also. Luther taught that God has created men and women to be equal and that the Holy Spirit came to men and women equally through baptism.[9] Thus this understanding of the priesthood of all believers expresses the equality of all believers and their equal right and responsibility to serve God.

Role of Women in the Reformation

During the Middle ages the reformers gave rise to the idea that it is not only the nun, monk and priest who are in celibacy have a 'Higher calling' but also the married and those in parenthood also have a worthy calling.[10] This was so because down the centuries the church understood the purpose of marriage as reproduction and providing as acceptable outlet for sexual desire but the reformers gave a fresh understanding of loving faithful companionship. Reformation recognized and celebrated the value of women status as wives and mothers.[11] They also provided women an opportunity to receive education (through the established schools where they were geared with skills toward reading the Bible, managing a household and teaching the faith to their children[12]), exercise leadership and be a supportive community.[13] Thus, women of the Reformation played a significant role not only in society but also in the church.[14] They had many roles but this paper attempts to highlight few important roles played by these women in a very significant way.

6 http://www.firstthings.com/web-exclusives/2016/10/the-priesthood-of-all-believers by Timothy George.

7 St. Peter in I Peter 2:9 says, 'You are a royal priesthood and a holy nation.' The Apocalypse says," Thou has made us to priests and kings by thy blood" (Rev. 5:9-10).

8 Altmann, *Luther and Liberation*..., 47.

9 http://faithmatters.us/women-in-the-protestant-reform

10 http://faithmatters.us/women-in-the-protestant-reform

11 Bainton, *Women of the Reformation* ..., 10.

12 www.livinglutheran.org/2015/09/women.Reformation/ Women and the Reformation: Then & Now.

13 Baiton, *Women of the Reformation* ..., 11.

14 Church is namely, holy believers and sheep who hear the voice of their Shepherd. "The Smalcald Articles," in *The Book of Concord*, 315. For Luther these two elements enter into the definition of church: the congregation of believers and the Word of God. Altmann, *Luther and Liberation*, 61. Firstly the church was originally and fundamentally the community of those who shared faith in Christ. Where there was only one baptism, only one gospel, only one people, all equally Christians and all equally priests. Secondly the church is brought forth and shaped by the Word of God. Where the Word of God is, there the church is.

1. Discerning the Will of God

Our lives on this planet are brief and therefore we ought to acknowledge God and His desires in our lives. God created us and redeemed us. We therefore have an obligation to fulfill His will as His workmanship and His children. Like Jesus, our spiritual food should be to do the Will of Him who has called us "out of darkness into His marvellous light". God loves us and desires what is best for us; since His will for our lives is "good and acceptable and perfect". God's will involve our obligation to others. God has entrusted each of us with the stewardship of a unique sphere of influence. We as ambassadors of Christ touch the lives of believers and unbelievers.[15]

a. Mission of Providence

Women all through the centuries are involved in the mission of providence. In Numbers 27:1-11 we read about the daughters of Zelophehad whose names were Mahlah, Noah, Hoglah, Milcah and Tirazah. The faith of the five women possessed to the promised inheritance. The sisters wanted to provide a land for the family. Since their father did not have a male child the young women came forward to write a new chapter in the history with courage and determination. And they were successful through their faith in God they promulgated a new and permanent law to secure inheritance for any daughter.[16] Just as these young women the women in the Reformation also wrote new chapters in the lives and families of the Reformers. They were able to be successful because these women discerned God's will at every stage of life. Martin Luther who was not that interested in marriage gave heed to his decision on hearing the words of Katherina Von Bora of her willingness to marry him.[17] Katherina is best known of all women of the Reformation. She was born in 1499 and her marriage to Luther brought many changes in the life of the couple. They began to live in love and harmony. She provided for a family by being the mistress of a household, a hostel and a hospital. Luther as a professor had a salary but it was inadequate. Katherina as the daughters of Zelophedad stood for her family, Katherina herded, milked and slaughtered the cattle made butter, cheese, brewed, planted and reaped.[18] She provided for a large household of babies, children, students, guests, refugees and servants. She resolved to make the household self-sustaining. She did some remodeling in the Black cloister with a bath, laundry and brewery.[19] It also carried with it a small garden yielding peas, beans, turnips, cabbage, lettuce, cucumbers and melons. An orchard was developed which supplied cherries, pears, apples,

15 http://bible.org/article/discerning-will-God

16 Fausset, A. R., *Bible Dictionary* (Grand Rapids: Zondervan Publishing House, 1966).

17 Bainton, *Women of the Reformation* ..., 24.

18 Ibid., 32.

19 Ibid., 33.

peaches, nuts, grapes, mulberries and figs. Her livestock included eight pigs, five cows, nine calves besides chicken, pigeons, and geese.[20] Katherina emerges as a woman of character and courage, sensible, non-sentimental, hard-headed, tender, determined and usually right.[21]

b. Mission of Protection

Women by nature are involved in the mission of protection. Esther was the queen of king Ahasuerus. She was a Jewish captive but because of her beauty she found favour in the eyes of the king. She was exalted to this position during the time when the Jews were to be destroyed. But Esther gained courage and determined to protect the Jews. In Esther 8:1-17 we read Esther discerned that she had to protect her people. She did it cleverly and meticulously. She took the risk and thus saved the Jews from being destroyed. The same spirit of Esther we see in the women in the Reformation, they through their courage and determination were protecting their family as well as the people of the land. Katharina protected her husband Luther when he was depressed and sick through ways of love and care. Katherina Zell protected her husband who was excommunicated from the church because of his marriage to her. As it was a claim that the priests should not marry, she stood a vigorous defense using the scriptures and strong wit of clerical marriage and denounced the celibate priest. The Church according to Luther was a place of healing. He frequently admonished the community to love those in need and to protect the vulnerable.[22] According to I Cor. 12, there is a mutual responsibility of the members of the Christian community as the Body of Christ. Thus in this the church as an instrument in precariousness and in love fights the battles of evil.[23] The church becomes the place of healing. That's what Esther did to Jews and also Katherina Zell in Strasbourg. She protected the church when the secessionists threatened to split the reformed community. She along with Zell acknowledged Christ as the true Son of God and the sole Saviour of the humankind.[24]

2. Relying on the Word of God the Bible

The Word of God is the central revelation for all believers. The Word of God not only teaches us the way of Salvation but also guides us in a way we should live as God's children. "Thy Word is a lamp to my feet and a light to my path." God designed His Word to equip us to accomplish "every good work" that is, to fulfill his purposes for our lives. Bible is of fundamental significance to Luther (Sola Scriptura) and its study led to his personal liberation, his rediscovery of the gospel and for the work of Reformation.

---

20 Ibid., 33.

21 Ibid., 42.

22 Altmann, *Luther and Liberation*..., 65.

23 Altmann, *Luther and Liberation*..., 65.

24 Baiton, *Women of the Reformation* ..., 65.

a. Mission as Conversion

Mary was a humble young woman from Nazareth. The place was a small town in the middle of nowhere. No significant people lived here. Mary was betrothed to Joseph who was of the house of David. In Luke 1:28 we read Mary was praised by the Angel of God, at which she was troubled but yet she believed and had faith in the Word of God which we can see in Lk 1:47-55 where Mary offers praises to God which is filled with scriptural truths from the Old Testament. Mary gave birth to Jesus the Immanuel (Matt 1:23). In the Sixteenth Century Martin Luther through his doctrines on *Sola Fide, Sola Gratia, Sola Scriptura* and *Solus Christus* gave birth to faith in different individuals. The Reformation led to conversions of different people in various arenas. Elizabeth Cruciger was a nun had faith in Christ through the writings of Martin Luther. She was a Lutheran woman hymn writer and poet. Elizabeth of Brunswick was an instrument after her conversion to Christ in establishment of the Lutheran Church in Lower Saxony. Ursula Von Munsterberg was an instrument in having Luther's writings for the Nuns to read. Through this act of hers many of the nuns left monasteries and followed the teachings of Luther.[25]

b. Mission of Intercession

As Christians we have the privilege to intercede for others. In Mark 7:25-29 we read of the Syro-Phoenician woman from the Gentile territory. She approached Jesus for a help for her daughter. She was a mother with a desperate need. Through her faith in God and persistence her daughter was healed. Katherina Zell was a woman of the Word; she trusted God's Word and devoted her life to encouraging others in their faith and in a consistent and faithful understanding of the Scripture. Because of faith in the Word of God she was able to pray for others, she wrote letter to the suffering women of the community of Kentzingen, who believe in Christ, encouraging them to stand firm in their suffering for Christ's sake. The letter was full of exhortations and encouragements from the Word of God. She also wrote hymns and songs. These women were the representation of the people in the presence of God where they carried on their privilege and duty of all believers to pray for one another in the name of Jesus Christ.

3. Proclaiming the Good Works of God

a. Mission as Witnessing

Witness is the key aspect in the life of a Christian. It points the way to God. The ultimate aim is to make known God to all people and nations so that they may have an opportunity to enjoy fullness of life as God intended. We are a part of respective nations and are a sign of God's goodness to the native land, people and culture. In Numbers 15:20-21 we read of Miriam, one among the leaders of the

25 http://lutheranReformation.org/history/faithful-women-Reformation

Hebrew women. Her leadership was seen through her example. After crossing the Red Sea, Miriam stood as a witness. She proclaims the wonderful deeds of God. She took the tambourine and danced. Her song says that women are important and have a role to play in the salvation which God provides. Women in Reformation were living witness of the Protestant faith. They responded to the Word of God. The teachings reached through worship, sermons, hymns, art, renewed religious practices, books, pamphlets, personal contacts and table conversations. They witnessed their faith through their homes and domestic vocations. Their calls often included as managers of parsonages that became centers of cultural life as well as gathering place for many religious events. A few women witnessed through their writings namely, Olimpia Morata an Italian Classicist and a confessing Protestant through her amazing writing, explicit passion for learning and her confident in her understanding of the Word and God pursued her religious duty to encourage and teach other women to right living and spreading Christianity. Argula Von Grumbach rooted her confession on the principle 'sola scriptura' and her thorough knowledge of the scripture made her to write truth statements. Katherina Zell, a powerful writer and a voice in her context in Strasbourg served the church with her charitable acts, as well as her many pastoral writings including a hymnbook for catechetical and lay proclamation purposes.

b. Mission as Service

In Mark 10:45, we read that 'The Son of Man came not to be served but to serve.' Service is an important component of Christian mission. Mark 1:29-31 talks about the healing of Peter's Mother in law. She was sick. Jesus came took her by her hand and she was healed. After her healing she began to serve Jesus. Serving can take various forms making a delicious meal, caring, sharing, encouraging, supporting financially etc. The women in Reformation served God through various ways. They had been limited in religious sphere but in the family and society they had a lot to contribute through their service. They were included in the priesthood of all believers as they excercised their faith through their actions. Katherina Von Bora ministered to her husband's diseases and depressions. She had a great skill with diet, herbs, poultices, and massage. She also served to the children at the Augustinian Cloister, the refugees who stayed there, and also to her maid servants. Katherina Zell involved herself in service to ministers who were forced to leave Kensingen and fled to Strasbourg, she fed them with food and arranged for their stay. She also ministered to their wives who were left behind in Kensingen to stand firm in their faith through the bible verses.

Implications for Women Today

The Reformation brought about some changes for women. Based on the Word of God, the issue of inequality between men and women socially and spiritually was discussed, the Reformers largely held to the notion that men and women were spiritually equal. Seeds for social and spiritual change were sown during this period, but it must be admitted that there was not as much development as some may allege.[26]

Inequality still exists today though women have overcome; the churches are still patriarchal in their thinking. The reformers teaching speak to us today though women were silenced during Reformation but it has paved the way for women to be in various spheres of ministry such as preaching, teaching etc. Reformation was the grounds for some women to speak; even those who acknowledged the categories of subordination found within the theology of the Reformers. Others spoke up due to the wielding of Reformation theology against Roman Catholicism. Still others felt that sola scriptura had led them to discover real, biblical grounds for women to teach. The Reformers' teaching on "priesthood of all believers" sowed the seeds for greater gender equality.[27]

Let us be challenged through these women who serve as living testimony of the gospel that continues to create faith and transform lives even after 500 years of Reformation. The powerful message of God's grace through faith in Jesus Christ is a life giving treasure that we are called to share.[28] The Presiding Bishop of ELCA, Bp. Elizabeth A. Eaton reminds us: "We are church…., we are church together, and we are church for the sake of the world."[29] The 'WE' includes all-men and women. These women were faithful in their vocations God had given to them as His daughters. They supported the Reformation and the church by serving the Lord as Christians in the Priesthood of all believers clothed in the righteousness of Christ, consecrated by the Holy Spirit for the purpose of God to serve Him in the world through varied ways as faithful wives, daughters, mothers, writers and musicians. They are examples of piety, service, generosity, faithfulness and obedience to the Word of God.[30] As women let us live His message and be in tune with the needs in the church and society, through partnership and participation.

Conclusion

The Reformation in Europe during the Sixteenth Century was one of the most important epochs in the history of the world. The Reformer's principles *sola fide, sola gratia, sola scriptura* has far reaching impact on our lives today. The sacrifices and the courageous application of the Word of God by the Reformers

26 Karen Spierling, "Women, Marriage and Family," in *T & T Clark Companion to Reformation Theology*, edited by David Whitford (New York: T&T Clark, 2012), 178-196.

27 Mary McKinley, "Dentiere, Marie," in *Handbook of Women Biblical Interpreters*, edited by Marion Ann Taylor and Agnes Choi (Grand Rapids, MI: Baker, 2012), 155-159.

28 www.livinglutheran.org/2015/09/women.Reformation/ women and the Reformation: Then & Now.

29 www.livinglutheran.org/2015/09/women.Reformation/ women and the Reformation: Then & Now.

30 http://lutheranReformation.org/history/faithful-women-Reformation

to every area of life, needs to be rediscovered. As we are celebrating the 500 years of Reformation let us respect women and regard them as equal as all Christians including them in the Priesthood of all believers and seeing the worth of all their services in extending the Kingdom of God.

7

Care against Commodification in the Context of Free Market Economy Reflecting on Pastoral Care with the Spirit of Reformation

Livingstone Arputharaj

Introduction

Pastoral care like any other discipline has gone through drastic changes in understanding its functional and ideological basis in the course of history. One cannot, however, ignore that pastoral care is a vital function of the community of faith. It becomes the channel through which church attends not only to the distress of the individuals and the communities but also engages in nurturing justice and peace to the entire creation of God. Nevertheless, pastoral care has been understood in a way that reduces its function merely to offer comfort to individual sufferings ignoring the socio political factors.

Recently, there has been an increasing awareness that pastoral care should break its shackles and realise that healing can occur only when it sees the wider aspects that impact the wellbeing of individuals and community. Therefore, I would like to critically look at the role of pastoral care in a context where the ideologies of free market economy have a great role in impacting the society in almost every aspect possible. How are we suppose to envision pastoral care in a context where millions are denied basic needs, rights and dignity while the nation boast of growth and prosperity?

One cannot find a more apt juncture to reflect on this thought than the 500th Anniversary of Reformation. What is even more significant is that the Lutheran World Federation has mindfully decided to reflect on the theme 'Liberated by God's grace' which has challenging sub themes that question the commodification of creation, human beings and salvation. Inspired by this, I have taken efforts to critique the principles of free market economy that in many ways have reduced God's creation as mere commodities. It is in such a juncture the spirit of reformation calls us to envision pastoral care as a healing force that challenges and stands in contrast to the values that dehumanise and distort God's creation.

The Spirit of Reformation: A Protest against Commodification of Care

The door of the Castle Church in Wittenberg witnessed the spark of pastoral care that stood against the monopoly and corruption of the very institution which is supposed to be facilitating care and compassion towards God's creation. Pastoral care was at the heart of Reformation. It is a definitive move to vehemently challenge the church structure that commoditized God's grace and salvation for personal gain. It is a pastoral activity that confronted the structure that was instituted to be the channel of God's healing touch and care.

The late medieval period was a context where the economic system was experiencing a shift from feudal system to the early forms of capitalism.[1] Robert Kolb describes it as an age of insecurity and violence.[2] It was a time where the community of faith, especially the church as an institution, needed drastic reformation. Church was plunged into economic interests and political power abuses. The church that was supposed to be a source of healing and care was that of an oppressive force exploiting people and became a stature of injustice. It just reflected the feudal hierarchy and its economic and political interests in both its structures and function.[3]

Many clergy class within the institution thrived in their business of selling indulgences. It is the church hierarchy that enjoyed the income by claiming monopoly over God's salvation. Church positions and authorities were seen as sought after profit minting power hubs. The hierarchical positions of the church were treated as commodities for sale rather than highly held pastoral offices with the supreme responsibility of care.[4] The Papal court was enjoying a lavish life style and became a center of corruption and political plots.[5] Martin Luther stood against papacy and its abuses in the name of divine. He condemned their greed and the desire to accumulate wealth at the cost of lay people's ignorance. He concluded that the elite clergy class of the church has reduced gospel to a commodity in the market. He challenged the understanding of church as a hierarchical structure.[6] As Bernard M. G. Reardon points out, for Luther church is a community of faith where each and everyone belongs to the body of Christ holding equal status.[7] Reformation

1 Walter Altmann, *Luther and Liberation: A Latin American Perspective* (Minneapolis: Fortress Press, 1992), 8.

2 Robert Kolb, *Luther's Way of Thinking* (Trivandrum: Luther Academy India, 2006), 5.

3 Altmann, *Luther and Liberation...*, 6.

4 David H. Eaton, "The Economists of the Reformation: An Overview of Reformation Teaching Concerning Work, Wealth and Interest," *Sage Open* 3/3 (2013): 2.

5 Robert Kolb, *Luther's Way of Thinking...*, 6.

6 Altmann, *Luther and Liberation..*, 5.

7 Bernard M.G. Reardon, *Religious Thought in the Reformation* (London: Longman, 1981), 73.

was an attempt to restore the principles of reign of God in the community of faith. Its spirit is one that condemned the monopolisation of power, exploitation of common human beings and commodification of gospel and care.

One cannot but see Reformation as the pastoral care activity that stood against the structures of economic, ethical and moral corruption within the ecclesiastical community. It is act that protested the economic exploitation of the common people in the name of religion. Luther and the spirit of Reformation stand against the attitudes where an individual or an institution attempts to grow at the cost of their neighbour's wellbeing.

Even as we reflect on Reformation in its context, we have to honestly accept the fact that reformation today calls for approaches that are different, at times that even conflict with the mind of the then Reformers. One may be tempted to raise questions with regard to the ideologies and stand points of reformers that may seem inapt for us today in our own challenging contexts. Nevertheless, we have to understand their contexts and the challenges that it posed in their times. What is more important for us today is to be kindled by the spirit of Reformation which then was a vital force to bring changes within the church. It inspires us to challenge and bring transformation and healing to the entire cosmos. The attempt here is not to eulogise Luther and romanticise Reformation but to see critically the need of the hour with the spirit of Reformation.

Distressing Social Realities of our Times

One cannot deny the unprecedented progress of technology and communication in this world of free market economy. It has opened up vast avenues of information exchange and opportunities for many. India is boasted to be in the run to procure the title of being the fastest growing economy of the world with its GDP growth rate, in the near future. Governments keep on promising a brighter and better day as the slogan '*Acche din aane wale hain*' (good day is coming) implies. But the question that pricks us today is 'does the promise of '*Acche din*' (good day) include the poor, the vulnerable and the groaning nature or is it going to be the privilege of the few'? Can we allow the technological developments to blind us to the ground realities of exploitation and displacement of the poor?

How are we suppose to understand the suicide of over 2000 farmers within the last 2 years in the Marathwada region in Maharashtra, India. Most of them were small scale farmers with few acres of land. Notwithstanding the failing monsoons, one cannot ignore the major role played by the economic policies that shows no mercy for those with lesser capital, small scale investors and those who are daily labourers. On the other hand, it is this same neoliberal economic policy that has given space to the agricultural seed giant Monsanto to comfortably establish its monopoly in seed business resting in the same state. What is even more ironical is that the ongoing severe drought was used heartlessly by the private water selling companies as an opportunity to reap exorbitant profits.[8] God's creation and grace in the form of seed and water has been monopolised by few and are commoditised to exploit and abuse the very source.

How can we ignore the fact that one in every seven to ten indigenous people are displaced in the name of developmental projects and industrial giants who are comfortably minting profits? Recently Coal India Limited has decided to increase the coal production in tribal belt of Chhattisgarh, Jharkhand and Odisha. This will result in thousands of indigenous communities losing their land along with their identity and culture. What remains hard to digest is the fact that the NDA government has conveniently amended the forest act and thereby making tribal land acquisitions less complicated.[9] Many states have successfully removed the provisions for social impact assessment and consent clauses for acquisition of land in their bills for "public purposes" and "industrial corridors." The responsibility to ensure the right to live safe and secure have taken low priority for the governments to serve the demands corporate giants. Such policies and amendments are always justified in the name of development and progress.

One cannot ignore the possibilities that globalisation and free market has offered to downtrodden communities in creating awareness of one's own right and massive communication facilities. However, several cases akin to the above raise serious questions on the fairness of the policies and the underlying principles that drive the free market economy.

With my limited expertise in the field of economics, I would attempt to dwell deeper and critique the foundational principles of the market economy that stand against the just and sustainable economy and are in many ways stand in stark contrast with the kingdom values.

The Invisible hands of Injustice: Free Market Economy and its Philosophies

One of the main functions of an economic system is to control the production based on demand, the resources available and also to utilise the labour force efficiently so that every member of the system will be able to have a decent livelihood. As Steven Kates puts in simple terms, *market* refers to the process of business interactions. It is process in which, based on the supply and the demand the products, are sold and purchased respectively.[10]

---

8 Neerad Pandharipande, "Marathwada's Drought: In the midst of severe economic downturn, private water sellers reap profits in Latur," *First Post*, April 8, 2016, http://www.firstpost.com/india/marathwadas-drought-in-the-midst-of-severe-economic-downturn-private-water-sellers-reap-profits-in-latur-2717106.html (Accessed on 30.08.2017).

9 Amnesty International. *"When Land is Lost do we eat Coal?" Coal Mining and Violations of Adivasi Rights in India* (Bangalore: Amnesty International India, 2016), 4f.

10 Steven Kates, *Free Market Economics: An Introduction for General Reader* (Cheltenham: Edward Elgar, 2014), 18.

Free market economy is one in which individual and groups who own and run the business decide on what and how much is to be produced. Their decisions depend on their ability to create and sense the demand opportunities. The owner is free to make decisions related to produce value assignment, volume of production and rate of production.[11] Free market proponents claim that the market is democratic as it gives individuals the freedom to compete in an open and free platform. Thus, the private firms or individuals own the means of production and what is produced and the value is determined by the producer and the consumer basically depending on the demand and supply. The free market believes that the efficiency of its economic functionality is checked by the competition thereby allowing just practices. Adam Smith, who is considered as the founder of modern economic theory, refers in his book 'Wealth and Nation' as the 'invisible hand' of the market that "when individuals act on self-interest trying to work for their own gain and profit, it will eventually lead to the growth of the society as a whole. Thus, if everyone is given the freedom to act on their own in deciding the trade rules, both the producer and the consumer, then eventually it will result in the profit for all and will maintain equilibrium."[12] The market thus assumes that all human beings are governed by self interest and thus will always engage in what is best for themselves, their family, their relatives and the community. It thus envisions an interference free trade '*laissez faire*'.[13] Thus, it presupposes that the combination of individual freedom available to everyone and their inherent drive of self interest will automatically result in combined growth of the society and higher living standards of each and every individual.

However, in reality it is observed in many cases that any unchecked power can and will be oppressive and discriminative in nature. It is the same principles that it boast off as maintaining just economy that is distributed to every one's best, allows monopoly of the rich, exploitation of the poor and the vulnerable and abuse of God's creation and its resources. Definitely in a democratic and just society, an individual should have the freedom to realise and exercise their potentials. However, it should not in any way deny or exploit the freedom and basic rights of the fellow citizens. The less privileged have no security in a free market. Free market is yet another manifestation of Darwin's dehumanising ideology of 'survival of the fittest'. Thus the idea of freedom and democracy are fictitious in a capitalistic world. As Michael O' Flyn points out, in a capitalistic world there can be no rule by the people rather it is always by the few powerful

---

11 Ibid., 10.

12 As cited by Sharon Beder, *Free Market Missionaries: The Corporate Manipulation of Community Values* (London: Earth Scan, 2006), 6-7.

13 'Laissez faire' is a French term that literally means 'leave alone' that was used to refer the Free Market notion of interference less trade. Kenneth S. Friedman, *Myths of the Free Market* (New York: Algora Publishing, 2003), 2.

elite.[14] In order to prove this fact, let us highlights the principles that drive the free market economy.

The Driving Forces of Market

One key principle that can be delineated from the aforementioned philosophy of market is the drive towards promoting 'individualism' and 'autonomy'. It boasts of giving the freedom to the individuals to make their own choices. In promoting self interest, it conveniently allows the greedy elite to monopolise and devour the vulnerable. The market promotes self interest of any form unchecked by any objective body of interest.[15] Individualism will never promote common good when left uncontrolled rather it makes survival a question for many. In the pretext of autonomy, greediness and selfishness are promoted as prerequisites and essential values in a free market economy. Cooperation, collective values and mutual support are deemed as unnecessary and unwise by the free market.[16]

The other primary principle on which the market functions is 'competition'. One's success depends on one's ability to compete in the market.[17] Market shows no mercy to the weak and the vulnerable to be a part of its economy. It is unfair to expect a poor local vendor who produces in his/her own small farm to fix prices to compete with a multinational giants. A lot of local industries suffered when India relaxed its trade policies for the fact that they were unable to compete with Chinese firms that bring materials much cheaper. Competition can be only fair when the competitors are reasonably equal in their ability to compete.

The goal of every individual and corporation in the free market is to make the maximum profit to prove that you are successful. The few who are able to compete and own the production and the labour and follow all strategies to maximise profit begin to accumulate wealth. Thus, profit becomes the primary motive in free market economy even if it is at the expense of others. To maximise profit, market economy has increasing 'consumption' as its strategy where the demand is increased in ways that are devious and unjust. This vicious circle of increasing the demand and increasing the production to sustain the growth rate has led to depletion of resources beyond the need to cater the greed of the few.

When corporate giants compete with a single goal to maximise profit and there is no little check by the government, it provides greater chance to exploit the human resources and to plunder the nature. The resources that are to be shared by everyone are then deplored for private interest. They fail to recognise the needs of others who live in this planet and there is no concept of sustainability.

---

14 Michael O'Flynn, *Profitable Ideas: The Ideology of the Individual in Capitalistic Development* (Leiden: Brill, 2009), 105.

15 Edward Dommen, *How Just is the Market Economy?* (Geneva: WCC Publications, 2003), 15.

16 Sharon Beder, Free *Market Missionaries...*, 8.

17 Dommen, *How Just is the Market Economy?,* 14.

In the course of being driven by competition, profit and self interest, free market becomes an impersonal one.

And the resultant effect is that wealth gets accumulated in the hands of the few who have greater control over the way the market functions and over its consumers. The market economy falls in their hands and they define its course. More importantly, the values that govern the market permeate into the socio-cultural and moral fibre of the society. Market values define human values, culture, human behaviour and life styles.

The success of the market is its ability to disguise in various forms that covertly perpetuate inequality in the name of development, advancement and even empowerment. In Paulo Freire's words, the charity works of multi-national giants that engage themselves in saving environment, funding NGO's for the empowerment of the marginalised can be seen as an expression of 'false generosity' to divert the mass from the dark side of their exploitative nature. These are used to legitimise and perpetuate exploitation.

Impact of Market Values in Society

The values of consumerism, individualism and profit oriented self drive have started to root themselves in diverse facets in our day to day life. The free market economy even has successfully assigned values to human labour. Its classification of labour as skilled labour and unskilled labour is a blatant example of its unjust valuation. The low wages a farmer gets and the exorbitantly high wage a software engineer gets is justified in this classification. Economic system has reduced our human bodies into working machines. The work culture has annihilated the creativity and independence and has resulted in commodification of our bodies, our behaviours and our skills. Human Labour is commoditised to such an extent in the free market that the elite capitalistic class are free to do whatever they decide on it.[18]

As Peter H. Sedgwick points out human identity in free market economy is mostly construed as mere consumers, even in disciplines such as health care and education that are conceived to be more personal and compassionate in nature.[19] The free market has successfully taken the monopoly of all modern communication channels including media and education to indoctrinate its principles and ideologies. Business interest is often linked with the public interest through media, charity activities and many other related channels. Media has become a major ally of the free market capitalism encouraging consumerism. Through media free market economy perpetuates commodification of almost everything. Even the very expressions of love and relationships are reduced to exchange of commodities. Human relationships are projected to reflect the greedy economic model of 'Quid Pro Quo'. Even knowledge and ideas are patented,

---

18 Michael O'Flynn, *Profitable Ideas...*, 104.

19 Peter H. Sedgwick, *Market Economy & Christian Ethics* (Cambridge: Cambridge University Press, 1999), 200.

treated as property of a few and are used to extract profit and accumulate wealth. These practices are justified in the name of rights and freedom of individual.[20] One cannot be blind to such progressive monopolisation of resources, values and beliefs by the dominant.

The ideology of competition, individualism and profit has deeply penetrated even in systems which were once hailed as ethically and morally having high standards viz. health care and education. Education systems are being controlled by the market. They inculcate market values and ideologies from childhood. They define the demands and scope of fields, and students become mere consumers of education. The educational institutions have become mere industries producing working human machines to cater the neo capitalist market economy. These values have inherently wounded the eco system that sustains our survival. Research shows that the last thirty years we have used up about one third of planet's resources.[21] With its policies more focused on self interest and profit market ignores the wellbeing of the future generations. Thus we see the values of market have permeated across the fabric of every social institution.

The Spirit of Reformation: A Challenge to Market Values

The values of self-interest, profit centeredness, competition of the market first and foremost stand in contrast with the values of the reign of God. They are very similar to the greediness and corruptive structures of the late medieval ecclesiastical and political structures. They were being challenged by the thoughts and values of reformation. Martin Luther's talks, writings and sermons were critical of the unjust economic and political interests prevalent in his times. In Martin Luther's time, the rich considered their wealth as something that they deserve as God's blessing whereas marginalised were considered disadvantages as a result of their sin and laziness. Kathryn cites one of Luther's sermons on the 'Rich man and the Lazarus' as a direct attack on the market values of greed fuelled by self interest. But for Luther, Kathryn states that if one claims to follow Christ one must be willing to share the burden of their neighbours in times of their need.[22] Luther's economic views showed concern towards the needy and the poor. It was not in favour of profit making at the expense of others.[23] Today's market in the name of self interest and freedom permits unjust means of gaining profit at the cost of the vulnerable and the poor. The market with its manipulative tools of media creates excessive demand and consumption. Martin Luther in his writing on *Trade and*

20 Michael O'Flynn, *Profitable Ideas...*, 151.

21 Suzanne M. Wilson, "God and the Markets: Reading the Signs of the Times," in *God and the Financial Crisis. Essays on Faith, Economics and Politics in the Wake of Great Recession,* edited by Gary D. Badcock (New Castle: Cambridge Publishing Company, 2016), 116.

22 Kathryn D'arcy Blanchard, "If you do not do this you are not now a Christian," *Word & World* 26/3 (2006): 300ff.

23 Altmann, *Luther and Liberation...*, 111.

Usury condemns strongly the unjust practice of individuals manipulating the product values on demand. Such greedy members of the society, for him, see the need of their neighbour as an opportunity to exploit them. He equates them to thieves and robbers. In the name of *laissez faire,* market has allowed the corporate giants to monopolise the market as well as have allowed their strong influence in the arena of politics and governance.

Martin Luther was also starkly against the large trading companies who establish monopoly in the market by thwarting any competition by selling things cheaper than their competitors. For him such greedy people 'are not worthy to be called human beings.'[24] One may argue that reformation had very less to address the governance and public sphere and was limited only to the Church but clearly its notions condemned any form of exploitation within and without the ecclesiastical structure. The spirit of Reformation challenges our faith community to protest against the disseminated values of the market.

A Critique on Pastoral Care Practices in a Context of Market Economy

Pastoral care, no doubt has been influenced by the all pervading and persuading forces of market economy. The shift towards clinical paradigm has made pastoral care to be more individualistic thereby failing to understand the social factors that are the root causes for the distress of communities and individuals. As Stephen Pattison opines pastoral care has conveniently ignored the causal factors for human distress that are beyond the individual's control.[25] The relationship that the wellbeing of an individual holds with the society, family systems, public policies, institutions and ideologies are often ignored in pastoral caring practices.[26] It has tried to bind the wound without even attending to the root causes of its continuous persistence. Often, sadly, pastoral care instead of promoting wellbeing has become an agent of perpetuating suffering and injustice by being blind to the dehumanising agents. In the name of privacy and confidentiality, oppression and abuse have been allowed to prevail unopposed.

Pastoral care has mostly been understood as the monopoly of either clergy community or professionally trained counselling personnel. In the pretext of professionalism, pastoral care recently has tilted towards overemphasising credentials thereby failing to recognise the care and creative healing present within the community at large. There is also a failure to acknowledge that pastoral care is a community activity and each and everyone are sources of care, compassion and justice. Pastoral care practices have blindly adapted western models of care and

---

24 Altmann, *Luther and Liberation...*, 102.

25 Stephen Pattision, *Pastoral Care and Liberation Theology* (Cambridge: Cambridge University Press, 1994), 208.

26 Bonnie J. Miller-McLemore, "The Living Human Web: Pastoral Theology," in *Through the Eyes of Women. Insights for Pastoral Care*, edited by Jeanne Stevenson Moessner (Minneapolis: Fortress Press, 1996), 7.

counselling, in turn have served as agents perpetuating free market philosophies. Care receivers are often reduced to their problems that need to be solved by professionals rather than taking into account their experiences and contexts as a whole. The professionalization of care has converted caring professions to focus more on time slots, rules and regulations, guidelines, ethical boundaries and profit acquired than genuine care.

Reforming Pastoral Care as an Expression of Justice and Compassion

The spirit of Reformation calls us to return from a highly mechanical consumerist understanding of religious care to a genuine and empathetic engagement with the lives of the people. The function of pastoral care not only be reduced to just healing the wounds inflicted by the demonic forces but also to empower the creation to stand against the structural injustice that is perpetuated. Liberation Theologies to a greater extent have challenged the pastoral practices that are highly individualistic and calls to engage in standing against the oppressive and unjust structure that cause distress. Pastoral theologians like Clinebell, Larry Kent Graham, Stephen Pattison and Immanuel Lartey have emphasised the importance to line our practices in a communal contextual paradigm. They have helped us to realise that concepts of justice and compassion intertwine in pastoral care practices. Pastoral care thus is endowed with the responsibility of unearthing the underlying dynamics of oppression, injustice and brings a holistic healing to God's creation. Pastoral care has the swim against the forces of commodification to bring meaning and value in the lives of people.

From Personal Care to Prophetic Care

Pastoral care should be sensitive to the social and structural dynamics of the issues that individuals and communities are facing. Pastoral care at the individual and personal level can in no way be undermined. However, a pastoral care that ignores the communal and contextual dimension of the issues fails to bring true healing in spite of its efforts to empathise at a personal level. The market tries to objectify and fragment individuals and treat them as entities independent of their context and communities. It is pastoral care that has to heal the impact of fragmentation and objectification. As Kathleen J. Greider points out communalization and contextualisation are no longer options in the understanding and practice of pastoral care.[27] As Larry Kent Graham opines pastoral care should embrace psycho systemic thinking where it becomes a prophetic agent in establishing justice.[28] Pastoral care should be about breaking silence, the silence of 'fear of

27 Kathleen J. Greider et al., "Three Decades of Women Writing for Our Lives," in *Feminist & Womanist Pastoral Theology*, edited by Bonnie J. Miller-Mc Lemore and Brita L. Gill-Austern (Nashville: Abingdon Press, 1999), 22.

28 Larry Kent Graham, *Care of Persons, Care of Worlds: A Psychosystems Approach to Pastoral Care and Counselling* (Nashville: Abingdon Press, 1992), 18.

freedom' that comes from the scars of deep rooted oppression in human psyche. It's about giving the courage to the wounded psyche. It should assist victims to fight against oppressive forces and should facilitate in creating workable alliances of communities that support and sustain this pursuit of justice.[29]

From Comforting to Compassionate Resistance[30]

The very term Protestant Reformation signifies that resistance has been an inseparable element of Reformation. In order to care for the souls Reformers had to confront and resist the anomalies of the institution that hosted the souls. All along the way, empathy and listening skills have been given so much importance and over emphasis in pastoral care. Comforting people in their sufferings and helping them to cope with their struggles were deemed as its primary functions. Pastoral care was served as the 'opium of the masses' rather than empowering them to stand for their right. It is here pastoral care has commodified human beings as mere problems to be solved with learned skills. Pastoral care has to move beyond empathising with individuals to rooting out the structural causes of the problems. As Bonnie J. Miller points our pastoral care should not only play a role of comforting people but also should confront, disturb and provoke people. It should not only facilitate venting off emotions and feelings but also should make people feel guilty and responsible for their actions that affect their neighbour's wellbeing. As Bonnie J. Miller states pastoral care in such a context demands compassionate resistance. This highlights the inherent function of pastoral care to confront the violent, abusive and unjust structures.[31] It is this that brings genuine self-worth and meaning to individuals and communities.

From Caring Individual to Caring Communities

Reformation affirmed the power of faith in each and every believer that brings them closer to Divine grace and forgiveness. The spirit of Reformation demands our caring practices to confront the notions and values of individualism and self-centeredness perpetuated by the market. Pastoral care has to breakaway the blindfolds of professionalism and individualism to see the bounty of healing potency that lies within our interconnectedness as communities. The family systems perspective affirms that growth of any individual is effected in larger communities and does not happen to an individual in vacuum.[32] In the past as

29 Ibid., 54.

30 Bonnie J. Miller-McLemore, "Feminist Theory in Pastoral Theology," in *Feminist & Womanist Pastoral Theology*, edited by Bonnie J. Miller-Mc Lemore and Brita L. Gill-Austern (Nashville: Abingdon Press, 1999), 80.

31 Bonnie J. Miller-McLemore, "Feminist Theory in Pastoral Theology,"..., 80.

32 Paula Buford, "Women and Community: Women's Study Groups as Pastoral Counseling," in *Through the Eyes of Women: Insights for Pastoral Care*, edited by Jeanne Stevenson Moessner (Minneapolis: Fortress Press, 1996), 296.

Kathleen points out, the role of the clergy in caring has somehow undermined or even ignored the care that the community or the congregation has been rendering to one another and to the society at large.[33] Bonnie J. Miller in highlighting the work of Roy Steinhoff Smith brings out his notion of congregation as caring communities.[34] The community of faith has to acknowledge the 'congregational nature of pastoral care.'[35] Church should facilitate networks of caring communities which will be an essential reflection of the healing potency of the body of Christ. Pastor should play the role of a facilitator to mobilise the healing forces that lie within lay people and communities. It is in communities people find their strength to come out and confront their oppressors and it is in communities people find their brokenness healed. It is here pastoral care stands as an instrument that helps to understand the interconnectedness of human beings and the ecosystem providing healing and growth together. It is only then Church as caring community will be able to realise its role in the lives of farmers who are in the edge of their survival and the tribal communities who have been deprived of their lands. It is when we realise our interconnectedness then we challenge the commodifying ideologies of market. Pastoral care becomes a tool that restores dignity and value to individual and community experiences and identities. It is then pastoral care emerges from the experiences of communities themselves and not from ideologies and skills prescribed by market that are alien. The marginalised communities themselves become the source of healing and foundation of the concept of care.

Conclusion

The 500th year anniversary of Reformation calls the community of faith to be reminded of the need and necessity to remove the blind folds that prevent us from experiencing the empathy and compassion of God the creator. Reformation is a call to value God's creation and to fight against commodification of God's grace and bounty. Reformation also calls us to realise that pastoral care is endowed with the power to heal the wounds created by the market in the society by commodifying human beings and nature. For pastoral care is a vocation that manifests these divine healing aspects. As reformation rejuvenated and aligned the Body of Christ to journey in the path of faith, and shook off the barriers that have kept church away from being a healing presence to God's creation, the spirit of Reformation calls us to address the structures that prevent God's creation from experiencing God's compassion and justice. It calls the church to be a source of care and compassion to the entire creation.

---

33 Kathleen J. Greider et al., "Three Decades of Women Writing for Our Lives," in *Feminist & Womanist Pastoral Theology,* edited by Bonnie J. Miller-Mc Lemore and Brita L. Gill-Austern (Nashville: Abingdon Press, 1999), 46.

34 Kathleen J. Greider et al., "Three Decades of Women Writing for our Lives,"..., 14.

35 Ibid.

8

Sola–Fide
A Dalit Reading

Samuel Logan Ratnaraj

Introduction

Dalit Theology is a musing on how God is present in the sufferings and seclusion of the oppressed people in the church and society. By doing so, it gives hope, courage and energy for the Dalits to face the oppression and to counter it. Similarly the Lutheran theology that arose in the context of oppression increased the faith of ordinary folk who are deceived and threatened by the authorities of the church by false perception of God, Judgment and authoritative traditions. During the time of Luther the poor and innocent people were made to feel guilty of their sins, psychologically they were made to believe that they were sinners. Based on the Scriptural foundations, Luther condemned the church for its blind following of traditions and re-examined the teachings and traditions of the church.

Today after 500 years of Reformation many false notions and myths are forcibly imposed on the Dalit Christians that made them to believe that they are impure and rejected by God. Even though, Christianity liberated the Dalits from several oppressions, the psychological discrimination continues to plague the Christians in the church. Therefore, considering such situation of the Church and in the light of the celebration of 500th Anniversary of Reformation, an attempt is made in this article to present the Lutheran doctrine of "Justification by faith alone" as a message of hope and solace for the discriminated and oppressed Dalit communities. It is divided into two parts. The first part discusses the notion of Divine rejection by the Dalits and how the teachings of Luther may help them to overcome from that oppressive thinking. The second one is a reflection on how the Lutheran doctrine of *Sola Fide* can be a help to overcome from the belief of suffering as natural on the basis of *Karma* theory.

Understanding of Divine Rejection by Dalits

In India, social stratification based on caste identity continues from birth to death. The stigma of untouchability creates in them the consciousness of alienation and often they feel that they are rejected. In most of the villages of south India the Dalits are not allowed inside the temples and houses of the dominant community. Separate glass system for the Dalits in the tea shops is prevalent even now. This exclusion of the Dalits is imposed on them by the dominant high caste people. Dalits have a history of humiliation and ill treatment from the hands of the so called high caste people for a long period. Oppression, depression, dehumanization and exploitation mark the lives of the Dalits.[1]

The church buildings that are laid out in the shape of a cross, the Christians of so called upper caste origin sit in the central part of the church and the Dalit Christians are given seat on the wings just to avoid the Dalits to see the Alter and the Sacramental elements as it might pollute the alter and the sacramental elements. The Dalits have to partake communion only after the upper caste people. Even there are separate cups used for the Dalits in some churches.

Though the caste society treated the Dalits as cursed by virtue of *karma* and *dharma*, the counter myths of the Dalits over against the myths of the dominant caste people, project them as sacred and privileged. The Dalits are forced to think that they are "no people" to God. However, the understanding of Divine rejection by the Dalits is very complex in nature, because they believe in exclusion defiantly and at the same time the Dalits are very firm in saying that they are not excluded by Divine, they are God's own children. They firmly believe that only the human agent is responsible for their rejection and strongly believe that God also partakes in their exclusion.

Dalits believe that God will not reject or exclude any human beings, whether it is oppressor or the oppressed; God in turn waits for the people to repent and reconcile so that they all may live in harmony. This explicitly shows that the Dalits are not looking for any hierarchical ruling in the society, but just an egalitarian society where there is no longer Jew or Gentile, slave or free, male or female, for all are one in Christ.

Luther's theology vehemently critiqued the Institutionalized church for being oppressive to the poor and needy by propagating false beliefs among the people. In Jeremiah Anderson's words:

> Luther's theology in reality served as watch-dog for the teachings and happenings in the Roman Catholic Church. Luther never hesitated to call a spade a spade. The interpretations of a sinful nature of life as expressed in the doctrinal aspects of the church caused much hindrance in the intra and inter - personal life and had influence on the corporate

1 Elungkiebe Zeliang, "Rereading of the Bible from Dalit Perspective," in *Dalits Speaking Experience,* edited by Elizabeth S. Balasundram (Delhi: ISPCK, 2005), 43.

> life and a life of relationship with God. That forgiveness was an offer made free and equal by God's grace through faith surely did leave an impact on the life of the people. Till then, the church dictated terms for this forgiveness through monetary matters, thereby swelling their own coffers but emptying the spiritual and economical coffers in the hearts and lives of the people.[2]

What we can infer from this is that the Reformation teachings which was very liberative and transformative inspires the Dalit theology to empower the Dalits through its powerful articulations against the age old traditions that oppress the people. It helps them to overcome the false beliefs that the institutionalized church imposed on them, and affirm their faith and hope that they are not rejected by God forever.

Sufferings of Dalits Justified

In classical Hinduism, actions (*Karma*) and duty (*Dharma*) were the dominant concepts. *Karma* as the accumulation of good and bad actions would influence a person's destiny.[3] Hinduism advocates good works (*dharma*) as a path to attain salvation. It further says that the present suffering of individuals is because of the bad deeds the individual had done in the past. Salvation, according to Hinduism, could be achieved in three ways namely *Karma marga* (way of works), *Gnana marga* (way of devotion) and *Bhakthi marga* (way of devotion and love of God).

In the context of Dalit sufferings, it is justified that the cause of inequality in the society is because of *karma* or the deeds of an individual. In other words, Dalits are responsible for their sufferings. It is not something which has been imposed on them but due to their *Karma*. Does is not sound ridiculous? Yes, it is indeed so. But how to overcome such predicament? How to remove such belief and consciousness, which linger in the minds of the Dalits that they have to work for their salvation. In fact, Dalits are in no way responsible for their plights. It is the religious belief and teachings that branded them so. For example, the Brihadharanyakha Upanishad, Chapter 4, Bhramana 4, Verse 5 says, "The doer of good becomes good; the doer of evil becomes evil. One becomes virtuous by virtuous action, another becomes bad, by bad actions."

This shows that the sufferings of Dalits are justified by the religion which took control over their daily lives and branded them as outcaste and created a guilty consciousness in their mind. The influences of the law of *karma* not only affected the Hindu Dalits but also spilled over to Christianity and influenced the mind of Christian Dalits. Since a similar concept and teaching of 'sowing and

2 Jeremiah Anderson, "Context Theology of Martin Luther and a Contextual Search for Relevance to Dalit Lutheran Theology in India," in *Gurukul Journal of Theological Studies* XXII/2 (June 2011): 13.

3 R. Pierce Beaver and Jan Bergman eds., "Hinduism" in *Eerdman's Handbook to the World's Religions* (Grand Rapids: William B. Eerdmans Publishing Company, 1994), 190.

reaping' is found the Bible, the *karma* theory easily was converted to new faith. Hence, in the light of this state of justified sufferings of Dalits, it is attempted here to reflect on the famous dictum of Martin Luther's *Sola-Fide* as we are in the year of 500th Protestant Reformation and derive implications for the emancipation of Dalits.

The Context of Reformation Period:

Pope Innocence III, wrote a book on "The misery of human existence" in which he stated: "We are born in order to die." In that book he picturizes the context of Medieval Europe, mentioning large number of deaths because of warfare, famines, outbreak of diseases, extreme cold, floods and terrible locus swarms. One third of the population in Europe died in the Fourteenth Century. In addition, during the end of the Fifteenth Century, syphilis appeared as the other great epidemic disease along with Black Death caused by the rats. The Black Death could strike down a healthy person within no time. The plague was perceived widely as God's punishment for humankind's sins. As a result of this, Flagellation was practiced among people. The Flagellants were religious zealots of the Middle Ages in Europe who demonstrated their religious fervour and sought atonement for their sins by vigorously whipping themselves in public displays of penance. This approach to achieving redemption was most popular during times of crisis. Prolonged plague, hunger, drought and other natural maladies motivated thousands to resort to this extreme method of seeking relief.

Works of Mercy to the Mass for the dead: Transition of Church

While many died of the plague, those who survived could not practice the traditional funeral rites. The church created fear, among the people by raising a question, *"What will happen when we die?"* This was one of the most challenging questions of the people during medieval times. There was a shift from 'works of mercy' to 'mass for the dead.' "Catholicism at the end of the Middle Ages was in large parts, the 'cult of the living in the service of the dead.' "People in the middle ages reflected on life after death, and strongly believed that all of rituals and related impacts endured for eternity.

This religious quest occupied the greater part of the lives of most ordinary people. The church, its institutions in the form of the parish church, the monasteries, and the more imposing basilicas and cathedrals, towered over the petty dwellings of the common folk. In medieval Christendom, one eventually knocked anywhere and everywhere into people whose lives were bound up with the service of the church either in its spiritual or temporal side. The village parson, a travelling monk, pardoner or summoner, were quite familiar sights.[4] It is no exaggeration to state that from the initial sacrament of Baptism to the final one of extreme unction, from cradle to grave, the church dominated every phase of a

4 C.T. Thomas, *Martin Luther and the Reformation* (New Delhi: ISPCK, 2012), 18.

Christian's life. With the decline of the Roman Empire and with the evolution of Catholic Church as near universal phenomenon in amplitude, power and wealth alongside there grew much profiteering in the provision of its sacraments and services.

Fear of Condemnation Begets the Sale of Indulgence:

In the prevailing atmosphere of widespread illiteracy and ignorance among vast swathes of its lay masses, there was an undue reliance on the spiritual benefits of pilgrimages, worship, amounting to idolatry, of sacred relics and belief in false doctrines. The infamous sale of indulgences was just the straw that broke the camel's back. This desperate situation called for a latter day Martin Luther – turned – Hercules to cleanse the system.[5]

Luther objected the selling of indulgences in his *95 Theses* because he felt that it was wrong to promise that souls would be relieved from purgatory through a simple monetary contribution, and he also felt that the Pope did not have the right to grant a pardon on behalf of God. John Tetzel was assigned to sell the Indulgences in Saxony area. Tetzel used a catchy slogan to attract the buyers "As soon as the coin in the coffer rings a soul from Purgatory springs." Luther believed that the corrupt Church was selling worthless pieces of paper to the poor people for the sake of financing to build the St. Peter's Basilica. Therefore, Luther realized the importance of establishing an image of God which could be helpful for the people to come closer with great faith in God as the people had great fear in God and the church cleverly utilized the fear of people to make profit out of it.

God of Majesty versus God of Compassion & God of Terror Versus God of Forgiveness

The theology of Luther emerged out of Luther's struggles that shook the foundations of medieval Christendom. The wrestling of Luther on the picture of God as a Judge and God as a gracious God helped him to develop his affirmation of *Sola–Fide*. His reading on Psalm 22 brought an illumination in his thinking. "My God My God why have you forsaken me" was the turning point for Luther. Christ experienced forsakenness, abandonment, alienation and estrangement from God. God is pure, man is impure. God is strong, man (sic) is weak. But Christ was not impure, Christ was not weak. Why then was he forsaken? The answer must be that he who was without sin for our sake became sinful and so identified himself the iniquity of us all, and to sense such a solidarity with mankind (sic) as to share in the estrangement from God. What a picture of Christ is this! The judge upon the rainbow has become the derelict upon the cross. He is still the judge and must be, so long as truth judges error and right judges wrong. But in

5 Ibid., 19.

the very act of judging the sinner he has made one with the sinners assuming his punishment and sharing in his very guilt.[6]

Luther identified a new picture of God. He sensed the import of the miracle of divine forgiveness. It is miracle because there is no reason for it according to man's standards. That is why Luther so decried reason and by reason he meant the measure of man's mind. Forgiveness from the human point of view makes sense because humans need forgiveness and ought for that reason to forgive. But God has no need of forgiveness. One would assume that God would consume human in God's anger but it is not so, and that is the incredible wonder of God revealed in Christ. Luther said, "God came on Sinai with terror, but now in forgiveness."[7] God of Majesty becomes God of Compassion, and God of Terror becomes God of Forgiveness for Luther.

"Sweet Exchange" Between Christ and Sinner

Luther considered justification by faith "the summary of all Christian doctrine" and "the article by which the church stands or falls." God accepts Christ's righteousness, which is alien to our nature, as our own. Though God does not actually remove our sins—we are at the same time righteous and sinful - he no longer counts them against us. To use Luther's words, it is a "sweet exchange" between Christ and the sinner: "Therefore, my dear brother, learn Christ and him crucified; learn to pray to him despairing of yourself, saying 'Thou, Lord Jesus, art my righteousness and I am thy sin. Thou hast taken on thyself what thou was not, and hast given to me what I am not."[8]

From the time of the first lectures on Psalms, Luther depicted the conscience as capable of judging, like God's judgment, the individual as a whole. He who acknowledges his basic sinfulness and his inability to merit salvation has conformed his judgement of himself to that of God. This conformity, in turn is also the basis of a divine judgement which does not condemn the person. This idea of Luther gave some kind of solace to the people who lived in guilt.

Credence and Trust: Two Sides of Faith Coin

The Lord of anger is the God who comes with great compassion to God's children. The only obligation for humans is to believe and accept this truth. Luther says "Credence and trust, these only are required, for by faith and only by faith we are saved."[9] Luther made strenuous efforts to find a gracious God. In the words of Luther, "Faith is not what some people think it is. Their human dream is a delusion. Because they observe that faith is not followed by good works or a

6 Roland H. Bainton, *Reformation of the Sixteenth Century* (Boston: Beacon Press, 1963), 34.

7 Ibid., 35.

8 Timothy George, *Dr. Luther's Theology* - http://www.christianitytoday.com/history/issues/issue-34/dr-luthers-theology.html (Accessed on 25.10.2016).

9 Bainton, *Reformation of the Sixteenth Century*..., 35."

better life, they fall into error, even though they speak and hear much about faith. "Faith is not enough," they say, "You must do good works, you must be pious to be saved." They think that, when you hear the gospel, you start working, creating by your own strength, a thankful heart which says, "I believe." That is what they think true faith is. But, because this is a human idea and a dream, the heart never learns anything from it, so it does nothing and reform doesn't come from this 'faith,' either. Instead, faith is God's work in us that changes us and gives new birth from God. (John 1:13). It kills the Old Adam and makes us completely a different people. It changes our hearts, our spirits, our thoughts and all our powers. It brings the Holy Spirit with it. Yes, it is a living, creative, active and powerful thing. Faith cannot help doing good works constantly. It doesn't stop to ask if good works ought to be done, but before anyone asks, it already has done them and continues to do them without ceasing. Anyone who does not do good works in this manner is an unbeliever. He stumbles around and looks for faith and good works, even though he does not know what faith or good works are. Yet he gossips and chatters about faith and good works with many words. Faith is a living, bold trust in God's grace.[10]

The road to faith that Luther took is theological because he does not start from the stand point of human psyche in terms of the conflict between spirit and nature, but brings the person face to face with himself in the mirror of God's word. Luther means that in the incarnation of his son – in his cross and suffering – God holds up a mirror in front of us one in which we recognize how God sees our condition even though we might see it quite differently.[11] At this juncture, a person does not judge himself/herself but is made aware of God's judgement over him/her. Here he/she sees himself/herself as God sees him/her as so lost that no law, no "ought" no ideal, no good intentions and no good work can help him/her. Therefore God puts aside law and sends his Son as Paul says: what was impossible for law is possible for God, who sent his Son as a merciful and saving God.[12]

Sola-Fide: Banish Guilt Consciousness

The sick person knows the sympathy of his sickness, but it is the doctor who first gives the correct diagnosis. In the same way, a person is by nature a sinner, but only comes to recognize this fact through the Holy Spirit when he/she first sees himself/herself as he/she really is and when he/she recognizes the root of his/her sickness while at the same time embracing the only possible cure. Luther calls this recognition-*becoming sinner*. He does not refer to the sins that a person commits,

10 An excerpt from "An Introduction to St. Paul's Letter to the Romans," in *Luther's German Bible of 1522* , vol. 63 Translated by Rev. Robert E. Smith (Erlangen: Heyder and Zimmer, 1854), 124-125.

11 Hans J. Iwand, *The Righteousness of Faith According to Luther* (Oregon: WIPF & STOCK, 2008), 31.

12 Ibid., 32-3.

but rather the recognition that breaks in on a person as to who he/she really is. What Luther means here is that *sin has to be believed* as much as *righteousness has to be believed.*[13]

In becoming a sinner we believe that God does not come near our sick bed to scoff at us or to abandon us. We learn under his healing hand to grasp, at first gradually, that sin is really a sickness unto death and we are already free of sin when we begin to recognize how deeply we are lost in it. For just our delusion indicated the victory of sin over us, so also he the recognition of our sinful nature is a sign of our victory over sin. By this, the theology of *Sola-Fide* banishes the guilt consciousness from people and helps them to overcome the guiltiness from which they suffered for decades.

The Concept of Dharma and idea of Sola Fide:

The issue of suffering and inequities in human life is justified by the *karmic* theory which affects the life of the Dalits and Women in our society. The law of cause and effect says that a person who plants mangoes, mangoes shall he/she eat: who plants thorn-bushes, thorn shall wound his/her feet.[14] *Karma* is intimately related to a matter of merit and demerit; it can be perceived not as the cause but as the effect of merit or demerit because it is conceived somewhat as a metaphysical force which is responsible for the retribution of one's actions. Good and bad action produce merit and demerit, respectively; they in turn produce good and bad *karma*; and again *karma* produces the appropriate retribution for the action. Therefore, "one's fate is determined by one's *karma*," "one's life fate is the consequence of the karmic force produced by all of one's past action." Whether a person's life is in a condition of suffering or happiness, rich or poverty, every event in his life is viewed as retribution for the past action caused by *karma*; in turn this *karma* can be perceived as a metaphysical force produced by his past action and behaviour. This understanding of life based on *Karmic* theory gives no hope for the Dalits, Women and other marginalized groups.

However, Luther's *Sola-Fide* gives an assurance to the marginalized group as it talks of Salvation as a grace of God which is freely given. For example, in the three parables of the lost coin, lost sheep and lost son, the lesson which Christ teaches is that a person is lost and helpless and he/she cannot save himself/herself. God seeks the lost sinner, forgives, gives his righteousness and saves a person.[15] "Faith is the way in which, even while living in the midst of earthly life, we transcend it and live in God, in the fullness of salvation."[16] The experience of God's forsakenness

13 Ibid., 34.

14 L. De La Vallee Poussin, "Karma," *Encyclopaedia of Religion and Ethics,* ed. James Hastings, vol. VII (New York: Charles Scribner's Sons, 1991), 675.

15 James C. Gamaliel, *Dharma in the Hindu Scripture and in the Bible* (Delhi: ISPCK, 1999), 44.

16 Paul Althaus, *The Theology of Martin Luther,* Translated by Robert C. Schultz (Philadelphia: Fortress Press, 1966), 47.

was necessary for Christ himself who had worked out our redemption without any help from the outside, even without the help of his father.[17] Jesus' cry, though an expression of deep agony, was not a cry of despair. It was still an affirmation of the relationship with God. Dalits' sufferings and cries still have not led them to a complete hopeless situation but a ray of hope and trust in the God.[18] For the Dalits, women and marginalized group this assurance of Luther's teaching gives a great impetus to live in the world that puts them down saying, 'it is out of their fate they live an awful life.'

Hope filled Lutheran Theology

Today in our churches Law has taken over the place of Gospel. Grace and love are replaced by hatred; compassion of Christ is replaced by the adamant behaviour of selfish corrupt leaders. Money is valued more than humanity, and disguised self-righteousness of the church leaders are glorified over God's righteousness. We have safely arrived once again in this rotating world to the world of Luther in which God is pushed to the fringes and corrupt leaders to the centre. This context forces us to become Luther rather than Lutheran.

Even after 500 years, Luther's famous dictum "*Sola-Fide*" gives lot of hope and meaning to life. The churches in this century are filled with more of non-Christian teachings; the belief in *Karma* theory in-filtered into the churches. Caste consciousness hardened people's heart as the *karmic* theory has gone deep down into the Indian Churches in this Twenty First Century. The *karma* theory legitimizes oppression against Dalits and makes them to accept it without resistance. The psychological impact of this system has lowered the self-esteem, increased the self-hate, confused and despaired the Dalits, women and other marginalized groups. In this context, the affirmation of Martin Luther that "by faith only we are justified" brings good news as it banishes the guilt consciousness as sinners and gives space for us to have a sweet exchange with Christ.

17 V. Devasahayam, "The Nature of Dalit Theology as Counter Theology," in *Frontiers in Dalit Theology*, edited by V. Devasahayam (Chennai: ISPCK/GURUKUL, 1997), 67.

18 Ibid., 63.

9

Re-Vitalising Dalit Religious Tradition in the Light of the Impact of Luther's Reformation

Jeevaraj Anthony

Religion plays and has been playing a major role in reviving members of every community. October 31, 1517 is the day when the German Augustinian monk Martin Luther nailed his *95 Theses* to the main door of a Catholic church at Wittenberg. It was the day when he finally broke his silence against the abuse of ecclesiastical authority over the affairs of humankind in that portion of the world known back then as Christendom. A renewed religious understanding came against the dominant powers and authority of the church. In the same manner we see Dalit leaders and Movements continue fighting against the dominant exploitation of Brahminism in the context of India. The laws and the scriptures of the Brahmins provide sanctions for both the hierarchy of castes and low status of Dalits in this hierarchy. For example, in Rg Veda Mandala 10, the foundation been laid to take power to marginalise the Dalits.

Later, it was Manu who insisted to bring the dichotomy between purity and pollution. It was not only the Dalit communities who had been marginalised and oppressed, but even their deities and religious tradition too. Therefore, the Dalit liberation is meant liberation from the Brahmin religion and religiously sanctioned degradation.[1] Near the end of the Nineteenth Century, when the Modern Dalit movement began, Dalits were still stigmatised, segregated and uneducated, living in poverty and almost total dependence on high caste people. Since the Dalit communities are spread all over India and their culture is richly diverse the topic limits to the religion and culture of the Dalits in South India alone. The focus and attempt in this paper is mainly to see possibility of re-vitalising the features of Dalit Religious Tradition in the light of the Impact of Martin Luther's reformation.

1 John C.B. Webster, *Religion and Dalit Liberation: An Examination of Perspectives* (New Delhi: Manohar Publishers, 1999), 12.

Features of Dalit Religious Tradition

The characteristics that describe the Dalit religious tradition are that it revolves around the worship. Dalit religious tradition is not only the collective art of dismantling reassembling dominant caste Hindu patterns of meaning for the sake of them, but it is also symbolic manifestations of their very own experience of the Divine. There are no hierarchy of deities. Every deity are given preference in the Dalit community worship. This a unique and significant characteristic of Dalit religious tradition.

1. Dalit Deities (Pluralistic)

Despite the number and variety of Dalit deities, several typical characteristics of these local deities have to be noticed. David Kinsley gives some of them. First, they mostly are female. Speaking of South India, Henry Whitehead says that "Dalit deities with very few exceptions, are female… All over Southern India…, the Dalit deities are almost exclusively female. Dalit Community had recognized the feminine dimension of the deities and it is evident in the fact that in most cases deities manifested their self in the form of feminine. In Tamil Nadu, it is true that most of them have male attendants, who are supposed to guard the shrines and carry out the commands of the gods and goddess; but their place is distinctly subordinate and almost servile."[2]

Second, these deities, goddesses for the most part, capture the primary interest of the Dalit Community and tend to be worshiped with more intensity than the great gods of the Hindu Pantheon. Although the great gods are acknowledged to be in charge of distant, cosmic rhythms, they are only of limited interest to most Dalit Community, many of whom traditionally were not allowed within the precincts of thc temples of these deities in the first place. The Dalit goddess, in contrast, engages the Dalit Community directly by being associated with their local, existential concerns. He/she is perceived to be their deity and to be concerned especially with their well-being and that of their Dalit Community.[3]

Finally, these Dalit deities are often directly associated with disease, sudden death, and catastrophe. When the Dalit Community is confronted by disaster, particularly epidemics, the local goddess is usually said to be manifesting herself. She bursts onto the Dalit Community scene along with disaster that threatens the stability, and even the survival of the Dalit Community. Furthermore, she is perceived both as inflicting these diseases and as protecting the Dalit Community from them.[4]

There are so many gods and goddesses in the Dalit communities. This understanding of gods and goddesses are according to the context of the own

2 David Kinsley, *Hindu Goddesses: Vision of the Divine Feminine in the Hindu Religious Tradition* (Delhi: Motilal Banarisdas Publishers, 1986), 197-198.

3 Ibid., 198.

4 Ibid.

Dalit Community. They are plural and they are polytheistic.[5] In the context of Dalit life, one of the most significant and powerful divine presences is their deity, a deity who is especially identified with the Dalit community and toward whom the Dalit Community often have a special affection. It is not uncommon, in fact, for there to be several *deities* in the village, each of whom may have a specialised function.

1.1. Dalit Deities in Andhra Pradesh and Telengana

There are number of Dalit deities in Andra Pradesh and Telengana. For example, *Durgamma* – the most powerful goddess whose shrine is to be visited first in processions, and she is responsible for the welfare of the village. *Poshamma* is a goddess of smallpox. *Uradamma* is the goddess of the particular Dalit village. *Katte-Maisamma* is Protectress of the village tank bund. *Mutyalamma* is goddess of chickenpox. *Mattadi Poshamma*, a protectress. *Balamma* – the fertility goddess and the protectress of children.[6]

1.2. Dalit Deities in Tamil Nadu

In Tamil Nadu, all the devotees who worship various goddess call all the feminine deities as *amman* (mother). In the Dalit villages, the Supreme Being is referred to as Sakti. The general belief of the Dalit communities is that, the Sakti has been revealed to them in seven manifestations as seven virgins who are called to be seven sisters. *Marriamma* been responsible for chickenpox and rain, *Ellaiyamma* is a border goddess who protects from any danger. *Gangaiyamman* is considered as the responsible for water resources. *Sethukallselvi*, *Thandumari*, *Thulukanathamman*, *Padavattamman* are few other goddess who are worshipped in Tamil Nadu. They also worship Goddesses *Mariamma*, *Yellamma*. *Kaamma*, *Morasamma* and *Matangi*. *Somalamma* and *Moosamma* as well as some male gods like *Ayannar*, *Karuannaswami* and *Pandi* and so on.[7]

1.3. The Seven Sisters

In all Dalit villages of South India, the Seven Sisters are the most prominent among Dalit deities. They have one younger brother called Potu Razu. His name seems to be the same everywhere, but the names of the Seven Sisters vary even in localities quite near. In the region of Andhra Pradesh, the names of these seven sisters are *Poleramma*, *Ankamma*, *Muthyalamma*, *Dilli Polasi*, *Bangaramma*,

5 James Massey, *Indigenous People: Dalits* (Delhi: ISPCK, 1994), 113.

6 P.Y. Luke and John B. Carman, *Village Christians and Hindu Culture* (New Delhi: ISPCK, 2009), 34.

7 Bartholomaeus Ziegenbalg, *Genealogy of the South-Indian Gods* (New Delhi: Unity Book Service, 1984), 137.

Mathamma, and *Renuka*[8] Of these, *Poleramma* is the best known and be found in almost every village. As the worship of the Seven Sisters is typical of that of all the Dravidian deities, some of the unique characteristics of Dalit religious traditions and rites are worth noting here.

2. Scriptureless

Dalit religious tradition has no scripture. Because it is a very Dynamic one it does not have any exact structure but contains of egalitarian values.[9] It does not have any scripture like other streams of Hinduism. However, they may have some sort of stories related the deities, who are worshipped by the whole Dalit Community. The nomenclature of the deities is of vernacular language. Narratives are mostly in folklore and oral tradition.[10] The myths and religious traditions of Dalit deities, however, often cast males in disruptive role and equate the Dalit deity with the civilised, orderly and refined realm of the Dalit Community.[11]

3. No Priest

The Dalit religious tradition doesn't have any priest as such. They believe in the possession of spirit or the dissension of spirit will come on any member of the Dalit Community. When they say "swami varum."[12] During the worship they play typical sound by the mouth and also beat drum. During this time they long for the deity to possess someone among the community and prophesy. There is no priest in any one of the worship. It is conducted by the people who encounter the possession of deity on them, but deity can dwell on anyone. The equality is practiced because they believe that either male or female whoever gets the possession of deity, will be the priest for few years.[13]

4. Non Vegetarian

Non vegetarian is offered to the deities which is universally a common practice of all the indigenous religious sects. At the festival time, many animals are sacrificed to the deity. In many Tamil Dalit communities, the rice and blood are made up into little balls and thrown up in the air, where, as the people firmly believe, they are seized upon by the deity to whom the sacrifice is offered.[14] The priest or priestess was to spill the blood of the cock over the sheaves invoking the names of

8 W. T. Elmore, *Dravidian Gods in Modern Hinduism: Study of The Local and Village deities of South India* (Hamilton, N.Y. : Author, 1915), 19.

9 James Massey, *Indigenous People ...*, 114.

10 Ibid., 114.

11 David Kinsley, *Hindu Goddesses...*, 203.

12 James Massey, *Indigenous People ...*, 114.

13 Ziegenbalg, *Genealogy of the South-India Gods ...*, 145.

14 Henry Whitehead, *The Village Gods of South India* (London: Oxford University Press, 1916), 100.

different goddesses. The belief of the people is that the blood is consumed by the spirit of the deity in the priest.[15]

5. Dwelling of Deities

Most of the Dalit deities are not icons or idols. They are mostly weapons shapeless stones called *modikallu* or just some of the icons and idols. Ordinarily, the people do not attach any holiness either to the place of worship or the symbols they have only during the festival, when the whole community is present they acquires holiness.

6. Social Integration

In every Dalit festival, the whole Dalit Community are called for a meeting by beating the drum. All come together and suggestions are asked regarding how would the festival be celebrated. Anyone can give their opinions and all the opinions will be taken to consideration, if it would be better for the whole Dalit Community. They take the decision as a community and all respect whatever is decided in the meeting in order to celebrate the festival as community. The Dalit Communities sacrifice a he-goat called as *Kada Vettu*. This is very significant from other sacrifices. Because, in the *Kada Vettu*, the worshippers who bring the goat do not offer for their own well-being, but also for the wellbeing of their kinsmen and women. They invite everyone for this occasion, and together they cook the sacrificed goat and eat together and celebrate the festival. Such communion of the people in food is the basic element or component of the family values. During the festivals by the sharing of food they emphasise the family and community value.

7. Festivals

Festivals are celebrations, usually having an ordered and ritualised character. Festival gives communal expression to the meaning of that process, in a shared affirmation of value and commitment.[16] In the month of *Aadi* the Dalits have their most important festival called *Aadi Thiuvizha* (Aadi festival). This festival links to all the deities to all the Dalit villages and to their female deities. The selected priest for the festival along with few youths come before the shrine with drum beating. In the Dalit Communities, the worshipper of the religious tradition, share the food and worship together. Their festivals are not individualistic but corporate one in which anyone can be a part of.

7.1. Mariamma Festival

India has always been a land of villages and in the context of village life, the most important and powerful divine presence is the *gramadevata*, a deity identified

15 Ibid., 103.

16 John Bower, ed., "Festivals and Fasts," *The Oxford Dictionary of World Religions* (New York: Oxford University Press, 1997), 340.

with the village. Village deities are numerous and some of them are known throughout a region. One these deities is the goddess *Mariamma* (also called Mari, Mariamman) who has devotees all over South India. *Mariamma* is an ancient goddess, whose worship probably originated in the tribal religious tradition of Dravidian India before the arrival of the Aryans and the Brahman religion.[17]

The village belongs to the goddess. Theologically she was there before the village and in fact she created it. The goddess protects the village and is the guardian of the village boundaries. Outside the village there is no protection from the goddess. The relationship between the village and the goddess is primarily for the village as a whole and not for individuals. *Mari* can mean *sakti*, power, and *amma* is mother, so she is the mother-power of the village.[18]

7.2. Matangi

At many festivals an important role is played by a *Matangi*, a low caste woman who is unmarried and holds the office for life. She is a living symbol of the goddess and becomes possessed by the goddess, dancing wildly, using obscene language, spitting at devotees, and pushing people around with her backside. The festival reverses social norms and the Matangi's behaviour, which would ordinarily be highly polluting, is purifying and people seek out her spit and insults.

7.3. Kolupu Festivals

7.3.1. Mathamma Kolupu

The community of Madigas in the Chittoor District of Andra Pradesh celebrates festival known as '*Mathamma Kolupu*' - a seven day communal festival celebrated every year between the months of April and August in every Madiga habitation. The dedicated girls serves goddess *Mathamma* by participating in the week long annual *Mathamma* festival popularly known as '*Kolupulu*'. The dedicated girls are expected to dance in ecstasy during the festival.[19]

A *Kolpula* woman sits facing the light inside the enclosure, and she stares steadily at the light. All the goddesses were thought to appear to her through that light. Outside the enclosure, the *Baindla* priests stand and invoke the goddess, beating their special drums. The *Kolpula* woman goes into trance, closes her eyes, and is taken possession of by one of the goddesses. The people outside break a coconut, kill a chicken and pour a portion of toddy on the ground where the sacrifice takes place. The women's face is washed with toddy. Before she becomes unconscious she utters the name of the goddess.[20]

17 http://www.philtar.ac.uk/encyclopedia/hindu/ascetic/mariam.html (08.08.12, 7:15pm).

18 Ibid.

19 http://www.ashanet.org/projects-new/documents/409/organizationdetailsandproposal.html (08.08.12, 06:07pm).

20 James Elisha, Liberative Motifs in Dalit Religion, http://www.religion-online.org/showarticle.asp?title+=2451(06.08.12, 5:36pm).

7.3.2. Ankamma Kolupu

The main characteristic of the ritual called *Ankamma Kolupu* is that a midnight worship (puja) is performed by making a colourful Rangoli with wheat flour, turmeric powder, *kumkum*, black charcoal powder, etc. During the worship, singers recite ballads based on local stories about heroes (*Ravaddevaraju* in Telugu, *Veeran* in Tamil). The climax comes at the end of the ritual, when the devotees sacrifice a goat and its blood is spilled in order to appease the goddess. Other rituals like the *Devara Kolupu* or *Veerla Kolupu* are normally performed on some special occasions by individuals or by the community as a whole.

8. Thee Mithi (Fire Walking)

Fire walking, called *Thee-Mithi* in Tamil is one of the popular rituals associated with deity *Mariyamma* in whole Tamil Nadu.[21] In some areas it also known as *poo-mithi* walking on flowers.[22] It is no doubt a primitive rite, which does require a considerable amount of devotion, courage and dedication. All people walk through the fire with a smiling countenance, and even those who start with some hesitation and fear end up with smiles and peace. No one is able to say what makes such different types of people do it and bear the burning heat, but they do it and nobody has complained of any burning of the soles of the feet.[23]

The fire walking ceremony is generally on the last day of the *Mariyamma* festival of ten days.[24] The arrangement of the fire pit require expert skill.[25] Any one cannot make the fire. It is traditionally men of the carpenter class in the rural area who are skilled in this through hereditary practice. The persons in charge beat down the logs a uniform size, so that the top surface is generally even, without any small fires and is a glow of bright red, without any white or black surface.[26]

An Appraisal

Luther's Reformation may be summarized as follows: First, it enabled the believer to understand the essence of faith by distinguishing the Law from the Gospel. Second, it replaced the previously-held view of a severe and harsh God with that of a loving God. Third, it enabled each believer to examine his/her own conscience, and to assume personal responsibility for his/her own actions. Besides, Luther's principle of 'distinction and integration' in guiding the religion-state relationship; the critical perspective provided by the 'Theology of Cross' in shaping theological thought and expression are some his great contributions. Also the hermeneutical

---

21 M. Arunachalam, *Festivals of Tamil Nadu* (Tiruchitrambalam: Gandhi Vidhyalayam, 1980), 197.

22 Arunachalam, *Festivals* ..., 300.

23 Ibid., 197.

24 Ibid., 298.

25 Ibid.

26 Ibid., 299.

key found in the doctrine of justification by grace through faith, over against emphasising work-righteousness that paved the way to corrupt practices in the ecclesial and the societal life and thought, is a great tools of Scriptural interpretations towards liberation and transformation of Church and society. Also his strong emphasis on the equality of all believers through 'Priesthood of all Believers and the understanding of the church as *Communio Sanctorum* derived from the co-inherent communion of the Trinity[27] are great help to understand and challenge the contemporary Church.

Like Luther, Dalit heroes and martyrs symbolise the Dalit protest and continue to inspire the Dalit towards the goals of liberation and equality from the oppressive dominant structures. Though the Dalit religious tradition through its nature had been emphasised here, one truth had been hidden today, is the deities had been given the colour of Brahminical Hinduism. The *Mariamma*, *Ankamma* and all goddess are merged and now called as avatars of Sakti, i.e., Parvati; where the goddess been independent before had been made dependent to male dominant as the Siva had become the husband of them. The virginity of the Dalit goddess been abused by the dominant Brahmin gods.

As it was earlier, all the rituals were done by an elderly person of particular Dalit Community. At present some of these rituals are brahminised and some are declining from Dalit Community life. For example, now the Brahmin priest are called to commemorate the festivals of the Dalit deities in the language called Sanskrit. The community oriented life is gradually vanishing from the lives of the people, through the Brahmin influence to many temples for the deities. The Dalits deities were sat on an open space where anyone can come and approach them without hindrances, which establishes the relationship between the deity and devotee. Dalit deities are no more sitting in a place where they like, the entry of the Dalit is denied by the so called caste people who even does not know about the god or goddess who been imprisoned on four walls called temple. Revitalising the Dalit Religious Tradition is a protest against the dominant Brahminism which has commercialised everything and restricted the community to come together to worship their deities freely and openly.

Dalit Deities are now worshiped in an alien language and time,
Dalit Religious Tradition awaits for Reformation…

27 R. Sahayadhas, *Hindu Nationalism and the Indian Church: Towards an Ecclesiology in Conversation with Martin Luther* (New Delhi: Christian World Imprints, 2013), xxi.

10

The Teaching of 'Priesthood of all Believers' in Today's Pluralistic Context

J.M.P. Thomas Birla

Introduction

The concept of 'the priesthood of believers' have varying interpretations of what the concept means, but we all treasure the biblical truth of the priesthood of believers. In this paper, I would like to highlight its origin, understanding and role of priesthood in the Old Testament. Then the transformation which took place within the role and responsibility of priesthood in the New Testament has been discussed. The paper also explored some of the select reformer's interpretation and the reformation which took place in the Church. An attempt has been made to point out false interpretations and to reaffirm the proper interpretation of the concept 'priesthood of all believers'. Finally, an effort has been made to see the contemporary relevance of the teaching on 'Priesthood of all believers' by Luther in today's multi-religious context.

Concept of Priesthood in Old Testament

In the Old Testament, Priesthood involves lot of responsibility and privileges. During that period, a priest holds a significant place in the temple and in the worship of God. When Israel has constructed its first sanctuary at Mount Sinai, it was then the ordained priests begin to appear in the history of Israel. The whole nation of Israel is considered as a "kingdom of priests" (Exodus 19:6), but within Israel, Aaron and his sons were chosen by Yahweh as his ministers in the house of God. They got the privilege to "stand and serve" (Deuteronomy 10:8; 18:5) at Yahweh's altar. They were almost become the household servants in general and the stewards of King Yahweh in particular. There is a reason for comparing them as household servants because the duties of the Aronic priests are mostly related to serving the community. Their priestly duties involve establishing the holy space, and then they guard it by standing at the entrance to prevent trespassers on the sacred ground. As it was pointed out by the Torah scholar Jacob Milgrom in his Studies in Levitical Terminology, "doing guard duty"[1] is one of the key responsibilities of Levites and priests (Numbers 1:53; 3:5-10; 18:1-7).[2] If anything that is unclean entered the sanctuary, then it would kindle the anger of Yahweh which would fall against Israel. Therefore, it was the priestly guards who were responsible to maintain the health and safety of the nation.[3]

Priests also cleaned house. As Milgrom pointed out, since the Israel's sin and uncleanness has been "registered" on the sanctuary;[4] the priests has also cleaned the house of Yahweh by performing the sacrificial rites, sprinkling the blood of bulls and goats.[5] It was believed that Yahweh would leave his house and abandon the people, if the house became defiled. Therefore, the priests served the people of Israel by serving Yahweh. Priests served Yahweh's table by offering "bread"[6] (Ezekiel 41:22; 44:16), (cf. Leviticus 3:11; 21:21-22). They also offered incense every morning and evening (Exodus 30:7-8).

Thus, by serving Yahweh the priests served the Israel. They not only served the literal "house" of Yahweh, which is the Temple but also served the metaphorical "house" of Israel. They taught them and judge the people of Israel; they also acted as the custodians of Israel's belief and customs.[7] By teaching Torah to the people (Leviticus 24:8), they trained Israel to distinguish pure and impure forms of behavior and so helped them to be holy as Yahweh their God was holy.

They not only cleansed the house and served the people of Israel but more importantly they restored the broken relationship between Yahweh and his people. They have strengthened the worshipers to fellowship with God. They offered praise and thanksgiving on behalf of the people. Therefore, not a single priestly service was for the priests alone but for the Israelites whom they represented. Priests were responsible for certain aspects of worship, such as the sacrifice of animals. They served as mediators between the people and God. The High Priest, the head priest, was the only one, however, allowed to enter the Holy of Holies in the Jewish temple. This especially sacred place was separated from the rest of the temple and from the other priests and worshippers by a great curtain or veil.

---

1 Peter J. Leithart. https://www.firstthings.com/web-exclusives/2010/10/priesthood-of-believers (Accessed on 13/9/17).

2 http://www.valpo.edu/ils/assets/pdfs/05_wengert.pdf (Accessed on 20/8/16).

3 Eric Gritsch, "Vocation," in *The Oxford Encyclopedia of the Reformation*, vol. 4 (Oxford: Oxford University Press), 245-246.

4 Peter J. Leithart. https://www.firstthings.com/web-exclusives/2010/10/priesthood-of-believers (Accessed on 13/9/17).

5 http://founders.org/fj03/the-priesthood-of-all-believers-and-the-quest-for-theological-integrity/ (Accessed on 15/8/16).

6 http://www.wlsessays.net/files/BrugPriesthood.pdf (Accessed on 13/8/16).

7 http://humanitas.org/?p=2517 (Accessed on 25/8/16).

Concept of Priesthood in New Testament

With the life, death and resurrection of Jesus, priesthood has a new perspective. The focus is shifted from the sacrifice of appropriate animals, because Christ sacrificed himself as a Lamb of God and paid the penalty for sin. This was a once-and-for-all act. In Jesus Christ the old priesthood has been replaced with a new priesthood (Hebrews 4-5, 7), Christians by the virtue of being united to Christ has become the priests and kings in him (Revelation 1:6; 5:10). All that the Aaronic priests did exclusively at the tabernacle, believers now do in reality without any hindrances and divisions. And, just as the Aaronic priests served Israel by serving in Yahweh's house, in the same way Christian priests serve the church by serving God.[8] Instead of sacrificing animals the believers now sacrifice praises to God through Jesus, the bread of life. More than offering incense, the believers now offer prayers in God's house, and through practices of forgiveness and love the believers clean the house of God. By using the gifts given by the Spirit, each member of Christ's body contributes to the edification of the whole.[9]

At the crucifixion of Jesus, the great veil in the temple "was torn in two from top to bottom" (Matthew 27:51 NIV), indicating that Jesus, the great High Priest, now mediated between God and humankind. The gulf between God and humankind has restored once and for all by Jesus Christ. Indeed, all who believe in Jesus become priests with direct access to God. Human mediators are no longer needed. We can go directly to God in prayer, confession, praise and worship.[10]

Concept of the Priesthood of all Believers

Martin Luther, a leader in the Protestant Reformation, is well-known as an exponent in propounding the concept of the priesthood of believers. Luther's posting of the 95 Theses on the Wittenberg church door, a call to disagreement has actually marked the symbolic starting point for the Reformation. As Luther has boldly stood against the corruptions of late medieval Catholicism, "priesthood of all believers" had become one of the great slogans of the Reformation. Luther has challenged and questioned the Roman Catholic Church's emphasis on the special role played by the Roman Catholic priests. Every Christian is a cleric, Luther proclaimed in one of his earliest treatises, The Freedom of a Christian, and those who "are now boastfully called Popes, bishops, and lords" are in reality "ministers, servants, and stewards, who are to serve the rest in the ministry of the word" servants of the servants of God. Priesthood of all believers has become the core doctrinal principle of the churches in the Sixteenth Century Reformation. This doctrine has clearly asserts that all humans have equal access to God

---

8 Avery Dulles, *The Priestly Office: A Theological Reflection* (New York: Paulist Press, 1997), 21.

9 http://www.firstthings.com/web-exclusives/2010/10/priesthood-of-believers (Accessed on 23/8/16).

10 http://www.baptistdistinctives.org/resources/articles/the-priesthood-of-the-believer-or-of-believers/ (Accessed on 12/8/17).

through Christ, the true high priest. This introduced a democratic element in the functioning of the church that means all Christians are equal. The ordained clergy thus were the one who leads and represents the entire congregation, preaching and administering the sacraments. Luther insisted that every believer was a priest, with direct access to God. He did not call for the elimination of the role of pastors but indicated that all persons, not just pastors, had a priestly function.[11]

Luther's Work and Arguments

The 27th of Luther's 95 theses states, "They preach man, who says that the soul flies out of purgatory as soon as the money thrown into the chest rattles."[12] Luther was objecting to the idea of issuing the letters of indulgence in exchange with monetary gains by priests who represents the institutional hierarchy. It introduced the idea that an appropriate sacrifice for sin will be offered by the intervention of certain selected people separated to the priesthood became a barrier to the common Christians under the Sixteenth Century Roman Catholic Church. It actually denies an immediate and direct access to God through faith in Christ. Martin Luther fought to overturn the tables of such clerical abuse by emphasizing justification by faith alone 'Sola Fide', the doctrine of the priesthood of all believers and other bold theological arguments. Luther taught that "as fellow priests with Christ we have access to God and may do all things which we see done and figured in the visible and corporeal office of priesthood. We are worthy to appear before God, to pray for others, and to teach one another."[13] This understanding of the concept of the priesthood of all believers went hand in hand with Luther's teaching on justification by faith.[14]

Luther pointed out two estates which exists within the church, the worldly (or secular) and the spiritual (including priests, bishops and monastics). Luther begins his argument against this "doctrine of the two estates" by completely destroying the distinction in the Christian church. He wrote,

> For all Christians are truly part of the spiritual walk of life, and among them there is no difference except because of the office alone, as Paul says in 1 Corinthians 12[:12ff.], that we are all part of one body. Nevertheless each member has its own work so that it serves the others. This each person does, because we have one baptism, one

11 http://www.britannica.com/topic/priesthood-of-all-believers (Accessed on 10/8/2017).

12 *Luther's Work*, vol. 48, 46.

13 *Luther's Work*, vol. 25, 238.

14 http://founders.org/fj03/the-priesthood-of-all-believers-and-the-quest-for-theological-integrity/ (Accessed on 22/8/16). Bernhard Lohse, *Martin Luther's Theology* (Minneapolis: Fortress Press, 2011), 288.

> Gospel, one faith and are equally Christians. For baptism, Gospel, and faith alone make a spiritual and Christian people.[15]

Luther's point becomes clear in his citation of 1 Corinthians 12 that we are all part of one body. Thus, holding an office within the one body of Christ can never be a claim to power but a powerful claim to weakness, to service. This is not simply "fulfilling certain functions" or "lording it over the laity" but rather a self-emptying and a laying down of one's life. Thus, this text cannot mean, "anyone can be a pastor," but rather, "all of us are members of the one body of Christ and individually servants to each other in our respective offices."[16] But misappropriation of these terms turns everything on its head and replaces service with power-grabbing and the unity of Christ's body with the disunity of individualistic spirituality. Paul Rorem puts it, that the priesthood of all believers means in actuality the priesthood of no believers.[17]

Having said that, however, it is important to realize that Luther does insist that, by virtue of our baptism, we are all priests, that is to say, we are all Christians. However, this did not imply for him a democratization of the Christian church or a defamation of the pastoral office. Instead, it was an attack on the papal claim that, by virtue of the power to consecrate and ordain the selected order of men, the pope and his bishops could create a separate spiritual stratum within the Church.[18] If we read in this light, Luther's comments that follow make sense,

> That the pope or bishop anoints, ordains, consecrates, or dresses differently from the laity, may make a hypocrite or an idolatrous oil-painted icon, but it in no way makes a Christian or spiritual human being. In fact, we are all consecrated priests through Baptism, as St. Peter in 1 Peter 2[:9] says, "You are a royal priesthood and a priestly kingdom," and Revelation [5:10], "Through your blood you have made us into priests and kings.[19]

It is the papal claim that, by virtue of ordination, a bishop may transfer someone into the "spiritual" Christian estate that instigates Luther's concept on priesthood of all believers. The claim itself simply makes hypocrites or "olgotzen," a delightful, Sixteenth Century German word that means "an oil icon depicting

15 http://www.firstthings.com/web-exclusives/2010/10/priesthood-of-believers (Accessed on 23/8/17).

16 *Luther's Work*, vol. 35, 100-101.

17 http://www.baptistdistinctives.org/resources/articles/the-priesthood-of-the-believer-or-of-believers/ (Accessed on 24/8/17).

18 Hans Schwarz, "Martin Luther's Understanding of Vocation in Light of Today's Problems," *Lutheran Theological Journal* (May, 1996): 4-12.

19 http://www.trowelandsword.org.au/Contents/Back%20Issues/Feature%20Articles/2000s/2010/ArchF201002art1.htm (Accessed on 22/8/16). Bernhard Lohse, *Martin Luther's Theology* (Minneapolis: Fortress Press, 2011), 287.

a god."[20] Thus, Luther realized that our baptism may consecrate us as priests but does not authorize us to exercise the pastoral office.

It's Relevance in a Pluralistic Society

Unfortunately, the priesthood of the faithful has been stained by fusion with modern individualism. Some have taken "priesthood of believers" to mean that every believer has an absolute right of private judgment about morals and doctrine, the liberty to interpret the Bible with complete autonomy. While others say that "Priesthood of believers" means that believers can do very well without attachment to any church. This was not Luther's view. Priestly ministry was ministry within and to the church. To be a priest means to be a priest for someone. "The fact that we are all priests and kings means that each of us Christians may go before God and intercede for the other," he wrote in a preface to the Psalter that, "If I notice that you have no faith or a weak faith, I can ask God to give you a strong faith". Timothy George captures Luther's viewpoint in one sentence: "Every Christian is someone else's priest, and we are all priests to one another".[21] But for Luther, the priesthood of believers was not an excuse to abandon the church, but rather described the shape of life in communion with the body of Christ and the family of faith. It was not a call to individualism, but summoned individuals to serve God, others, and the common good of the church. It did not free the believer from obedience to authority or leaves him/her free to do as he/she thought best.

Luther mentioned only about Christians in his concept of the priesthood of all believers. However, in a pluralistic Indian context, Luther's idea of the 'Priesthood of All Believers' could be broaden by including the people of other faiths too. In the Sixteenth Century, how the spiritual matters are privatized by the select few and alienated the rest of the church. In the same way, today the spiritual matters such as God, salvation, heaven, healing etc. are privatized by the church and trying to alienate the people of other faiths. It also went to the extent of questioning the credibility of the faith of our brothers and sisters who affiliated themselves to different religious traditions. In this context, the concept of Luther particularly 'Sola Fide' Faith alone serves as a bedrock foundation. Their faith in God, which reflects in their deeds and words, qualifies them as a believer. It is God who qualifies them by Grace alone. The church acts a judge, plays the role of God against the people of other faiths. The church cannot limit the boundless grace of God that includes every true believer irrespective of their nature, style and form of worship.

The reformation was a result of various ritualistic and unchristian practices of the church. In other words, practices that are against the word of God kindled the reformation in the church. In our multi-religious society, quite often the

20 http://www.valpo.edu/ils/assets/pdfs/05_wengert.pdf (Accessed on 23/8/16).

21 http://www.firstthings.com/web-exclusives/2010/10/priesthood-of-believers (Accessed on 23/8/17).

church looks down at the people of other faiths and it aims to 'save the lost ones'. A clear introspection would reveal a different aspect about church itself; where there are many idols such as money, power and position etc., caste system rooted in the church, church is divided based on denominations, doctrines and assets, a shift from mission and evangelism to marketing the brand Christianity. Here the question is who is a true believer? "Not everyone who says to me, 'Lord, Lord,' will enter the kingdom of heaven, but only the one who does the will of my Father who is in heaven." (Mt. 7. 21)

There are many people of other faiths who accept Jesus as their saviour but remain in their religious traditions and did not come under the institution of church. There are people of other faiths who experience God in the form of Krishna, or Allah and live according to the will of God. The spirit of Luther's reformation may lead to the 'Churchless Christianity.'[22] When Luther talks about the priesthood of all believers, it doesn't mean the elimination of priestly office. In the same way, Churchless Christianity doesn't mean the elimination of Churches, whereas the purview of Christianity is not limited to the institution of the Church alone. Thereby, it includes every true believer and the grace of God is manifested.

Conclusion

The doctrine of the priesthood of all believers cannot be denied by anyone since it is in line with the word of God. At the same time, equal importance must be given not to trivialize the meaning with modern individualism or theological minimalism. It is a call to ministry and service. It bridges the gap between the clergy and laity of the church. This could instigate us to take this forward to unite and bridge the gulf between Christians and the people of other faiths. It helps us to analyze ourselves 'Are we true believers?' Church always plays a significant role in imparting the love of God to the world. But Church cannot confine the love of God within itself. God can save a person who is outside the church too. If God is willing to save a person who is outside the church; who are we to stop it? Therefore, all believers could join hands in fulfilling the will of God. It means every true believer can serve as prophets, priests, sons and daughters of God according to their training and vocation.[23]

---

22 http://www.missionfrontiers.org/issue/article/christ-followers-in-india-flourishing-but-outside-the-church (Accessed on 28/8/16).

23 http://www.trowelandsword.org.au/Contents/Back%20Issues/Feature%20Articles/2000s/2010/Arch F201002art1.htm (Accessed on 23/8/16).

11

Impact of Lutheran Reformation in India and Ziegenbalg's Mission in the field of Inter Religious Dialogue

S. Thomas Kennedy

Introduction

We got freedom nearly seventy years before. In this short time India was able to build her own version of democracy, infrastructure, governance, legal systems, delivery mechanisms, satellite to Mars, education and health care. Things change when we start to think. German Lutheran mission exercised a profound influence on the emergence of modern India. The impact of their work through education, empowerment, eradication of social evils, introduced the moral ethics on the basis of human values and dignity and uplift of the downtrodden people was possibly of greater importance than their proselytizing effort.

Dr. Daniel Jeyaraj who is a historian and great authorities on Ziegenbalg's mission said that "Christian mission established multifaceted relationships not only between human beings and God, but also among human beings across cultures and nations so that they can learn from one another and grow together. The Royal Danish-Halle mission, also known as the Tranquebar Mission (1705-1845), created living relationships among the peoples in India, Germany, Denmark, Great Britain and other countries". This mission which originated purely as religious encounter, later involved into a vibrant and intensive multicultural dialogue influencing lives in two continents.

Here Ziegenbalg is the key to understand many features about Tranquebar Mission. He was not merely a pastor and preacher but also a linguist, scholar, one who engaged himself in dialogue with people of other faiths and indologist printer, translator and publisher. But given the under- development in all possible directions as a nation. In the history of India the Eighteenth Century German Lutheran missionaries have contributed a great extent in various realms. They invested pioneering projects in the past. These investments do not siphon any revenue to the respective places of origin.

1. Historical Background of German Halle Pietism

Like all religious movements, German Pietism was, at least in part, a reaction to the spiritual and political climate of its day. Any attempt to understand the theological emphases of Arndt, Justinian von Welz, Spener and Francke must therefore be preceded by an overview of the religious and political climate in which they lived.

Pietism is a type of religion which emphasizes human emotions and actions rather than precise doctrinal statements. It implies some kind of extreme position. It was a religious and educational movement that sought to rekindle the reformation through mystical and spiritual rebirth of its followers. Followers of Pietism believed that Christians should work for the betterment of humankind instead of leading contemplative life. Ronald J Gordon explained the meaning of Pietism, in his article 'Pietism and Brethren in Seventeenth Century: "A movement emanating from Lutheranism that emphasized the need for "religion of the heart" instead of the head, yet combined with a strong commitment to express this inner experience in daily life. It was characterized by ethical purity, inward devotion, charity, separation from worldly interests, and even mysticism. Followers were known for individual piety and rigorous adherence to the teachings of Christ. Leadership was more empathetic to adherents instead of being strident loyalists to sacramentalism. A later and more radical version of pietism known as Separatism questioned the necessity of religious denominations.

1.1. The Religious Situation in Germany

Pietism did not try to undo or disown the reformation, but it tried to complete the reformation. The Church had a reformation in doctrine; now it needed a reformation in life. Elements of Pietism can be traced with continuity to early Christian teachings of Gregory of Nyssa, Macarius, and Ephraem of Syria. But the largest movement of Pietism was birthed in Germany through spiritual pioneers who wanted a deeper emotional experience rather than a preset adherence to form (no matter how genuine). They stressed a personal experience of salvation and a continuous openness to new spiritual illumination. They also taught that personal holiness (piety), spiritual maturity, Bible study and prayer were essential towards "feeling the effects" of grace.[1]

1.2. Religious Background of Tranquebar

This little colony provided a peculiar socio-religious setting for the first Lutheran Pietist missionaries and Indian Lutherans. Its population consisted of worshippers belonging to Indic religions such as **Shaivism** and **Vaishnavism,** popular *Bhakti* movements, Islam and Roman Catholicism. The followers of ***Shaivism, Vaishnavism*** and *Bhakti* movements alone had fifty-temples; the Muslims had two mosques, and the Roman Catholics worshipped in their church. The DEIC,

1 James A. Scherer and Justinian Welz, *Essays by an Early Prophet of Mission*, 28.

the ruler of Tranquebar, acknowledged the supremacy of the King of Denmark and represented in that capacity the Danish Lutheranism.

Most of the household servants of the Danish officials were Catholics (Tapasses). It was very common for the Danish soldiers who were Lutherans to marry Catholics girls. Due to this factor the Danish authorities at Tranquebar were tolerant towards Catholics.[2]

2. Ziegenbalg's Contribution in the Field of Inter-Religious Dialogue

The arrival of the Tranquebar mission initiated a transformation process, which in decisive areas changed the religious, social and cultural patterns and sketched out some main tracks, which can be followed continuously through the next 300 years, thus constitute a key to understanding of present day Tranquebar. This transformation process was not initiated only through cultural encounters between Europeans and Non- Europeans or between Christian missionaries and non-Christian Tamils. A description of the development process based solely on the basis of such simplified dichotomies does not do justice to the complexity of social life in Tranquebar.[3] The Christian missionaries did not interact with a homogenous Tamil population, and were confronted with a multi-faceted society with distinctly divided caste and religious communities, political and economical interest groups. Hence, they entered into a complex pattern of cross- cultural communication and interaction that formed the particular development in Tranquebar.

Traditional research into the history of missions has focused on how the missionaries tried to win the native population for Christianity, and the cultural consequence of creating enclaves of Christian communities with in Indian settings. However, this perspective is eurocentric and the development is described as a one way communication from missionaries to converts. Recent research has pointed out that the process involved a much higher degree of reciprocity between missionaries and converts. The result of this dialogue was not that European Lutheran Christianity struck root in south India, but rather that its special Indian variation emerged.[4]

Ziegenbalg served as the meeting point where the west and the east, Church and society, faith and action, ethics and spirituality, rich and poor, men and women, different classes in Europe and different castes in India, educated and illiterate met with each other and got collaborated. He attempted this integration in a pluralistic society in India where he faced many difficulties and tiny encouragement. This kind of unique nature of Ziegenbalg paved the way to

---

2 Jospeh Thekkedath, *History of Christianity in India*, vol. II., 198.

3 Heike Liebau, Andreas Gross, Y. Vincent Kumaradoss, ed., *Halle and the Beginning of Protestant Christianity in India*, vol. III., 1025-46.

4 Robert E Frykenberg, *Christians and Missionaries in India: Cross–Cultural Communication since 1500*, 2.

many social transformations in India. Ziegenbalg's contributions have led India a century ahead than all other nations in Asia.

For Christian, dialogue is nothing new. Jesus Christ was in dialogue with the people of other faiths and also with God. Martin Luther held dialogue, dialogues with intellectuals and commons and the outcomes of these deliberations were published in the form of book called "Table Talks". So, the Christian faith is dialogue par excellence. Dialogue is more than merely polite conversation. It is spirit, a mood, an attitude towards neighbours of other faiths. Religion should act as the agents of peace and unity in the world that is full of conflicts of every kind, economic, social, racial, political and cultural. But fortunately they have turned to be source of conflict, violence and bloodshed. So it is the need of present context to promote dialogue and collaboration between religions which is an inevitable condition for peace among people tried of religious fundamentalisms. Religions are playing vital role in forming people's attitude and thought. Religions are for life and for living.

Ziegenbalg was far ahead in theologizing amidst south Indians religion three hundred and eight years ago and had set an example to be emulated by the theologians of present times. So he was the pioneer of interfaith dialogue in Eighteenth Century. The Rev. Mark S. Hansonspoke in the seminars and consultations exploring Ziegenbalg impact on Indian Christian Mission:

The eyes of 140 member churches in 78 nations, representing 66 million Lutherans, are now upon this city as the whole Lutheran World Federation joins with you in thanking God for 300 years of Protestant ministry in India. We will give thanks these days for the great variety of gifts of Ziegenbalg but more for the fruits of those seeds that he planted as they have flourished in a diverse culture and an Indian context." He praised the Lutheran churches in India for three centuries of coexistence in a society of multiple religions and classes. "You have much to teach us about what it means to be Christians in a pluralistic context. How do we hold in tension respectful dialogue with persons of other faiths, engage in mission that is holistic, and yet continue to proclaim the gospel of Jesus Christ. He said that "we in other parts of the world are looking to you to be our teachers.

He delivered in his preaching at New Jerusalem Church, Tranquebar during the Ter-Centenary worship:

> Ziegenbalg's ministry was noted for several contributions to Indian culture, such as the translation and printing of the Bible in Tamil, production of the first Tamil grammar book, and his pioneering work in herbal medicine. Speakers noted that missionaries of his time were known to require obedience to their beliefs and customs, while Ziegenbalg first learned Tamil and Tamil philosophy. "We live in a divided world, yet our witness as Christians is that we are one. Unity does not mean sameness. We embrace the other not to make them like us. Ziegenbalg did not come to make Tamil people Germans or

> Danes. The 18th century missionary did not teach the Tamil people European customs but taught them to take pride in their own ways. The ministry of Jesus was one of reconciliation, based on friendship rather than domination.

The Rev. Rafael Malpica-Padilla, executive director, ELCA Global Mission, Chicago, served as a panelist on Mission to the Oppressed said:

> Ziegenbalg's greatest contribution was his perception of the Tamil people. In addition she said "Ziegenbalg engaged the Tamils as people. Ziegenbalg relied on the gifts and skills of the local people who taught him the Tamil language. He sat with the young children on the floor and practiced writing the letters in the sand. Ziegenbalg's ministry was one of accompaniment with and among the Tamil people.

Ziegenbalg realized to understand the religions of Malabar without prejudice. He convinced that even these Malabar religions can teach many good things to the Europeans. This conviction never changed his faithfulness to the Gospel of Christ because he had fully understood that the main task of disciple of Christ is not only converting people to Christianity but also to serve as ideal pastor to bring a total transformation in the society.

3. Church Response to Inter-Religious Dialogue

Discussion with the other religions is actually essential to survival, necessary for the sake of peace in the world. The world is not getting any smaller: the migration of peoples, new methods of communication, and the vast expanse of knowledge about others are increasing rather than diminishing. Addressing our response to other religious traditions is both unavoidable and valuable as the church attempts to understand the reality that surrounds it. In a society that has become increasingly diverse and complex, what it means to be religious in this society has shifted. The church, like other religious groups, must reconsider its role in the midst of a changing society.

Here we see that how to spread the outcomes of inter-religious dialogue and evaluate its impact; the opportunities and challenges involved in conveying the outcomes of dialogue to wider society; the role of key actors from religious, social and academic circles in disseminating inter-religious dialogue; the importance of involving women and young people in promoting the wider acceptance of inter-religious dialogue.

Dr. Mohammad Reza Dehshiri, Vice-President of the Islamic Culture and Relations Organization, Tehran, also shared his vision for dialogue:[5]

---

5 http://www.oikoumene.org/en/resources/documents/wcc-programmes/interreligious-dialogue-and-cooperation/interreligious-trust-and-respect/communique-from-wcc-and-cid-inter-religious-dialogue-meeting (Accessed on 14th August 2017).

- The basic requirement includes commitment, co-operation and comprehensiveness.
- Its methodology should be reciprocal, respectful and representative.
- Its approach required participation, proclamation and promotion.
- Ways for dialogue included exchange, education and evaluation.
- Dialogue needs to involve people in mutual understanding, offering an incentive approach, and be an authentically indigenous dialogue from generation to generation.

The church could see pluralism as a problem and choose to be separationist, claiming its own superiority and vowing to remain unmoved by society or the church can follow its call to transform the world and choose to be an active and vital part of society. The church must recognize the necessity of growing in its understanding of and relationship with other faith traditions. The gospel calls Christians to live as neighbors with those who surround them, learning to love and minister even to those with whom they wholeheartedly disagree. If the church will have any impact on its society, the church must learn to live with its neighbors, not merely in toleration, but in a respectful relationship that seeks the best for all parties involved.

While interreligious dialogue is necessary for the church to assert a meaningful voice in society, it also offers rich possibility for the church. As it recognizes its situation in a world of abundant diversity, the church must overcome its fear and mature in its own understanding of the presence of other religions as an opportunity rather than a problem a chance for church renewal, building relationships, growing in understanding, and expressing the love and grace of the Christian message in a way that is non-confrontational and open-minded. Interreligious dialogue provides the greatest of opportunities for the church to grow in appreciation of the abundance of other traditions while maintaining the integrity of its own commitment to the gospel.

Dialogue is the best means of overcoming misunderstandings and fostering mutual appreciation and peaceful coexistence between the adherents of different religions in today's multicultural world. Dialogue at the theological and philosophical level may result I' significant gains in mutual knowledge, understanding and insight about each other's religion; it is also very important to seek to spread the fruits of such personal encounters to the members of wider society. We will make every effort to spread peace, friendship and peaceful coexistence among the adherents of different religions by encouraging various forms of dialogue: conceptual, joint social action and in daily life. The need to work strategically with various forms of media, to share the results of inter-religious dialogue, was underscored.

As Ziegenbalg did, we have to emphasize the importance of encouraging young people to actively take part in inter-religious dialogue and of ensuring that future generations promote the value of peaceful coexistence and respect for their fellow human beings, irrespective of their religion. We need to encourage the active participation of women in inter-religious dialogue at all levels, recognizing women's previous initiatives. As Ziegenbalg approached, we have to agree that effective dialogue can constitute a significant means to counteract the words and actions of those who incite religious hatred or seek deliberately to dishonour what is sacred to others. We need to encourage inter-religious dialogue in all sectors of society with the aim of involving all in ensuring justice, equality, non-violence, welfare, friendship and compassion in society.

4. Communal Harmony and Peace

India is a land of Unity in diversity. High mountain ranges, vast seas, large river-irrigated lands, countless rivers and streams, dark forests, sandy deserts, all these have adorned India with an exceptional diversity. Among the peoples there are numerous races, religions and languages. The modern Indian civilization has been nourished and developed by multiracial contributions. From times immemorial, diverse races migrated into India through land and sea routes and get themselves settled here. In course of time they are absolutely absorbed in India's social life. In the historical period, diverse branches of the unique ethnic groups the *Persians*, the *Pallavas,* the *Kushanas*, the *Greeks*, the *Sakas*, the *Huns*, the *Portuguese*, the *Arabs*, the *Turks*, the English and the European races came to India, and enriched Indian ethnicity and culture by their contribution to the same. India is the place of reunion of many religions and languages of the world. Here the Hindus, the Sikh, the Christians, the Muslims, the Jews, the Buddhists, the Jains and the Parsees live together. Besides this, the aborigines living in the jungles or in the hill areas have various ancient religious customs which they carefully observe. Again, in different regions and among different races, social customs and usages assume different shape and character.

5. Diverse Languages and Unity in India

The Indian people composed of several racial elements have a range of languages among them. Official accounts confirm that more than two hundred languages are present in our country. Each region has its own language. In our society, it is the responsibility of every individual to preserve harmony and protect individual rights. But recent day Tamil Nadu was rocked by bomb blasts and discovered a huge quantity of explosives.[6] Over the years India has been a place of peace and communal harmony. But we see that political leaders killed, churches were demolished and people were displaced due to communal violence. The context against which such violence is occurring is a noticeable change in the communal climate across the country.

6 *Frontline, March 20, 1998.*

5.1. Communal Violence and the Denial of Justice

Independent India established a governmental structure committed to secularism and democracy. Its constitution guarantees equal treatment before the law to all individuals regardless of community background. Victims of communal violence in India suffer a range of violations of internationally recognized human rights. These include the right not to be arbitrarily deprived of life, the right to equal treatment before the law without discrimination, and the right not to be subject to coercion which would impair the freedom to have or adopt a religion. Ethnic, linguistic, and religious minorities are guaranteed the right to enjoy their own culture, to profess and practice their own religion, or to use their own language. Furthermore, under international human rights law states are obligated to prohibit by law any advocacy of national, racial, or religious hatred that constitutes incitement to discrimination, hostility or violence.

5.2. Need of Social Integration and Communal Harmony in India

India has set an important example of communal harmony to this world. India is the only country of the world where people of all religion and beliefs have been living peacefully for a long time. It is important to note that even during the reign of British EIC and Tranquebar Mission; there was no tension among the various religious people. India, a multi-religious, multilingual and multi-racial country has always enjoyed the essential unity of culture amidst diversities that kept her people united. After independence, narrow religious, regional and communal feelings attracted the country. The apparently mindless communal tensions and bloody riots that take place occasionally create a sense of mistrust among the two principal religious communities involved in clashes. The country pays a heavy price for such disturbances through loss of life and property.

India is a vast country where people of different religions and communities live side by side. In India, national integration alone can be the foundation of a strong, united and prosperous India, especially in these days of extremism and terrorism. The fact remains that regardless of divisions and distinctions, caste or creed, we have lived together for thousands of years. In every walk of life we find that it is our unity that gives us strength. A united country is respected in the eyes of others. Unfortunately today, instead of unity there seems to prevail some disunity that hinders national harmony in India. Most of the time the, quarrels are between Hindus and Muslims, but sometimes a few other communities have also clashed with each other. Moreover, social and economic inequalities are also responsible for the disunity prevailing in the country. The absence of a truly and widely acceptable common national language has made national unity difficult.

As Schwartz, a peace maker contributed to our Indian society, it is important to accept that there is a need for unity in India and of commitment not to a party, not to a particular religion but to the nation as a whole. We have to form strong and durable links to create national unity to avoid disastrous consequences. We conclude that India is a land of Unity in Diversity.

Conclusion

Ziegenbalg and his successors derived their intercultural insights from important German and Tamil sources, and also incorporated them in their writings and implemented through their noble ministry. In collaboration with Tamil Christians they produced Tamil Christian literature, established churches and schools for both boys and girls, and trained fellow Indian workers to carry on meaningful missionary work with commitment. They insisted that Tamil Christians should learn to live as Christians and Tamil people within their own society by following Biblical values, priorities and concepts. Eighteenth Century German Lutheran missionaries' legacy invites us to live together, love each other, and break the wall of differences on the basis of colour, sex, caste, sex and religion towards service to soul and service to body.

Finally, what is most fascinating value is Ziegenbalg's method of encounter with Hindus. He was accessible to everyone and eager to engage in dialogue. His commitment to truth motivated him to understand the truth of others. He initiated meetings and correspondence, which proved to be enriching and to some extent transforming too. Ziegenbalg's pioneering attempts will be a constant reminder for generations to come of the need to learn, evaluate and move on making sense of mission and church life in multi- faith context such as India.

12

An Account of the Re–Formation of Tamil Society by European Lutherans and the Native Co-Workers

J. G. Jacob Sundarsingh

I. Introduction

The first Evangelical (Lutheran) intervention in the Tamil society had its beginning with the simple desire of an individual–Fredrick IV – the king of Denmark and Norway who wished to patronize the missionaries who would willingly proceed from Europe to his faraway colony in Tharangambadi (Tranquebar)[1] to evangelize his 'heathen' subjects. Though it was a very difficult task, without any prior training, with no experiences to be a missionary, with no models to follow, with no idea of voyages and with no good health, two German young students studying in Halle University, Germany – Barthtolomeus Ziegenbalg and Heinrich Plutchau accepted King's invitation and have sailed to Tharangambadi from Copenhagen. Finally they have landed in the small coastal village in the Coramandal coast[2] on

1 'Tharangambadi' is the name of a small coastal village in the Coramandal coast where the pioneer Protestant missionaries landed in 1706. 'Tharangam' and 'badi' are Tamil words. They mean 'waves' and 'singing' respectively. A 'waves singing' place. As the native people have called this village as Tharangambadi, all through this research, the usage of 'Tranquebar,' a colonizer's way of calling, though familiar and popular, is avoided. Geographically it is situated in the Coramandal coast nearly 250 kms south of Chennai. As it had direct trade relationship with many European and Asian countries like Ceylon, Burma, China, Rome, Portugal, Denmark, France, England, Holland and Russia from the 11th cent A.D. through the sea, it was called as the Queen of Coramandal Coast. G. Veerappa Pillai, *Tranquebar: Queen of the Coramandal Coast* (Madras: Popular Printers, 1953), 1–3.

2 The Eastern coast of present India from Kolkota to Kanyakumari on the shores of Bay of Bengal is commonly known as Coramandal Coast whereas the long shore from Goa to Kanyakumari on the shores of Arabian Sea is known as Malabar Coast.

9th July 1706. Because of this co – operation, later they began to be known as the pioneer Protestant or the Royal Danish – Halle missionaries.

The society in which they began their missionary endeavour was very complex because of many external and internal forces. Yet, having understood the needs of the major section of the society composed by the Dalits, they have inaugurated many programmes. All such interventions have surprisingly transformed and reformed the society thereafter. As faithful Lutherans and Pietists, the Royal Danish – Halle missionaries (1706-1841) have ventured to explore many new areas and those who followed them[3] have also adopted the legacy and the heritage of pioneer mission. They continued to minister in Tharangambadi region and in all other regions of Tamil Nadu with the same zeal, passion, commitment, expertise and love. Therefore, in this paper, an attempt is made to explain the significant changes the Lutheran missionaries have brought in the Tamil society. No doubt, the driving force for all such ministerial initiatives was the evangelical faith proposed by Dr. Martin Luther in the Sixteenth Century A.D.

II. The Factors that Characterized the Nature of the Eighteenth Century Tamil Society

The ***first and major factor*** or practice that significantly characterized the Tamil society was the observance and perpetuation of Caste system. The caste system introduced by the Aryan intruders in all over the country was prevalent in the Tamil society also. This practice has distinguished and discriminated people as 'high' and 'low' and as 'clean' and 'unclean'. It categorized people into four sections and declared that a major section of the community cannot be part of this categorization. It called them as *chandala, avarna* and as the fifth caste. Because of this declaration, it has denied them all privileges including their right to natural resources. By not allowing them to get educated and by withholding the privilege of education as the monopoly of 'higher' castes, it has made the major section of the society to remain as uneducated group. Instead, it has assigned them menial and unclean jobs. It did not allow them to change their jobs and asked them to live only in segregated settlements in villages. It called their dwelling places as '*cheries*'. It denied them dignity, honour, equality and the basic amenities of life like health care, sanitation, drinking water facility, etc.

As the Dalits continued to remain as the daily labourers and basic work force generation after generation producing food for the entire society, rearing the animals and in the up keeping the sanitary needs of the society, they did not own lands and their economic standard was very low. Despite the fact that they were the producers of food, they were denied access to natural resources like ponds, canals, rivers, roads and to enjoy the fruits of trees through lease. As they had

3 The Missions were: The English (England) – Halle (Germany) Mission (EHM) (1745 - 1841), The Leipzig Evangelical Lutheran Mission (Germany) (LELM) (1841 - 1919) and The Church of Sweden Mission (Sweden) (CSM) (1848 – 1919).

to struggle with the limited income of six months a year, their economic status never improved. They remained always as economically dependent on others for their survival. The health care provided to village women even during the time of pregnancy was very poor. Therefore, the Dalit women remained in still worst conditions.

Thus, the Dalits remained in the society as socially discriminated, religiously marginalized, ethnically exploited and as culturally unclean. They were also economically downtrodden and politically divided. While describing the conditions of Dalits or the 'untouchables,' Brijraj Singh writes,

> They (the 'untouchables') were so considered because it was believed that their traditional occupations were polluted and polluting, whether those occupations involved removing excrement, dealing with animal carcasses and hides or toddy tapping. Untouchables lived in separate sections of villages and marriage between them and caste Hindus was prohibited. But this did not mean that no relationship existed between them and the higher castes....The largest group of Untouchables was the *Paraiyar*, which sometimes came to be used as a generic term for all Untouchable *jatis*.[4]

The ***second*** characteristic of the society was the subjugation of women as secondary citizens and the treatment of them as filthy and unclean. Because of this attitude, the women were kept in the lowest strata of the society even lower than the Dalit male members. They were destined only give birth to children and to rear them along with performing domestic duties. They were never allowed to take part in decision – making bodies and their suggestions were always suppressed. They were denied education and were always made to feel about them as inferior.

The ***third*** factor that characterized the Tamil society was the two distinct geographical locations of Tharangambadi region and of the villages in its vicinity such as 1) The Coramandel Coast and 2) The Delta of river Cauvery. The native Muslims and the people belonging to *Chettiyar* and *Nadar* castes were engaged in inland and foreign trades. They were sailing to various countries such as Sri Lanka, Burma, China, Rome, Portugal, Denmark, France, England, Holland and Russia from Eleventh to Nineteenth Century AD itself and thus contributing to the revenue of the society.

Along with them, the fisher folk community has not only formed another major section of the society but also supported the economy of the entire nation. They have provided the ***fourth*** characteristic of the society. Because of its geographical location in the Coramandal coast, this region was occupying a significant place in the sea related industry for many centuries. As Vedaranyam[5]

4 Brijraj Singh, *The First Protestant Missionary to India: Bartholomaeus Ziegenbalg (1683 - 1719)* (New Delhi: Oxford University Press, 1999), 54.

5 Vedaranyam is also a natural animal and bird sanctuary.

and Kodiakarai are situated in the southern tip of Nagapattinam district they had closer contacts with Sri Lankan fishing community. Thus, until the recent past, the fishing communities of these two nations had closer relationship as they live in close proximity. When new harbours emerged in Chennai and Thoothukudi, the economy generated by Nagapattinam began to decline. Yet, the various sea – related trades undertaken by the fishermen of this region have continued and generated revenue to the national economy of the nation.

Fifthly, the traders began to come to Tharangambadi from European countries[6] in successive periods also began to characterize the nature of the society. In a short span of 300 kms on the Coramandal coast from Chennai to Velankanni, they were establishing their trading centres. After having settled in the towns, they built huge residential, official and religious buildings and named certain areas of the towns with their own names. They introduced their food stuffs and brought with them various items that began to change the ethos of the people.

The ***sixth*** factor was the various religious practices perpetuated by the various religious faiths and the shrines, temples and holy places such as 1) Saivism 2) Vaishnavism 3) Buddhism 4) Jainism 5) Roman Catholicism 6) European Protestantism (practiced by the officers and soldiers of Danish East India Company) 7) Islam 8) the religion of fisher folk 9) the Dalit religions having

6 The Portuguese were the first ones to land in Velankanni and in Nagapattinam in the Sixteenth Century. They were followed by the Dutch who also landed in Nagapattinam in 1657. Then the French followed them and got settled in Karaikal in 1739. The Danes came next. The English were also in their initial stage of undertaking voyages to places like Madras (Chennai) from early seventeenth century and to Cuddalore from 1624. A few historians were able to trace the arrival of such trading people from neighbouring countries of Asia even from the beginning of First Century A.D. The first Europeans to land in the Malabar Coast in 1458 were the Portuguese. Then in the Sixteenth Century a few more Portuguese traders came to Thoothukudi region and as a result of the ministry of Francis Xavier, at least 30,000 people embraced Christianity and became Roman Catholics. In the Sixteenth Century, a few other Portuguese sailors landed in Velankanni and established a shrine. So the origin of the Roman Catholic Church in Tharangambadi goes back to Sixteenth Century. Then, except for the French, all others who followed the Portuguese were from various Protestant European nations. Like the Portuguese, all of them came to the various coastal towns mainly for trade through sea, but were not interested in religious conversions. They had their trading centres mostly in the Coramandal coast and began to operate from such centres. The **Dutch** established their centres in Pulicat (1609), in Sadras (1647) and in Nagapattinam (1660). The **British** established their centres in Masulipattinam (1622), in Chennai (1639), in Cuddalore (1683) and in Calcutta (1689). The **French** established their centres in Pondicherry (1674) and the **Danish** established their centres in Tharangambadi (1620) and in Serampore (1676). The Portuguese Roman Catholics had their centres in Velankanni and Tharangambadi since the beginning of the Sixteenth Century. Cf., Wikipedia, *Karaikal*, viewed on 14th June 2010 at 4 pm; Udayakumar Victor Kanagaraj, *Tharangambaadiyil Airopiyargal: Or Aaivu* (Tamil) (The Europeans in Tharan-gambadi: A Research), A M.Phil., Thesis submitted to Bharathidasan University (unpublished), Tiruchirapalli, 2000; Wikipedia, Cudddalore, viewed on 14th Nov 2014 at 4 pm; Cyril Bruce Firth, *An introduction to History of Christianity in India* (Madras: CLS, 1974).

Ayyanaar, Kaaliamman, Ellaiamman and the *Mariamman* as their local abodes 10) the modern Hindu religious cults of the Puttaparthi Sai Baba, Melmaruvathur Bangaru Adigalar, Matha Amirthanandha Maayi, Baba Ravishankar and many other 'minor' gods and 11) the various tantric and mantric practices of the local superstitious beliefs.

Thus, the religious traditions that were introduced to this region in a latter period were considered to be the 'official' religious traditions and their dominant expressions had often excluded the major section of the society that hailed from the Dalit background in this region and denied them many privileges. In fact, they have discriminated them. After designating the natives as 'lower' castes and then claiming them as 'higher' castes, all new Hindu traditions prevented them to practice 'higher' religious traditions. Basically they denied the natives the privilege of entry into their worshipping places. Even in religious festivals, the Dalits were always excluded and were not granted equal status. Rather, they were asked to perform only menial duties. But, the Dalits began to realize this distinction only at a latter period. also have become popular among the people of this region. Apart from the Dalits, other neglected segments of the society such as the fisher folk, the scavengers and others have also developed their own religious traditions and have erected their own religious centres.

The ***seventh*** influence was by the traders, soldiers, those who were in the service of Danish East Indian Company and others who have accompanied the officers of Danish colonialism have developed illegal relationship with the native women and at one point a new community began to emerge with native girls who were unmarried mothers. These women along with their children were struggling to ascertain their identity and for their survival. Of course, the teachings of Kshthriya religions, the personal relationships emerged between the Western traders and the natives and the new job opportunities the Dalits got in the houses of Europeans and in the harbor have laid the foundation to the Evangelical missionaries to venture new areas with them. As Daniel Jeyaraj writes,

> In every aspect, the Danish colony of Tranquebar (1619 – 1845) was a place of multiple people groups, religions, cultures and traditions. In 1702, just four years before the arrival of B. Ziegenbalg (1682 – 1719) and H. Plutschau (1677 – 1746), the Danes in Tranquebar conducted a census. Accordingly, about 6,000 people lived in the walled city of Tranquebar, and about 30,000 people in the adjoining fifteen villages. In the midst of 100 Portuguese, 500 Roman Catholics and about 2,000 Muslims only twenty – four Danes lived in Tranquebar. The rest were Tamil people, who worshipped in fifty – one temples. Their major deities were Shiva, Vishnu, Brahma, and the members of their families including the "minor" deities such as male god Aiayanar,

and goddesses Mariyamman and Ellamman. Besides, the Tamils in Tranquebar represented ninety – six caste groups.[7]

III. The Interventions of Pioneer Protestant Church

1. The Assertion with Lands and Buildings

The pioneer Protestant missionaries have primarily bought lands to build churches, schools, boarding homes and even to bury the dead ones. This was the first revolutionary step that really empowered the landless and daily wage labourers. All along, for many centuries, these Dalits have been never gathered under any roof. That too they were never allowed to walk through and enter into the streets of the 'higher' caste people. But, the missionaries bought two significant lands in the King's street in Tharangambadi which was situated in the European quarter. The first one was a land to build New Jerusalem Church and the second one was an old bungalow called *The Seniorate* from where presently the Ziegenbalg Spiritual Centre is functioning. When people gathered in such buildings, they were always empowered with the assurance of God's abiding presence. The school buildings where the children began to learn languages, science, history, moral values, and other subjects, they have felt elevated as education and entry into schools were new phenomena in those days. Only representatives of dominant castes have admitted and trained their own children for their own benefits. But, it was Ziegenbalg who provided education to those who do not belong to his race, nationality and other parameters.

The third land was the burial grounds. Until his arrival, when a Dalit dies, the society used to arrogantly refuse to bury him/her with dignity and honour. Rather, it used to ruthlessly command that he/she should be carried on to the cremating place through crude and unleveled roads. He/she should be only cremated and not buried and the earthly mortals should be thrown in the rivers. Making of coffin boxes, carrying the corpse in decorated vehicles and the religious leaders performing last rites were forbidden. Ziegenbalg and his followers not only bought lands to bury the Lutheran Christians but also have buried them with prayer and liturgy after a solemn service in the church. Processions to the church for burial service and the conduct of service were introduced by the Evangelical missionaries.

2. The Confidence Implanted through Building Communities and Congregations

The Lutheran congregations established by the missionaries in and around Tharangambadi and later on in different places of Tamil Nadu became the basic units of ecclesiastical administration and the units of social transformation.

7 Daniel Jeyaraj, "Colonialism and Mission in Tranquebar – their Relationship to the "Hindus", 101.

Congregations were defined as a group of baptized 'believers', both men and women, young and old, who lived in a particular village or in a closer geographical proximity. Prior to their conversion, the Dalits living condition and their status in the society was unimaginable. It was in this context, the pioneer protestant church has established congregations in Tharangambadi region. Consequently, ***first and foremost***, the missionaries have owned the converts from Dalit background by giving them new Christian names and began to enroll their names and their family particulars in their registers. ***Secondly,*** they began to take care of them by providing them education, awareness and health care. ***Thirdly***, they began to serve them by standing beside them for their basic entitlements and ***fourthly*** they have made attempts to emancipate them from all their deplorable conditions. In turn, they demanded the converts to attend the divine services regularly and expected them to be loyal to church and to the new faith. They were taught to lead a different way of life than before and were instructed not to worship any 'idols' but to believe only in Jesus Christ. Many of their socio, cultural practices that were undergirded and sanctioned by hierarchical religious systems, were banned. Prior to the formation of congregations, the Dalits had no opportunities to gather them as one homogeneous group. In fact, they did not have the guts to do that against the will of their masters/landlords and they had no time for such gatherings because they were constrained to work from early in the morning until late night all through the year. Though they were paid unjustly, it was presumed that they should work like animals without demanding any extra pay.

When they became Christians, all these deplorable conditions began to change slowly. Though the missionaries were the official heads of all these congregations, they wanted to share their responsibilities with the natives. As Heike Liebau writes, actually the European missionaries were looking for persons who could take over the sensitive task of mediation between people and them. They required loyal persons who knew the country and the languages and who were willing to pass on the knowledge of Christianity they had acquired from them to their own people, as multipliers in the service of the European mission. Consequently, some of them have arisen from the congregations and have given them voluntarily to the service of the church whereas some were identified and were called by the missionaries for various tasks in the church's administration. In the course of Eighteenth Century and in the first decades of Nineteenth Century, there were about 500 Indians who were working in different capacities. They included catechists and/or evangelists, school masters, assistants, prayer – leaders, washer men, cooks, accountants, sextons, grave – diggers, book – binders and in a later stage also pastors and others.[8] They were broadly classified as "Workers of the Word" and "Workers in the External Establishments."[9] Though there were

8 Heike Leibau, "The Indian Pastors in the Danish – Halle and the English – Halle Mission," in *Halle and the Beginning of Protestant Christianity in India – Volume II,* 720.

9 Leibau, *Indian Pastors ...*, 720.

converts also from other castes who hailed from other regions, it was mostly the *Paraiyar* workers who have served in all these villages as others could not work among *Paraiyars* and could not get rid their casteistic mind – set even after conversion.[10]

Among all other workers, it was the supervising catechists who have contributing to the life of the congregations though others also were contributing. Most of them have lived among the people in their villages. The catechists have begun to teach the congregation members European Hymns, lyrics and other necessary Bible verses. They have taught them to pray, sing and to give offerings to God. They have meticulously served and/or safeguarded their 'sheep' as their shepherds. As Dennis Hudson quotes from Daniel Jeyaraj,

> The mission could not survive without Malabarian catechists...besides teaching Christian doctrine, they superintended the spiritual lives of Christians in the villages, visited the sick and needy, administered aid to the poor, conducted marriages and funerals, and preached sermons...Importantly, they could go where Europeans could not.[11]

Because of these developments, next to European missionaries, the catechists (and mostly who were also the teachers) were respected by the people. Having these two groups of people as their spiritual and administrative leaders, other workers and other ordinary members have begun to revere and respect them. Thus, the protestant Christianity has gathered the uncared, uneducated and unorganized people particularly the women as part of a big institution or organization called the church and provided select individuals from such 'lower' caste background to function as leaders and religious heads of their communities. It is indeed unthinkable and surprising to note how the missionaries have trusted and entrusted the responsibilities with those who have hailed from a very low background. So also, it is very surprising how these men got transformed and began to transform their own communities when such opportunities were given to them because all of them have hailed from very low background and were involved only in doing filthy and menial jobs. They were living even without the realization of their worth.

---

10 While writing about the significance of the ministries of these catechists, Heike Liebau quotes in her article a diary entry that talks about the appointment of a Tamil catechist in the Danish – Halle Mission in Tharangambadi dated 28th May 1707. Catechists from among the Indians are very necessary for the mission in order to work with the catechumen in the manner shown, to be sent out among the heathen, but also to visit the members of the congregations from time to time and to visit the sick every day. Neither the heathens nor the catechumen, and even the members of the congregation, venture to question a European preacher freely and to reveal their concerns. Therefore, it is very necessary to have loyal persons from their midst who can observe and tell us daily what is happening among these people and what questions the preacher should address. Leibau, *Indian Pastors* ..., 719.

11 Quoted in Hudson's *Protestant Origins* ..., 31.

The ***second*** important task of the missionaries after entrusting the ministries in the hands of native workers was purchasing of lands in all the villages where congregations were established and in such newly purchased lands, they have primarily built churches and schools for the people. Mostly, the buildings were built in the segregated corners of the villages known as *'cheries'*. Yet, in some places like Tharangambadi, Sirkali, Mayiladuturai and in Karaikal huge lands were purchased also in main roads that were designated as 'high' caste lands. These simple buildings and the divine services and other deliberations that took place in such simple thatched shed buildings have become the nucleus of all their activities. Many native people involved actively in the mission endeavour to uplift the society. All these unrecognized native workers also have equally committed them to the service of the church through the educational institutions and have contributed to the upliftment of the children.

3. The Declaration as God's People with the Provision of Holy Bible and Hymn Book

When we spiritualize the event of translating Bible into Tamil and the German Hymns, printing, publishing and distributing them to the natives, we may not understand the actual impact they have played in the society because giving Holy Scripture in the hands of people who were until then treated as unworthy, filthy, polluting and unholy was not an ordinary act. Inspired by Luther, Ziegenbalg also was giving it in vernacular of the recipients. Like German Christians, the Dalit Tamil Lutherans were also fortunate to receive God's Word in Tamil. So also, they were given the privilege of receiving the fiery and revolutionary songs in the form of Hymns. They have played a great role in Germany against all the ritualistic practices, theology, order of worship and religious beliefs of medieval Christianity. When the Dalits were forbidden to sing the *Indian ragas* arranged in Carnatic tunes, Ziegenbalg introduced these Hymns as the heritage of Lutheran church, thus counter acting to the accusations of the dominant classes.

4.The Awareness through Language and Education

Though the missionaries have committed them to the ministries of Word of God and of the Sacraments aiming at the conversion of 'heathen', when they have witnessed the heinous practices based on caste observance, they have realized the importance of providing education to the masses to which it was denied for many centuries. As Heike Liebau writes, soon after their arrival in Tharangambadi, Bartholomeus Ziegenbalg and Henrich Plutschau have set up their own school with a schoolmaster in their house and thus gained insights into local teaching methods. On their travels in the area around Tharangambadi they have looked for schools and talked with the village teachers.[12] On 27th August

12 Heike Liebau, "Faith and Knowledge: The Educational System on the Danish – Halle and English – Halle Mission," in *Halle and the Beginning of Protestant Christianity* – Vol. III, edited

1709 Ziegenbalg mentioned in his letter that in all cities, small towns and villages there were schools in which young people were taught to read and write. Yet, he has expressed his dissatisfaction with their performance.[13] During his time of arrival, in many villages there were no schools that helped to educate the children for future employment in the local accounts or administrative sections. Except few girls who were chosen to be the *devadasis* in the temples no girls were studying in such schools.[14]

The first mission schools were "house schools" opened by Ziegenbalg and Plutschau in 1707. Classes took place in the living quarters of the missionaries. Plutschau set up a "Portuguese" school in which Danish and German were also taught, while Ziegenbalg set up a Tamil school. The school was housed in a separate building only two years later. From 1710 onwards Grundler taught Tamilian children in his house in Poraiyar. Schools were established in all the districts under the care of the mission. In 1735, the mission had five schools in Tranquebar and others in the districts of Mayavaram, Tanjavur, Mahadevipattanam, Tiruppalatturai, Mannargudi and Marrawa.[15]

The primary task of mission schools was to directly recruit members for the local congregation, to train local mission workers and in end effect to plant Christianity firmly in local society.[16] Thus, the establishment of schools for boys and girls, boarding homes, orphanages, homes for children, seminary and other institutions by the missionaries have begun to bring in great social transformation as most of them who have served and studied in these institutions hailed from very lowly background. The missionaries with the help of already existing village teachers, some pundits and other volunteers have drawn the syllabus and started teaching the children though the students were neither able to pay for their enrollment nor for the salaries of their teachers. After getting educated, the Dalits had the opportunity to get involved in alternate jobs. Thus, the missionaries have catered to the needs of poor, neglected, needy and deserted people.

Though the initiatives to start, monitor, support and to educate the rural masses have emerged from the missionaries, it was predominantly the teachers cum catechists (in most of the cases) who have actually run the schools and other institutions related to educational ministry. These workers served as liaison persons between the missionaries, congregation members, students and their families. Most of them have started initially as mere catechists but later on they began to serve also as teachers in church run schools and institutions. In fact, no religious or political or social forums were taking care of the education of Dalits in the whole nation when the Lutheran missionaries began to establish schools for

by Andreas Gross and others, 1183.

13 Liebau, *Faith and Knowledge* ..., 1183.

14 Liebau, *Faith and Knowledge* ..., 1183.

15 Liebau, *Faith and Knowledge* ..., 1184.

16 Liebau, *Faith and Knowledge* ..., 1214.

Dalits. The colonial powers had no schemes to uplift the Dalits as they were not clear with their agenda what to do with caste distinction. It was in this context the Lutheran missionaries have established schools in the remotest parts of this region particularly in *cheries.*

5. The Protection and Accompaniment through Boarding Homes

The boarding homes have served as another important institution that not only empowered Dalits but also had great impact on them. The protection and the other benefits provided in these institutions, to both boys and girls apart from the formal and regular education imparted there provided them self – respect, hope for future, opportunities for economic development and self – confidence, various exposures to town life, interaction with students other villages, new status with a sense of dignity, self – respect and security for life and job. It also helped them to get emancipated from the shame attached to their caste. Thus, the residential learning systems firstly introduced by the evangelical missionaries that were continued by the following Lutheran missionaries became one of the significant motivating factors. Most of the latter day Dalit leaders and spokesmen like Panditha Ayothidasa Pandithar have insisted on the importance of educating the rural masses. But, the evangelical missionaries have laid the foundation and started the ministry from the beginning of Eighteenth Century itself.

When education itself was denied to students hailing from the downtrodden background, the pioneer missionaries have established not only schools but also boarding homes all over Tamil Nadu.[17] Though it was primarily admitting Lutheran boys from villages (in other words, the children of Dalit Lutherans), boys of other castes and other religions also have joined the institutions. The standard education provided in the school under the strict supervision and guidance of German missionaries like E. Shepper, the discipline with which the students were monitored, the values of life inculcated in them through the masters and wardens like personal devotion, cleanliness, punctuality, self – respect and respect for elders, the financial helps provided by the mission, the various opportunities provided to the village boys to learn new games, musical instruments and western music, to be part of students army wing (the National Cadet Corps) and the National Service Scheme, to know and understand the world, the society, the importance of education, the responsibility of them as educated youth and many other things have moulded them during their adolescent period and as a result

17 Such schools with boarding homes were started in the following places of Tharangambadi ecclesiastical district. They were: Tharangambadi, Porayar, Sirkali, Mayiladuturai and Chidambaram. Though all of them have served the poor rural masses, the TSM Primary School and Shiyali Central School established in 1896 (which was named latter on as Leipzig Mission Central School – L.M.C. Hr. Sec School) along with the boarding home situated in Sirkali are to be specially remembered as they have transformed the lives of most of the boys who have joined them. Some boys have studied their entire school studies in the Sirkali home right from their 11th year of age to the 16th year of age.

most of them have continued their studies in colleges with great interest though it was not that easy task in those days. They endured all sufferings and achieved their goals. While some became pastors and teachers in church schools, many of them began to occupy respectable positions in many other forums and offices.

6. The Dignity through Alternate Jobs

Since the beginning of his ministry, Ziegenbalg was keen not to employ his converts in the works that were assigned to them by the dominant castes. Rather, he wanted to discover the skills and abilities from them. Therefore, he has established a culture of sharing the work and delegation of authority with his fellow believers. Therefore, the Dalits were entrusted with greater responsibilities and surprisingly they were discharging them very faithfully. The co – operation existed between these two group of Lutheran workers have tremendously transformed the lives of many people. The first alternate jobs to Dalits were provided by Ziegenbalg to work in the first printing press in Asia in various categories such as makers of paper itself, printing dye, fonts, proof readers, printers, operators of printing machines, binders and others. It is really astonishing to note these persons who were employed first in the press have executed their work with much skill and expertise. They have proved to be worthy persons to the vocation. So also, the alternate jobs the catechists and Bible women carried on in this region are commendable. Because, after getting trained in the seminary, they have rendered yeomen services in the remotest parts of the villages. All through their lives all the Indian native workers have served as trustworthy representatives of the missions and as liaison persons between the missionaries and the people.

As the Lutherans of twentieth century also realized the need of providing higher education to the rural masses to engage and employ them in alternate jobs with dignity and honour, they have established few institutions. The most important one was **Tranquebar Bishop Manikam Lutheran (TBML) College, Porayar** which was established in 1972. Prior to the establishment of this Arts and Science college in this rural area, there were no opportunities for the village boys and girls to pursue such higher studies as ***Firstly,*** they were doubtful of getting admitted in such colleges. Therefore, they were hesitating. ***Secondly,*** they were not confident to pay huge fees to join such colleges. ***Thirdly,*** their economic status allowed them neither to travel every day from their villages nor to utilize the services of staying in hostels. ***Fourthly,*** there was not much scope for them to get employment opportunities. ***Fifthly***, the parents of the girls were not at all ready to send their daughters to faraway places for study.

The TBML College provided solutions to all these problems. At the first step, eminent professors who were already working in various colleges and schools were invited to be the faculty of newly emerging institution and this new step has provided the young people of this reason to pursue university education at their door step with the manageable financial commitment. The presence of professors, office staff and a number of students (both boys and girls) in the village has drastically changed the ethos of the village. Number of hotels, residential places, stationary and other shops began to emerge in this little village. Apart from pursuing courses with the university degree, the students were also given opportunities to participate in sports, games, fine arts, National Cadet Corps, National Service Scheme and many other clubs and organizations. When they were taken out to neigbouring states on 2 to 4 day tours, such trips have provided them opportunities to get exposed to other regions and cultures of the country. Above all, it has produced many first graduates from the rural families.

IV. Conclusion

In spite of many hurdles and shortcomings, the pioneer Lutheran missionaries and others who followed them were able to transform many traditional practices and the perspectives of both dominant as well as oppressed people. This became possible mainly because of their unshakable faith on God and God's Word as explained by Dr. Martin Luther. Therefore, along with the Bible, they have also translated the Spener's explanation to Dr. Martin Luther's Small Catechism.

Therefore, in spite of the problems Ziegenbalg was able to create, propose and execute a counter culture which challenged all past constructions. He was neither the first European nor the first Christian to land in Tharangambadi. Much earlier to his arrival, so many traders have landed in the small village. Many religious forces were already strongly influencing the minds of people in the villages. The co – existence of different people groups that differed within themselves in terms of their religious allegiances, ethnic, lingual, national and professional backgrounds did not change the several century old discriminating practices based on caste in all the periods in different forms. In other words, the heterogeneity of administrators and their administrative forms, a large number of natives have remained as untouchables and were poor. The conditions of women also were not improving. So, it was perceived that the new Lutheran Protestant faith would not bring any formidable changes in the society.

But, quite surprisingly, the strong belief and the bold venture of both European Lutherans and their native co – workers have brought in unimaginable changes in the lives and conditions of natives particularly in Dalits and women. They have definitely inaugurated a new era in the Asian rather Indian soil where 1) the Dalits were owned and loved, 2) the Dalits were treated with equality and dignity, 3) the Dalits and particularly the girls were provided opportunities to get educated, 4) the Dalits were declared as children of God and were given the Word of God freely, 5) the rights of Dalit girls were protected and their welfare was restored, 6) Dalits were not only allowed inside the religious places but were also entrusted the responsibilities of being God's ministers, 7) enormous number of lands were purchased for the use of Dalits, 8) Dalits were trained and provided alternate jobs, 9) the Dalits were taught to overcome the shame and guilt attached to their ethnic identity and finally 10) the Dalits were honourably buried.

All these bold ventures were achieved because of the joint venture of the Western Lutheran missionaries and their native co – workers who strongly believed in the transforming power of Triune God. Thus, they have not only evangelized the Tamil society but also have *reformed* and *re –formed* it as God desired it.

13

The Foreclosed System of the Orthodox Church's Caste Identity
A Christian Ministry Perspective
(A Tribute to Martin Luther and His Legacy)

George Varughese

Introduction

Pastoral care became a significant part of Luther's ministry both as a Reformer of the Church and as a parish priest. Luther's emphasis on pastoral care has continued in the Lutheran church and it shaped its *seelssorge* or pastoral care. It has three factors. First, the role of the pastor as a strong influence in the homes of parishioners. Second, the role of theology in which God works through God's Word and Sacraments, and third, the approach to life based on the two kingdoms, namely the kingdom of the Spirit in which God rules by grace and the other fallen world in which God rules by law. We are called by God in the kingdom of the Spirit to live out our call in the midst of the realities of the fallen world as political guardians to discern the signs of the times and to confront the systemic evils in the world.

This paper is not about Luther or his theology. But as the world marks the 500th anniversary of the Protestant Reformation, this is a tribute to Martin Luther and his great legacy by identifying and acknowledging the courageous reformers of my own Church, whose lives impacted the Church, radicalized its pastoral theology, and concretized its pastoral engagement in the society, as Luther did in his time.

The Indian Orthodox Church is an ancient church in India. It is believed that Saint Thomas, one of the apostles of Jesus Christ, established the church in 52 C.E.[1] Christianity took root in the "caste-ridden" Kerala society.[2] The local

1 David Daniel, *The Orthodox Church of India: History* (New Delhi: Rachel Daniel, 1986), 1.

2 Ibid., 36.

converts of the apostle, other than the Jews were high-caste Brahmins and Nayars.[3] Even after conversion, the high-caste Christians followed the customs and habits which they were used to before conversion. Church historian Daniel writes, "the Christianised Brahmins and Nairs retained their prerequisites even after change of religion" and "continued to preserve their customs and habits."[4] This helped them maintain their high status in society. However, the exclusivity of the church's caste identity changed with conversion of Dalits during the late nineteenth and early twentieth centuries.

During the early part of its history the Orthodox Church was not open to Dalits. An important issue that it faces today is its caste identity particularly in the context of exclusion of Dalits from its church Tradition.[5] The church claims that its Tradition and identity are inclusive. However, its failure to genuinely integrate Dalits into the Tradition is reflected in its high caste oriented theology, mission, and ministry among them. This paper introduces and analyzes the pioneering mission and ministry of two prominent reformers and committed Indian Christian missionaries and practical theologians (*karmayogis*) of the Indian Orthodox Church, namely Metropolitans Geevarghese Mar Gregorios of Parumala and Petros Mar Osthathios among Dalits and Dalit Christians in the Orthodox church.[6] I would argue that in spite of the effective mission and ministry of these practical theologians to integrate Dalits into the main stream of

---

3 The claim that the early converts of apostle Thomas were high-caste Hindus has been challenged by renowned Kerala historians like Elamkulam Kunjan Pillai who argues that *Varna* (*Brahmin, Kshatriya, Vaisya and Shudra*) into which classical Hindu texts divide India, entered the Kerala society with the incoming of Aryans between eighth and tenth centuries B.C.E. Elamkulam Kunjan Pillai, *Kerala Charithrathile Irulatanja Edukal* (Some Unknown Aspects of Kerala History) (Kottayam, India: Sahitya Pravarthaka Co-operative Society, 1963), 180. Due to the absence of contemporary records on persons and events relating to Apostle Thomas's arrival and further activities, there is much controversy regarding the reliability of this tradition. Despite the controversies, the community as a whole entertains little doubt about the truth of its origins in Thomas. This tradition has been handed down orally through several generations of St. Thomas Christians. Eventually, it was recorded by the Portuguese after the Sixteenth Century. Mathias A. Mundadan, *Indian Christians: Search for Identity and Struggle for Autonomy* (Bangalore, India: Dharmaram Publications, 1984), 3; Philip Kuruvilla, *Identity and Integration of the Orthodox Church in India: Diaspora Youth-A Vision Beyond Malankara* (Delhi: ISPCK, 2000), 22.

4 Brahmins are the high-caste Hindus and Nayars/Nairs are a *jati* or sub-caste. Daniel, *The Orthodox Church …*, 36.

5 Tradition (or Sacramental Tradition) means the total expression of the Orthodox faith rooted in the "knowledge of Christ, the teaching of the Apostles, the doctrines of the Saints and fathers, the practices of worship developed by the community of faith, its way of doing things and practice of love" and "Scripture." Paulos Mar Gregorios, *Introducing the Orthodox Churches* (Delhi: ISPCK; Kottayam, India: M.G.F. of the Orthodox Theological Seminary, 1999), 45.

6 Parumala Gregorios and Osthathios are well known in the church for their pioneer mission and ministries to the Dalits in Kerala in the late nineteenth and early twentieth centuries. Daniel, *The Orthodox Church…*, 473.

the church, the high caste culture and ideologies were implicit in their approaches to Dalits.

This paper, therefore, will demonstrate that the latter have contributed to their thinking and pastoral practice which lead the church to be viewed as an exclusive community with a foreclosed system.

Practical Theologians:

Metropolitan Geevarghese Mar Gregorios of Parumala (1848-1902)

Parumala Gregorios, also called Saint Gregorios, was probably the first Metropolitan of the church who had a "sense of mission" to non-Christians, especially to Dalits.[7] After his ordination as bishop in 1876, he took charge of the newly established Niranam diocese in Kerala.[8] It was during this period that the mission work of European Protestant missionaries flourished in South India. Their work among the Dalits created a "sensation among the high-caste Hindus and even among Syrian Christians."[9] Sabu Kuriakose observes that the work of the Western missionaries was "an incentive and eye-opener for mission projects in the Orthodox Church."[10] Their work motivated Parumala Gregorios to establish the "*Malankara Syrian Clerical Sangham*" (Society of Malankara Syrian Clergy) in 1892, with the purpose of initiating and strengthening mission work among Dalits.

Concept of Mission and Ministry

Upliftment of Dalits through conversion was the main objective of the mission of Parumala Gregorios. Although he vehemently opposed the aggressive model of mission employed by the Protestant missionaries, he adapted their methods of gospel work that were very effective among the high and low castes.[11] These laid

---

7 Sunny Thomas, *Behold a Saint: The Life and Times of Parumala Mar Gregorios* (n.p: Printaid, 1977), ix. Parumala Gregorios emphasized the work among the Dalits as that which "Christians ought to do." Parumala Thirumeni (Gheevarghese Mar Gregorios), *Oorslem Yathra Vivaranam* (Travelogue) (An Account of the Journey to Jerusalem), edited by Paul Manalil (Kottayam, India: Current Books, 1996), 92.

8 Thomas, *Behold a Saint* ..., 13, 18.

9 C. P. Mathew and M. M. Thomas. *The Indian Churches of Saint Thomas* (Delhi: ISPCK, 1967), 70.

10 Sabu K. Kuriakose, "The Religious Situation of Dalit Christians in the Malankara Orthodox Church: An Appraisal," (B. D. Thesis, Senate of Serampore College (University), India, 1991), 25.

11 On the one hand, Parumala Gregorios opposed the Protestant missionary efforts to convert St. Thomas Christians to their fold. So he called them "false prophets and ravening wolves who undermine the apostolic faith." On the other hand, he adapted their methods to do mission among Dalits. Thomas, *Behold a Saint*, 28. Webster comments that Protestant mission strategy which was not "caste specific" yielded good results leading to conversions of high and low castes. He notes the observation by Frederick and Margaret Stock that this method shows

the foundation for the church's mission and ministry among the Dalit community and later for the dynamic mission and pastoral care of Osthathios among Dalits.

Parumala Gregorios's concept of mission is integrally related to his understanding of the church. Deeply rooted in the Eastern Orthodox tradition, he believed that "our mother, the Church," who held her members together in one apostolic faith, tradition and ethos, had adequate resources to uplift Dalits.[12] He considered the Dalit issue not only as a social problem, but also as a spiritual and theological one. He was convinced of the strong relationship between theology and ethics, prayer and action.[13] His life and ministry as a practical theologian was such a living example of his convictions that in 1947 the Holy Episcopal Synod of the church canonized and proclaimed him as a saint.[14]

There are many salient features to the mission of Parumala Gregorios. He believed that Christianity transcended caste divisions, and that the Christian religion, as represented by the church, promised equality, freedom, and a better life for Dalit converts. So conversion was his key strategy to uplift Dalits. Grounded on this insight, and disregarding the strong objection of his contemporaries, he baptized and converted as many as 500 adults and 200 children from the *pulaya* and *pariah jatis* (sub-castes).[15] Another unique feature of Parumala Gregorios' mission was that, quite different from the Protestant missionary approach (which was individualistic), he tried every means to get the church involved in mission and ministry to Dalits. To make this a reality, he wrote pastoral letters exhorting the whole church about the need for evangelistic work among Dalits. He insisted that the church must also begin institutions for training priests to work among

---

an "unconscious elitist strategy." My point is that this "*unconscious* [emphasis mine] elitist strategy" is more *conscious* or explicit in the mission strategies of the Orthodox Metropolitans especially Parumala Gregorios. Frederick Stock and Margaret Stock, *People Movements in the Punjab with Special Reference to the United Presbyterian Church* (South Pasadena, CA: William Carey Library, 1975), 18-20, quoted in John C. B. Webster, *The Dalit Christians: A History* (Delhi: ISPCK, 1994), 36.

12 Thomas, *Behold a Saint...*, 28; Thirumeni, *Oorslem Yathra ...*, 92.

13 Another Metropolitan Geevarghese Mar Osthathios in the forward writes, "his [Parumala Gregorios's] religion was not vertical one, but also horizontal. He could combine in him the bipolar dimension of prayer and action, silence and speech, God and fellowmen [*sic*]." Thomas, *Behold a Saint...*, x.

14 John Punchakonam, "Malankara Orthodox Syrian Church: Parumala Thirumeni," available from http://www.indianchristianity.org/orthodox/parumala.html; Internet; accessed 27 February 2007.

15 Sabu K. Kuriakose, *The Religious Situation ...*, 25. *Pulaya* and *pariah* are *jatis* or endogamous units or sub-castes among the Dalits in Kerala. *Pulayas* are mainly landless agricultural laborers and *pariahs* deal with dead animals. Their touch and mere presence polluted the high castes. Mendelsohn and Vicziany observe that, "until well into the Nineteenth Century, the Pulaya laborers had been bound to their masters in a form of slavery that entailed being heritable and transferable." Oliver Mendelsohn and Marika Vicziany, *The Untouchables: Subordination, Poverty and the State in Modern India* (Cambridge: Cambridge University Press, 1998), 37.

Dalits. He set an example by continuing to train priests at his own residence. His efforts later developed into an institution known as "the Parumala Seminary."[16]

Parumala Gregorios believed that conversion would lead to both social and spiritual upliftment, which is summed up in the term "human dignity."[17] In a communiqué to the church issued after his return from the Holy Land in 1895, he wrote:

> As Christians we have a duty towards those in wretchedness, illiteracy and sin. The so-called backward classes have been long suppressed - branding them as outcaste and denying them their human dignity. We must take upon ourselves the duty of uplifting these men, educating them and saving them from sin.[18]

Conversion was the "duty" of high-caste Christians while Dalit Christians were the recipients of the ministry of the church.[19] Thus, within the same church Tradition an attitude of difference (high caste "us" and Dalit converts "other") gradually took shape. Once Dalits were converted there were internal issues which the church had to address because majority of the church members were from the high castes. Parumala Gregorios observed that conversion to Christianity did not obliterate the lower caste identity of Dalit Christians. He knew that the integration of Dalit Christians into the mainstream of the church was a serious problem. Fully aware of this systemic issue, Parumala Gregorios initially insisted on building separate churches for Dalit Christians and later integrating them with the larger church community.[20] Sabu Kuriakose records that Parumala Gregorios established the first church for Dalits in the Niranam diocese in 1893.[21] This was done with good intentions but as a consequence many Dalit Christians still worship in separate churches and have separate cemeteries for the burial of their dead! The empirical study of a small parish in central Kerala, which I did in 1998, revealed that these are the realities of present day Dalit communities in addition to the several forms of discrimination which they face in the church.[22] The issues which Osthathios faced during his ministry also indicate that the full integration of Dalit Christians into the mainstream of the church has yet to take place.

Another important limitation was that, in spite of Parumala Gregorios's pastoral concern for Dalit Christians, they were always considered recipients of care and support by the high-caste members of the church. As already mentioned,

16 Thomas, *Behold a Saint…*, 13.

17 Ibid., 27.

18 Ibid.

19 Ibid.

20 Ibid.

21 Sabu K. Kuriakose *The Religious Situation …*, 25.

22 George Varughese, "'Acceptance' in the Pastoral Ministry to Dalit Christians in the Orthodox Syrian Church." (M.Th. Thesis, Senate of Serampore College (University), India, 1998), 9.

most of the church's attention was focussed on what it could do for the Dalit converts. For instance, the concern was how to raise their social, economic and religious standards, rather than exploring their contribution to the church's Tradition. In Parumala Gregorios's mission his "elitist strategy" juxtaposed the religion of high-caste Christians with that of Dalit Christians. Hence, his concept of mission did not help the church to acknowledge and appreciate the rich life experiences and resources that Dalits brought to the church, such as their centuries-old history soaked in pathos, theology, community consciousness, and folk culture. Instead, this patronizing and hierarchical attitude enabled the maintenance of the high-caste Christian status quo and excluded Dalit converts from the Tradition of the church, in spite of its claims to be inclusive.

By continuing multiple forms of segregation within the church, the Dalit community was seldom recognized as a people with unique cultures and traditions. The major and complex task of making the church more inclusive by more fully incorporating Dalits was taken up by Parumala Gregorios's successor Metropolitan Petros Mar Osthathios.

Metropolitan Petros Mar Osthathios (1886-1968)

If Parumala Gregorios can be considered the pioneer missionary of the church among Dalits in Kerala, it was Osthathios who actually broadened the scope and gave a sense of direction and identity to the church's mission and ministry. After the time of Parumala Gregorios it was Osthathios who revived the Dalit mission and provided it with a charismatic leadership. In 1911, Osthathios began his career as a teacher in the Kerala state government service.[23] As a young man in his late teens, Osthathios was deeply engaged in the life of Dalits by personally visiting their huts, educating them, organizing night meetings, reading newspaper to the illiterate, and even encouraging his friends in this ministry.[24]

Two factors motivated Osthathios to enter full time ministry. First was his exposure to talks by an Oxford Mission's Anglican missionary, Father Holmes, whose message on God's call to mission during an Orthodox Student Conference at the Mar Dionysius Seminary in Kottayam, Kerala, India, in 1908.[25] This experience, according to him, "made an unworthy me as a permanent priest of the Messiah."[26] Second was a lack of interest on the part of the church for mission

23 Aniyan Kallath, *Karmelile Karmayogi* (The labourer in Carmel), (Kandanad, Kerala, India: Carmel Dayara, 1991), xv.

24 Ibid., 19-20.

25 Mar Gregorios Orthodox Christian Student Movement of India (MGOCSM) is the student organization of the church that originated in 1908 with its motto: worship-study-service. The MGOCSM's student conferences and inspiring messages of its annual sessions provided the groundwork for Osthathios to start "the Servants of the Cross" Missionary Society (Now known as Petros Mar Osthathios Memorial Charitable Trust) in 1924 to work among Dalits and Dalit Christians. Daniel, *Orthodox Church* ..., 482.

26 Kallath, *Karmayogi* ..., 54.

among Dalits. His vision was that the church should become a "missionary church."[27] The government authorities noticed his commitment to the Dalit cause and appointed him as a Special Officer for Dalit concerns in 1925, a job which a year later he left to serve a much "nobler vocation" which was mission work among Dalits as an ordained person in the church.[28] During his service as a priest of the church and later as a bishop, he gave full time attention to mission among Dalits within and outside the church.[29] These backgrounds equipped Osthathios to be a practical theologian and set his ministry apart as unique and different from that of his predecessor.

Concept of Mission and Ministry

Osthathios' concept of mission is grounded in the close relationship between theology and the worship of the church. He had the strong conviction that theology and mission should flow out of the worship experience of the church. Aniyan Kallath, his biographer, writes:

> Osthathios firmly believed that both worship and evangelization are equally important for the church's growth. He courageously pointed out the danger involved in the church's exclusive focus on liturgy ignoring mission work. Though others realized this truth, foreseeing the difficulties ahead, they remained silent.[30]

A key to his concept of mission was justice. He believed that "the church loses its mission and integrity when justice is denied to its low-caste members."[31] Anything less than justice was unacceptable to him; mere open-mindedness towards Dalits was not enough. Dalit Christians had been denied justice in the church in several areas. In spite of Osthathios's commitment to the church and its Tradition, he was highly critical of the practice of discrimination within the church and raised his prophetic voice against the ecclesial leadership and high-caste Christians. He vehemently opposed segregation in the form of maintaining separate churches and cemeteries for Dalit Christians.[32] Osthathios was also deeply hurt by incidents that took place even in Parumala, where Parumala

27 John Sankarathil, *Asthamikkatha Surian* (Biography) (Never setting sun) (Kottayam, Nalathra Printers, n.d.), 49.

28 Kallath, *Karmayogi* ..., 223.

29 Ibid., 260.

30 Ibid., 67.

31 Ibid., 69.

32 Ibid., 79; Churches that were earmarked for the Dalit Christians were called *pulapalli* (In the Malayalam language of Kerala state, *pula* means *pulaya* sub-caste; *palli* means church; therefore "church of the *pulaya* sub-caste"). Sankarathil, *Asthamikkatha Surian* ..., 32. The parish that I visited in 1998 was called "Mission church." That means the parish that formed out of the mission work of the high-caste members of the church. George Varughese, *Acceptance in the Pastoral Ministry* ..., 10.

Gregorios had worked for Dalit Christians. One such incident was the baptism of a *pulaya* baby which was performed "not inside the church but one furlong away" in a shed in a copper vessel.[33] Another event was that a Catholic priest administered the Eucharist to Dalit converts at the end of a bamboo stick for fear of pollution.[34] Osthathios opposed the classification of Christians as old and new Christians and the practice of addressing Dalit Christians as *puthu-christiani* [newly converted Christians].[35] According to him the word *puthu-christiani* has no meaning because "originally there were no Christians in India and all (Indian) Christians are converts."[36]

Osthathios's vision of the upliftment of Dalits was not confined to the church alone. His vision of Dalit social reformation included "freedom of worship" for Dalits irrespective of their religious backgrounds, "freedom of movement on public roads," "freedom to use wells and public places such as schools, hospitals, courts, markets, streets, cemeteries, work places, parks, places of worship," "freedom of education," "better medical care and better hygiene," and "temperance education."[37] To this end he joined hands with the people of his community to bring about holistic emancipation of Dalits.

As a practical theologian, Osthathios's approach was deeply personal and at the same time holistic.[38] He took the time and risked reaching out to Dalits in their own huts, engaging them in personal conversation. This unique approach not only gave him direct access to the deeper problems of Dalits but also gained their trust. His holistic vision of the upliftment of Dalits included the social, economic, educational, and spiritual spheres. Osthathios utilized personal visits to preach, teach, and counsel Dalit families in all these areas which enabled him to become one with them.[39] However, he had the strong conviction that in addition to all other needs, Dalits needed Christ for deliverance from their present state. He wrote:

> Even when I organized meetings . . . for the upliftment, and freedom of movement of the low caste people and during my appointment as a Special officer for the low castes, I realized that what they desperately needed was Jesus the Messiah. And there is salvation in no one else, for

33 It is not clear why a copper vessel was used. The fact that the baptism was performed not in the church itself is an example of how Dalits were treated. Kallath, *Karmayogi* ..., 78.

34 This incident did not take place in Kerala. However, it demonstrates the intensity of discrimination against Dalits. Ibid., 78.

35 Ibid., 79.

36 Ibid.

37 Ibid., 118-121; Sankarathil, *Asthamikkatha Surian* ..., 30-33.

38 Kallath records that Osthathios's method was based on "Personal approach or Individual Contact." He was also well recognized as a "social reformer" both within the church and in the society. Kallath, *Karmayogi*..., 85, 103; Sankarathil, *Asthamikkatha Surian* ..., 30.

39 Kallath, *Karmayogi* ..., 91.

> there is no other name under heaven given among men by which we must be saved (Mathew 6-12) [*sic*]. Eternal salvation is only through Christ, for the whole human race and for the depressed classes.[40]

Osthathios incorporated local cultural methods and resources to communicate with the converts. Using local resources proved to be very effective. In open-air gospel meetings and house visits he used local drums to accompany songs and picture rolls and tracts to tell biblical stories. At night he also carried hurricane lanterns for lighting meeting places and to read the Holy Bible to Dalits.[41]

Another important area of Osthathios's attention was "making high-caste Christians conscious of the need for mission among Dalits."[42] He was highly critical of the church hierarchy who opposed his ministry because of their discomfort with the awareness of caste diversity that his mission brought to the church.[43] For instance, on a public stage shared by many church leaders who gave their silent consent for separate churches for *pulayas*, he screamed, "If Lord Jesus would come today, his whip would first fall on the red cassocks."[44] To make the church in India and the public aware of the plight of Dalits, Osthathios frequently wrote in journals, magazines and newspapers. His vision of mission extended beyond the church in Kerala. To accomplish his vision for the whole of India, he made mission journeys to several Orthodox parishes outside Kerala.[45] Wherever he spoke his major theme was the "upliftment of the depressed communities."[46]

Training and educating workers to carry on the church's mission among Dalits was equally important for Osthathios. Adapting models from other church organizations, he established "*Sleeba Dasa Samooham*" (the Servants of the Cross Society) in 1924 with three major purposes: to make the proud high castes in the church "aware of the need for gospel work;" "to attract the illiterate and marginalized low castes to the 'true faith' and to sustain them in that faith", and

40 Original scripture reference is Acts. 4:12 RSV; Ibid., 72.

41 There are indications that in this regard Osthathios followed the evangelizing style of Protestant missionaries. The missionaries' methods of bazaar preaching, itinerating through villages, conducting open-air services in public places, visiting homes, distributing scripture portions and tracts usually in Indian languages, were highly successful and made a lasting impact in the mind of Osthathios. He formulated a new mission approach which incorporated the best strategies of the sister mission organizations and rejected others. Webster, *Dalit Christians...*, 36; Kallath, *Karmayogi ...*, 85; Sankarathil, *Asthamikkatha Surian ...*, 40, 45.

42 Kallath, *Karmayogi ...*, 85.

43 Ibid., 117.

44 "Red cassock" refers to Metropolitans who usually wear that dress. Ibid.

45 Sankarathil, *Asthamikkatha Surian ...*, 60-61; Kallath, *Karmayogi ...*, 154-163.

46 Ibid., 117.

"to train disciplined workers for the Society."[47] The Society continues its work among the Dalit members of the church to the present time.

Osthathios's philosophy and method of mission have several similarities and differences with that of Parumala Gregorios. An appraisal of his work will help explain to what extent high-caste ideologies influenced him and to what degree his approaches did or did not help the church understand the diversity within its Tradition.

Like Parumala Gregorios, Osthathios was very much rooted in the Orthodox Christian faith and tradition; hence he believed in the close relationship between worship, theology, and mission. However, his practice of care within the socio-religious parameters of the church was high caste-oriented. Osthathios was born in a high-caste Christian family in Kerala, India.[48] He was convinced that "the self-sacrificial mission of the church" was to redeem the souls of Dalits from "darkness and shadow of death" and "to bring non-Christians from devil's bondage closer to the true God."[49] He used a popular passage from the scripture to emphasize that much more than social upliftment "the depressed communities needed Jesus the Messiah."[50]

Osthathios projected his method of mission work and the Christian faith as represented by the church as being true and, therefore, was adequate to uplift Dalits socially, educationally, and economically.[51] He associated hygiene, temperance, and monogamy with Christian culture. In contrast, Dalit ways of life, and especially polygamy, were equated with that of the "land of the out castes such as Africa."[52] This comparison indicates that although he wanted to feel differently for the Dalits, his sense of caste hierarchy influenced his thinking and actions. The "elitist strategy" followed by Parumala Gregorios continued to implicitly govern the mission of Osthathios.[53] There is no indication of any effort on the part of Osthathios and others to acknowledge the life experiences, belief systems, and spirituality that had sustained Dalits for centuries. Because his strategy was based on a high-caste orientation it helped to perpetuate the caste system within the church.

In spite of his deep concern for Dalit Christians, Osthathios treated them as mere recipients and objects of care. His whole attention was to offer all that the church could out of its own great Sacramental Tradition and other resources. From his point of view, Dalit Christians, as an oppressed community, had nothing to

47 Since 2004 the name has been changed to "Petros Mar Osthathios Memorial Charitable Trust." Kallath, *Karmayogi* ..., 66, 85; Sankarathil, *Asthamikkatha Surian* ..., 22, 44.

48 Kallath, *Karmayogi* ..., 1-3.

49 Ibid., 367.

50 Acts 4:12 RSV; Sankarathil, *Asthamikkatha Surian* ..., 22; Kallath, *Karmayogi* ..., 72.

51 Ibid., 85.

52 Ibid., 351; Thomas, *Behold a Saint* ..., 27.

53 Webster, *Dalit Christians* ..., 36.

offer either the church or the society for their own emancipation. Their centuries of history, culture, tradition, and life experiences were totally excluded from the new life that they acquired through conversion and, therefore, from the Tradition of the church. The classification of high-caste Christians as the custodians of cultured Christianity and of Dalit Christians as the people with an uncultured religion and lifestyle set Dalits apart as the "Other" in the church community.

The most notable and admirable feature of Osthathios' mission was that, unlike Parumala Gregorios, he focused his attention not only on converting Dalits, but also on attending to the needs of those who had already joined the church. Even though it was still ordered by high-caste values, his approach toward integrating Dalit Christians into the church was more radical than that of Parumala Gregorios. Parumala Gregorios wanted to start with separate churches and schools for Dalit Christians and when they became more acceptable they could be assimilated into the church and allowed entry to the high-caste schools. On the contrary, Osthathios took a more radical approach and wanted the immediate acceptance of Dalit converts into the church. He also opposed labeling the Dalit converts as *puthu christiani* [new Christian converts] and fought with the church leadership and laity for their upliftment within the church and society.[54] Another unique feature was Osthathios's personal approach to Dalits and their problems, an approach unmatched in the history of the church's mission.[55] His personal interaction with Dalit Christians, including individual contact, accepting Dalit hospitality and personal visits clearly stand out as manifestations of his inclusive philosophy of mission and ministry. While Osthathios wanted them to be more a part of the church, it was his high-caste orientation, which ultimately kept Dalits in a second-class status because it did not incorporate their histories, theologies and practices.

Unlike Parumala Gregorios, Osthathios incorporated local methods and cultural resources such as bells, drums, and picture rolls, to communicate with Dalit individuals and groups. He adapted these practices from Protestant missionaries. He found these methods so successful that he was able to convert as many as 22,000 Dalits to the Christian faith.[56]

Freedom of worship within the church was another concern of Osthathios. While Parumala Gregorios showed affinity towards Syriac liturgy and encouraged it, Osthathios found that the exclusive identification with that dominant language was not only a symbol of "foreign language domination," but also a threat to the national identity of the church and an obstacle to the common people's full participation.[57] Moreover, Syriac, as the dominant language of worship in the church, was accessible only to clergy (who mainly belonged to the high castes

54 Kallath, *Karmayogi* ..., 79.

55 Ibid., 85.

56 Ibid., 262.

57 Ibid., 134-135, 137.

within the church). After a long period of opposition from the ecclesial leadership, Osthathios had the liturgy translated into the local language of *Malayalam*.[58]

These reforms have two implications for the mission work of Osthathios. First, it sheds some light on the way Osthathios envisioned the integral relationship between worship and practice. If praxis is to be meaningful, it has to evolve from worship in a way that makes sense to the participants. Second, it is a dynamic symbol of emancipation for the Dalit Christians. In Hindu religion the language of the high-caste Hindu scriptures, Sanskrit, was inaccessible to Dalits and "there were cases of active persecution of any low-caste person studying that language."[59] Thus, in the church context, Osthathios challenged the exclusive association of the dominant language with high-caste Christians that denies the diversity and the freedom of Dalit Christians to express their faith in Christ.

Both Parumala Gregorios and Osthathios were generally critical of the aggressive nature of the mission work of the western missionaries in Kerala society. However, it is known that they received the motivation, challenge, and basic philosophy of gospel work from mission organizations of the Roman Catholic and Protestant churches. The unique model which Osthathios carved out of these methods continued after his death and in the establishment of "Petros Mar Osthathios Memorial Charitable Trust" for ministry among Dalits.[60]

The philosophies and approaches to mission and ministry of both Parumala Gregorios and Osthathios govern the church's present ministry among Dalit Christians. It encourages accommodation, assimilation, and tolerance of the Dalit Christians rather than their genuine integration into the mainstream of the church. Therefore, the integration of Dalit Christians is seldom a concern of the present church leadership and clergy.[61] Hence, the Tradition of the church remains exclusive.

Conclusion

Parumala Gregorios and Osthathios, who were practical theologians and pioneers of the church's mission among Dalits, were genuinely committed to the cause of Dalits. Their work among Dalits motivates the Indian churches to rethink their mission and ministry among the Dalits and other marginalized today.

---

58 Ibid., 144, 149.

59 K.M. George, *The Silent Roots: Orthodox Perspectives on Christian Spirituality* (Geneva: World Council of Churches Publications, 1994), 14; Sathianathan Clarke, *Dalits and Christianity: Subaltern Religion and Liberation Theology in India* (New Delhi: Oxford University Press, 1999), 123.

60 Formerly known as "*Sleeba Dasa Samooham*," or the Servants of the Cross Society. Sankarathil, *Asthamikkatha Surian …*, 22.

61 A professor of the Orthodox Theological Seminary, Kottayam, Kerala, India Father John Mathews writes, "this (Dalit concerns) is not an area of prime concern for the church . . . ." Fr. John Mathews, Kottayam, Kerala, India to George Varughese, Iliff School of Theology, Denver, CO, USA, 3 July 2003, e-mail script in the hand of George Varughese.

However, their "elitist strategy" did not help to fully integrate the converts into the mainstream of the church. Dalit Christians remained as mere recipients and objects of care of high-caste Christians rather than as subjects of their own history and the Church's Tradition.[62] As a community, they were represented as having nothing worth offering to the Sacramental Tradition of the church and lived at the margins of the church.

Their mission and ministry were ordered by the Western missionary style and orientation and in the Indian context, the high-caste Hindu tradition with which the church has always identified itself socially and culturally. In other words, cultural and traditional diversities within the church have never been a positive value for these theologians so that they also excluded the silent and silenced traditions of Dalit Christians from their mission and ministry. As a result of the church's history, thinking and practice, Dalit traditions have never been acknowledged as an "infra tradition" worthy of scholarly writing and research and emulating in praxis.[63]

The high-caste ideology inherent in the practice of care, and the total absence of Dalit traditions in the total Tradition of the Church have contributed to the exclusivity of the Church's identity. However, till today the church has not yet fully acknowledged its own exclusivity.[64] In practice the church continues to consider Dalit Christians as the "Other," demonstrating that it is a foreclosed system in spite of its self-perception to the contrary.

62 Webster, *Dalit Christians...*, 36.

63 George, *Silent Roots*, 80.

64 The recognized church theologians such as the late Metropolitan Paulos Mar Gregorios, Dr. K.M. George, and the current bishop of the Mumbai diocese Mar Coorilos of the Indian Orthodox Church downplay and even deny the existence of caste issues in the church.

14

Understanding the Reformation and its Impact in the Protestant Churches with Special Reference to Lay Training in the CSI, Madras Diocese

N. Manova Santhosham

The "Priesthood of all believers" was the true teaching of Martin Luther who himself being a catholic priest witnessed the unruly and extensive oppressive administration of the Papacy. The result of his protest against the evil designs of the official church led him to reorient the believers of the church with his teachings of scripture relating to their faith and action. His teaching was promoted by his translation of the New Testament into the German language and with the advent of the printing press. The momentum of reformation spread like fire among the German people who were longing for freedom from the repression of the church. Martin Luther with the participation and true cooperation of the people of Germany made reformation a reality in his own time. Translating scripture into the mother tongue, educating and uniting the common people of his nation, interpreting the scripture to address spiritual issues, highlighting the false teachings of the Catholic Church, printing and distributing hundreds of tracts to be made available to the common people, introducing hymns in the German language, and building platforms to promote faith in God were a few areas on which Martin Luther concentrated to popularise the cause for reformation.

Training the laity, which had been a neglected mission of the episcopal church, was overwhelmingly executed by the reformation movement. The reading of the scripture in the mother tongue, inaugurated by Martin Luther in the early Sixteenth Century, had a direct effect in bringing about the fruits of reformation in Germany. The people were equipped and armed by the sword of the word of God to understand the need for revival in the church. Martin Luther believed that "Scripture alone" (*sola scriptura*) would educate the Christian community to protest against the atrocities of the leaders of the church. He wanted to build "faith community" being convinced that "Faith alone" (*sola fide*) would unite them as one family to stand against the evil practices of the church (for instance, indulgences). He was aware of the biblical teaching that "Grace alone" (*sola gratia*) would liberate them from all bondage.

The Sixteenth Century Reformation is not a past phenomenon that we have to contend with and only glorify its fruits, but reformation should be a daily matter. It is not a matter that is over and done with. Reformation should be happening every day; it should be eternal, and it requires consistent commitment by the believers in the church along with the leaders. Therefore continuing education, well formulated syllabuses, organised teaching, and scientific approaches in implementing the biblical and theological educational system are required to equip every member of the local congregation. In this context I want to mention three different programmes initiated by a Seminary, the CSI Synod and the Madras diocese (CSI).

Theological Education for Christian Commitment and Action (TECCA): 'Learning to learn'

Tamilnadu Theological Seminary situated in Arasaradi, Madurai, South India is a pioneering educational institution in Biblical and theological education. Ever since its formation the seminary has been committed to formulate a syllabus in order to teach people from both urban and rural backgrounds. With the invitation of local pastors, the seminary arranges a two-year TECCA course with two-day classes once a month. Both faculty and students are involved in teaching the students of TECCA who are from all walks of life and take up the course voluntarily. The seminary students are taught to help the students of TECCA to learn. This is a systematic course in which new songs, new orders of worship, new orders of service set to Tamil music, and social awareness on social action are taught along with Biblical and theological education. This seminary also witnesses for ecumenism as the Church of South India and the Lutheran Churches in India came together and formed the seminary in 1969. This is a sign of continued reformation in the churches and a sign also of commitment to it. The world theological community should be proud and happy at the enthusiasm with which the study programme of TECCA is continued.

Vision for Equipping Local Congregation for Mission (VELCOM): 'Taught to teach'

The programme called VELCOM was conceived by the then Moderator of the Church of South India Rt. Rev. Dr. P. Victor Premasagar, a theologian and a bishop committed to the cause of education of the common people in the CSI. He envisaged the concept of new education and teaching among believers of the church with a time-bound and result-oriented approach to gaining biblical and theological knowledge. This was initiated throughout the CSI churches in four southern states of India at the beginning of the 1990s. This was the first attempt by the official church, and it enjoyed the patronages of all dioceses in the CSI. Many seminars and workshops were conducted to popularise the need of this programme. All pastors with the guidance of the Synod were equipped with relevant study materials to create awareness among church leaders to understand the need for VELCOM and to embrace it. This programme has been an eye opener for many ordinary people of the churches who had no taste of preliminary and basic biblical education. It is unfortunate that the popular and very deserving programme did not continue. It doesn't mean that it lacked the support of the people or that it was irrelevant. But I should say that the church has allowed a good and relevant programme to go in vain. What else does the Church have to do to teach people and equip them for mission?

Laity Institute for Transformation Education (LITE): "Transformed to Transform"

Madras diocese has constructed a training centre for the laity to nurture them for theological education with a liberation perspective. The purpose of the institution is to educate the people of the diocese of Madras to be transformed and to transform the rest of the world. It serves to educate the people and qualify them to understand the present world so as to witness in their neighbourhood. Since 2013 ten different courses were introduced, and each course has 45-50 hours of learning. Systematic syllabuses were formulated to teach through deep biblical and theological education. Pastors with deep commitment in ministry and with adequate pastoral experience were assigned to formulate the syllabus. They were made to write lessons and given the opportunity to teach. The entire LITE building has been put into use to accommodate many classes during weekends. So far, 4500 students have been given certificates. I am proud to mention here that I was the first director for these courses and privileged to conduct the first seven courses until May, 2015. I was directly supervising the formulation of the syllabus and conduct of the classes which was a joy indeed. Let me mention a few courses: 1) Christian Discipleship; 2) Mission and Ecumenism; 3) Scripture and Interpretation; 4) Christianity and Caste; 5) Christian Theology: an Introduction; 6) Church Ministry and Sacraments. Centres for these courses were also expanded to several towns including Arakkonam, Tiruvallur, Walajabad, Chengalpet to facilitate rural people. This has been very successful, and many have taken part in it.

Apart from these courses, there has been a course in Pastoral Counselling and Spirituality with the help of the Department of Christian Study, University of Madras. Many have benefitted and commit themselves to the cause of the poor and exploited through the courses they have undergone. Let me conclude by quoting my own words which I made at my report during the 6th Valedictory and Convocation held at the LITE auditorium on 26th September 2014:

"The spark from LITE led to the realisation of the darkness of innocence and the slavery to superstition which kindled the thirst for liberation. This is nothing but a similar experience of the laity to the days of MARTIN LUTHER in the Sixteenth Century."

15

Luther's Call to Examine the Conscience

Florina and Gladston Xavier

Introduction

Luther was a revolutionary of his times. Probably if he had more charisma and claimed that he was son of God or a prophet, there may have been Lutheranity today. However, Luther as a doctor of moral theology decided to challenge the church and its practices. Have you ever wondered what would have been running in the mind of Luther before he actually wrote these *95 Theses*? Yes, we do know about the discussions he had with various people and the decision to further deliberate on his theses however, to have the nerve to actually challenge an institution is amazing. It needs certain conviction that he decided to do it despite all odds. There is growth only when "facts" are challenged. If Isaac Newton did not ask why the apple fell down, there would have been no sense of gravity. Some even question if Luther was much ahead of his times which may have been the reason for his excommunication, or was the church too ancient for its times? Thus whether ahead of his times or not, Luther's contribution created history and taught us a different way of looking at things.

We decided to write about Luther because of his daring act which is valid even 500 years later. We also decided to write about Luther because in our own way this is our theses too. When we say "our" theses, it is from those of us who are concerned about the church and the trajectory it is taking. This is yet another opportunity to challenge the church to get away from its hypocrisy its money mindedness and move towards more fulfilling things like love and care without conditions. While reading Luther's theses, it was clear that Luther was disillusioned with the church and the way it was conducting its affairs. In his limited capacity as a professor of moral theology, all he could do was, take the pen instead of the sword and write down what he thought was not worthy of the church. Thus was born the *95 Theses*. In the following pages we will look at just four of his theses, although all of them are relevant today, we choose four for want of words and for the context into which it is woven. We will examine it from a socio-economic angle within the sphere of the church and its people especially the marginalized and vulnerable. This will help connect the thoughts of Luther from yesteryears to the plight of the church even today. We will objectively look at what needs to change.

Thesis no. 3. Yet it does not mean solely inner repentance; such inner repentance is worthless unless it produces various outward mortification of the flesh.

A child cheated in his exam, was caught but apologized to the teacher, to which the teacher asked the child "are you really being contrite?" The child answered, "What does contrite mean?" it was not a philosophical question, but in this case let's look at its philosophical value. Are we being contrite when we say we are sorry, do we really mean it? How do we let ourselves, the person/people we have offended know that we are truly sorry. Does not making the same mistake again mean that we are truly sorry? What if I stole some money from the church and then apologized after using it up and never stole money from the church again. Did I really mean it, what about the people who I stole it from, does the forgiveness ring in them? Luther calls for true repentance which according to him is reflected in a change in life style. A popular healing program demands that the person seeking forgiveness needs to call the person they think they have offended, remind them of the mistake made and then seek their forgiveness. Often the one against who it was committed may have forgotten it but the sin remains in the heart of the sinner if there was no repentance. Whatdid Luther mean when he called for a change in lifestyle? We would interpret it as, not committing the sin again, making it up to the person/people against who it was committed. Find ways to regain the trust in yourself so that you will not commit it under similar circumstances. Restorative justice a new form of justice talks about not punishing the offender but giving the person achance to rewrite the wrong done. The man who kills the son of an elderly couple is asked to work and pay towards the maintenance of the parents and try to be a son to them. This may sound idealistic but it could be done, especially when we think of what our punitive justice system has done in creating more criminals. But the questions remains, is a man who decides to serve the family of his victim truly contrite?

Thesis no. 27. They preach only human doctrines who say that as soon as the money clinks into the money chest, the soul flies out of purgatory.

This is one of the most interesting theses, more so because Tetzel[1] promoted it. One of the reason for Luther writing the theses was a reaction to the actions of

1 Johann Tetzel, O.P. was a German Roman Catholic Dominican friar and preacher. In addition, he was a Grand Inquisitor of Heresy to Poland, and later became the Grand Commissioner for indulgences in Germany.

Tetzel. When money rings, souls springs – he said. Tetzel is as much relevant today for what he said as Luther is relevant for what he challenged. Of course the two go together, as long as there are people who believe that they can buy their way through, there will be anger people who will nail the churches and be excommunicated. A recent whatsap video showed a clip of an engineer in Telegana buying certificates to paradise. It reported that he paid a lakh for each of them. Although there was no chance to verify its authenticity it still says something about what people believe. He bought them for himself and his parents who were still alive. The emphasis here is an engineer and alive. Why hadn't education make him think? He was stupid enough not to wait for his parents to die but was willing to invest even before that. Neither a dead soul nor a one alive can be saved for putting money into the millions of hundis and dumb boxes and offerings kept in temples, churches and other places of worship. Demonetization was good for the Gods, maybe it was planned by them, and they needed the black money perhaps. Today, more than ever, we see people trying to write off their wrongs by letting the till ring.

Thesis no. 32. Those who believe that they can be certain of their salvation because they have indulgence letters will be eternally damned, together with their teachers.

Together with their teachers, Luther says, Those who believe their wrong teachings should not be forgiven. The one who shows the wrong way should be condemned to death. The one who leads you to evil should burn in hell. We are glad that Luther puts the blame not only on the believer but the one who leads us to believe. We think they carry a greater sin because of the great responsibility given to them. The church leaders need to know that not only in spiritual matters but in all matters of life, they are called to lead and if they don't lead us to the right way, they shall burn in hell. It may sound like a harsh judgement – aren't they also people, some might argue, but by virtue of becoming a pastor, a preacher a teacher, they make a solemn commitment that they are responsible for their people and so there is no escape. Church leadership today is being bought, we know of priests who pay money to the bishop to be in a certain parish. We know about the amount of money involved before and after elections and we are talking about church elections. Obviously if I have to spend millions to become the Bishop then I must sell indulgences to recover the money, whether it is building St. Peter's or the get away home, it is people's money that is wrongly got. All of us with responsibility be it parents, teachers, officers, pastors, we should remember that because of the position we are in we need to be a good example and lead people in the right way, if not we are all going hell.

Thesis no. 43. Christians are to be taught that he who gives to the poor or lends to the needy does a better deed than he who buys indulgences.

Nothing has changed in the last 500 years, even today Christians need to be taught giving money to a poor neighbor is better that flaunting the money before it goes into the offering. It has become fashionable to contribute to church buildings and various activities of the church. We know churches where names of the benefactor is written on the tube light or on the pew. Contributing to the church is today's modern way of buying indulgences. The church body may be angry with us to promoting this idea, of course the church needs money for maintenance and other functions to keep it alive. However, what we mean here is the millions of rupees of property and resources available with the church that is misappropriated. If only these can be channelized and people allowed to give to what they want, there will be less poor people in the world. First of all by giving to the church, our sins cannot be forgiven, we give because we hope that we will find favor with God if we give to build the church. What we forget is that there is really no need for a pompous church. If people need to pray they can pray anywhere, they just need a roof above their heads to protect them from the rain and shine. There are more sincere prayers being prayed from humble shanties than shiny churches. The need of the hour is to make sure that your neighbor has eaten. Clothing the naked, feeding the hungry and tending to the sick is relevant after more than 2000 years ago when it was said. We need to change our way of bettering ourselves in the eyes of God. If only we knew that God lives in our neighbors.

Conclusion

The above four theses can be summarized as the need for inwards repentance to be accompanied with an outward change in lifestyle, that the souls in purgatory (and neither ours) can be saved by money, and woe to those who believe and teach that salvation can be bought and finally a person who gives to the poor is seen better in the eyes of God than those who try to buy forgiveness.

The four theses that we chose may not be directly connected with each other since they each follow a different lead – true change, money, teachers and charity, however the point being that each of them are looking at ways in which we can make our lives better. The church is the center of Luther's theses, his challenge is to reawaken the church and let it live for what it was built. Today the same challenge is being placed in front of us, are we willing to let the church live by not building false churches with fake money, by truly repenting when we make a mistake, by helping the people who need our support and by being good leaders who can lead the church in the right direction.

If we think deeply about it, and this is not a new thought, we don't take anything with us when we die. We just need enough to live well and take care of ourselves and our families. But the problem arises when we want to save for our children and our grandchildren and our great grandchildren. The government also needs to take some responsibility for our greed. If structures and systems were in place we will not need that extra money to buy them and so we will not accumulate wealth. This may seem naïve, but that is the truth. The lapse is the government system is similar to the lapse in the church. If we pay our pastors less, how do we expect them to have a decent living? They then depend upon others to take care of their needs and this slowly goes into having more than what they need. Surely we can come out of this rut, it is not something that can happen overnight but takes time and effort. There should be cleansing of the churches and true repentance. When we say cleansing, we mean from corruption and any greed that is associated with it. The leaders and teachers who are more responsible and doubly condemned according to Luther should take it upon themselves to bring about the change. It requires a change of heart, lifestyle and attitude and only then it will be possible, but surely it is possible. If only we look into the eyes of our neighbors, if only we care enough to acknowledge the goodness of people around us, if only we stop being greedy and start by giving to the needy, if only we embrace the responsibility given to us whole heartedly making the best of the circumstances and reviving the church again. All this is indeed possible.

Websites that were looked up

http://www.luther.de/en/95thesen.html

https://en.wikipedia.org/wiki/Ninety-five_Theses

http://www.oocities.org/united_in_christ_3in1/95explained.pdf

https://www.reddit.com/r/AskHistorians/comments/1po2ej/which_legend_about_purgatory_was_martin_luther/

http://mediengeschichte.dnb.de/DBSMZBN/Content/EN/Printing/04-ablassbriefe-en.html

https://www.luther2017.de/en/wiki/stationen-der-reformation/letters-of-indulgence-comprehensive-cover-for-the-next-world/

http://www.historylearningsite.co.uk/the-reformation/the-95-theses-a-modern-translation/

16

500 Years of Reformation
Reviewing from the Catholic Perspective

"The things that unite us are greater than those that divide us." [Pope John XXIII]

Roy Lazar A.

Deviation from the Path

"Where was the church before the Reformation?" is akin to asking, "Where were you before you took a bath?" – to say that this short fictional conversation points out the status of the Church before Reformation will not be an exaggeration. However, the period of Reformation is now adjudged even by those who are on the other side as an attempt primarily to clean up the mess in which the Christian community found itself in the Middle Ages.

The 'Edict of Milan' in 325 C.E. and the following centuries of 'Pax Romano' created an unholy alliance between the secular society and the church. 'Power corrupts and absolute power corrupts absolutely'. And it happened in the church as well. Excessive wealth and political power diminished the initial vigour of the Early Church and the clergy became the main cause of scandal and destruction for. However, there had been numerous attempts to reform the Roman Church during this period, but they had always been curbed with an iron fist by the ecclesial authorities with the royalsanction. And there were also groups outside the Roman Church, like *the Albigenses* and *Waldenses* who challenged the practices of the Church openly but they were responded with bloody martyrdom. Church men like John Wycliffe, John Huss and Gerolamo Savonarola, etc., also spoke out against the papacy, auricular confession, purgatory, pilgrimages, worship of saints, relics, etc. who were termed as 'heretics' and a few of them were burned along with their writings. A few lukewarm attempts to reform the life of the church through various Councils such as that of Pisa (1409), Constance (1414-1418) and Basel (1431) ended up bearing hardly any change.

During these years reformed minded people formed themselves in to a pious society calling it *The Brethren of the Common Life* for the specific purpose of bringing reform in the church and also a few famous men who belonged to this group like John of Wessel, Erasmus and Thomas à Kempis tried their best through their spiritual writings. Earlier the radical life of Francis of Assisi who captured the imagination of many rich and educated youth of the period *en mass* unfortunately didn't bring positive changes in the administration and the life of the church. Everyone clamoured for change, renewal and reform but all were clueless of where and how to begin. Many a time the good things happen through the evil that we go through. The changes in the secular world especially due to the spread of Islam in Europe through military force and the outbreak of Renaissance ushered in also positive changes with the church. There rose a person who captured the moment and paved the way for historical change in the church. It would be unfair to history to claim that he was the spearhead of Reformation but it will not be an exaggeration to say that he played the role of midwifery for this great event in the life of church after 'the Great Schism' in the Eleventh Century C.E..

Reform or Rift?

The real change came like bolt from the blue with a lot of good will to reform than to destroy on 31 October 1517, which was like any other autumn day for Europe also for a sleepy little town, Wittenberg in Sachsen-Anhalt, Germany. But nobody dare to imagine that one of the important events in the history of Christianity as well as that of the Western world was to going occur on that day. A diminutive and laconic Augustinian monk believed to have nailed his *95 Theses* on the door of the Castle Cathedral, the Church of All Saints, in Wittenberg which broke the ice and set the ball rolling, calling for a radical change in the life of the Church especially the clergy. Martin Luther (10.11.1483 – 8.02.1546), a professor of biblical theology at the University of Wittenberg and a faithful monk and priest, clamoured for radical changes in the life of the Church. Similar to the vision of Francis of Assisi in Thirteenth Century, Luther too might have felt the call 'to renew the church'through the 'tower experience' he had as crisis in his faith. But the political and social situation of his time paved the way for the drastic division within the church, which reshaped the organisation of the Christian community not with military power but with a piece of paper titled, "Disputation on the Efficacy and Power of Indulgences."

There is a lot of uncertainty with regard to the number 95 and the place where Theses were pinned. Georg Roerer (1492-1557), Luther's secretary later mentioned in 1540 that the Theses of Martin Luther were nailed to the 'churches' in Wittenberg. Phillip Melanchthon who collected and published the works of Luther in 1546 speaks about the *95 Theses* but he came to Wittenberg only in the year 1518. Hence, there is no eyewitness either to the number of theses or to the location, where they were found; but history has become witness to effect of the daring act of raising a voice for change. After many attempts to make him heard about the aberrations especially in the life of the clergy and the sale of indulgences Martin Luther wanted to 'reform' the church and purify it of its malicious practices. Hence, he sent a letter to Archbishop Albrecht of Mainz and his *95 Theses*, as an appendix to it, in which Luther expressed serious concerns about preaching and the practice of indulgences occurring under the responsibility of the Archbishop and urged him to make changes. On the same day, he wrote another letter to Bishop Hieronymus of Brandenburg. With his *95 Theses* Martin Luther was calling for a 'disputation on the power and efficacy of indulgences out of love and zeal for truth and the desire to bring it to light'. Pope Leo X commissioned the German bishops in 1515, to use the Dominican order to sell indulgences in order to raise funds for completing the Basilica in Rome. The Dominican monk, John Tetzel, went around the continent preaching with his famous caption: *As soon as the coin in the coffer rings, even the soul of a monkey from purgatory springs.* For Luther this was the worst of all blasphemies that had to be stopped at all cost.

The *95 Theses* were written in a remarkably humble and academic tone, questioning rather than accusing. However, the second reading of the paper would reveal that the overall thrust of the document was nonetheless quite provocative. The first two of the theses contained Luther's central idea, *Sola Fide* and *Sola Scriptura* (faith alone and not deeds would lead to salvation and the Bible is the sole foundation of Christian faith). The rest of them vehemently criticized the practice of indulgences and voiced the popular indignation against the monumental work of St. Peter's Basilica in Rome at the cost the poor people's toil and money.

Consolidation of the Division

Pope condemned on 9 November 1518 Luther's writings as conflicting with the teachings of the Church. One year later a series of commissions were convened to examine Luther's teachings. The first papal commission found his theses to be heretical, but the second merely stated that Luther's writings were "scandalous and offensive to pious ears." Finally, Pope Leo X issued a papal bull in July 1520 that concluded that Luther's propositions were heretical and gave Luther 120 days to recant in Rome. All the efforts from the side of the Church in Rome to chastise Luther and to make him to withdraw 41 of his theses brought forth only negative results as the German princes and knights wanting to be free from Roman domination started rallying behind Luther. Thus Martin Luther became the flagship of wrecking the grand peace of the great Roman Empire. *Pax Romano* started to crumble little by little! On January 3, 1521 in the Diet of Worms Luther declared:

"I cannot and will not recant anything,
for to go against conscience is neither right nor safe.
Here I stand, I can do no other, so help me God. Amen."
(*Hier stehe ich und kann nicht anders! Gotthelfemir, Amen!).*

Luther refused to renounce his stand and the Papal nuncio, Girolamo Aleandro, declared Luther to be an 'obstinate heretic' and banned the reading or possession of his writings. Consequently Pope Leo excommunicated Martin Luther from the Roman Catholic Church on January 3, 1521 and on 25 May 1521 Emperor Charles V nailed the coffin with the Edict of Worms declaring:

> For this reason we forbid anyone from this time forward to dare, either by words or by deeds, to receive, defend, sustain, or favour the said Martin Luther. On the contrary, we want him to be apprehended and punished as a notorious heretic, as he deserves, to be brought personally before us, or to be securely guarded until those who have captured him inform us, whereupon we will order the appropriate manner of proceeding against the said Luther. Those who will help in his capture will be rewarded generously for their good work.

At the Diet of Speyer in 1519 the *Schmalkaldischer Bund* (Schmalkaldic League*)* consisted of German princes under the leadership of Fredrick III, the Wise walked out of the diet refusing to obey the imperial order to ban Luther's teaching and thus the name "Protestants' came into use identifying those who supported the teachings of Luther defying the papal authority.

In order to defend 'the Lutherans' against misrepresentations and to provide a statement of their theology that would be acceptable to the Roman Catholics Phillip Melanchthon presented on June 25, 1530 to the Emperor Charles V the summary of 'the Lutheran teachings' on faith, grace, sin, redemption and papacy, etc. in 28 articles, which is called the *Augsburg Confession*, which would later constitute the basic teachings of the Lutheran Churches. The Catholic theologians under the leadership of the Dominican Cardinal, Thomas Cajetan, condemned 13 articles of the confession, accepted 9 without qualifications and approved 6 with qualifications. But the reformers refused relentlessly to give up their position and manoeuvring sectarian division. Hence, the Emperor refused on 22 September 1530 to accept the reply of the reformers and confirmed his stringent measures to curb the so the called 'Protestants". Thus Reformation began with the ardent desire to reform the church 're-formed' it into many churches based not on liturgical practices as in the Eleventh Century but on ideological and administrative structures: Roman Catholic and Protestant Churches.

The Church in Rome was not prepared to face Reformation which has taken a political turn at the Diet of Augsburg as seven Lutheran princes and two principle cities rallied behind the reformers and putting an end to the Great Holy Roman Empire for which the Emperor was the secular head and the Pope the spiritual leader. It reacted with 'Counter-Reformation' as Pope Paul III called for the Council of Trent (1545-1563) to respond to the accusations of the reformers, who were many by this time. The Council said that 'some of the accusations were valid'. They are:

1. Abuse of Indulgences
2. Moral life of Clergy
3. Worldliness of the monastic life

Some were accepted as partially true:

1. Justification by faith alone (*Sola Fide*). Good works are also needed for a life of faith.
2. Scripture is the sole authority for teaching (*Sola Scriptura).* Apostolic tradition is also needed.
3. Validity of the sacraments especially Baptism and Eucharist (biblical), but seven for the Catholics.
4. Real presence of the Eucharistic (communitarian and temporary but for Catholics sacrificial and permanent presence).

Trent totally rejected the Lutheran teachings on the following:

1. Infallibility of Papacy and his apostolic succession
2. Need of ministerial priesthood along with common priesthood.

The result of Reformation and Counter-Reformation was nearly 450 years of bitter rivalry and separation and at certain periods marked by war and bloodshed. Though the *Peace of Westphalia* treaty ended the *Eighty Years War* between the Spanish Catholics and the Dutch Reformed Christians and the *Thirty Years War* between German princes the rift worsened and the relationship between the two churches relinquished into bitter chasm. Instead of looking at the dark side of history, let us look at the positive outcomes and trace down the stream of hope for unity that has brought closer the 'separated brothers and sisters' in the recent decades.

Outcomes of Reformation

It is true that Reformation has left an unbridgeable rift in the Christian community. However, there were also many 'blessings in disguise' also for the Roman Catholic Church. Its positive repercussions can be seen in the intellectual and cultural flourishing it inspired on all sides of the schism especially in the universities of Europe, in the church music, in the baroque art and architecture, in the field of biblical scholarship and homiletics and in formation of the clergy. Reformation has also paved the foundation, as Max Weber claimed, for cultivating 'the spirit of the capitalism and economic growth' raising up scientific temper and leading to the discovery of new colonies.

The remarkable 'blessing' especially for the benefit of the Catholic Church was the *Society of Jesus* formed in 1540, which spearheaded the counter-reformation. The Jesuit theologians tried to bridge the gap between Thomism and Augustinianism by claiming that man had freedom of choice but ultimately God was omnipotent and their pastors took up the education of the clergy as well as the laity within the Catholic fold. For example, Cardinal Robert Bellarmine from Milan and Cardinal Ximenes from Spain reorganised the formation of priests and the clerical discipline and also encouraged scholarship at schools and universities. Matteo Giberti popularised the *Oratory of Divine Love* founded in Rome in 1517 to foster good works in everyday life encouraging the lay people in ecclesial activities. Fr. Peter Canisius, a Dutch Jesuit priest, founded colleges all over Germany to spread Catholic education and he revived mysticism in the Catholic Church. The Jesuit missionaries started their voyages to the far eastern countries and landed on the shores of India and China. St. Francis Xavier brought the Gospel to South India and Matteo Ricci went to China. Gian Pietro Caraffa (later Paul IV) helped to form the *Theatines* in 1524, a religious order of priests working within the community but living in monastic austerity. The religious communities realised their missionary mandate and were forced to walk out of the borders of Europe looking for new pastoral fields. Reformation made the church missionary – once again after the period of the Apostles! The Euro centrism of the Christian faith and practice started to spread to other continents and it also brought into contact with other religions and civilisation that were more ancient than that of Judaeo-Christian or Greek-Roman civilisation.

Road to Unity

The longing for unity of all the churches in spite of the mutual accusations and inimical attacks was always sustained by many individuals since Reformation. There were a few visionaries who gave shape and structures to ecumenical efforts for unity. From the side of the Catholics, for example, Fr. Paul Wattson, who was an Anglican, later became Catholic began the *Church Unity Octave* in Graymoor, New York and Abbè Paul Irène Courturier introduced in Lyon a *Triduum Prayer for Church Unity*. The popular appraisal for unity among the Christians slowly started making inroads into Vatican and began loosening the shackles of bitterness and hostility.

Pope John XXIII issued on 25 January 1959 a directivein which he expressed his intention to call for an ecumenical council for which he desired to invite all the churches and ecclesial communities or 'all those who bear the name of Christians but are separated from the Apostolic See to find more easily the path by which they may arrive at unity for which Christ prayed for'. '*Aggirnomento* (let us renew)' and '*Ecclesia semper reformanda (church is ever to reform)*' – such slogans became bywords of the Roman curia, which reflected the mood of the entire Church of the decade. Hence he created the 'Secretariat for Promoting Christian Unity' to promote the cause of ecumenism.

The Second Vatican (1962-1965) promulgated on 21 November 1964 the decree on ecumenism *Unitatis Redintegratio (UR),* which recognised the 'means of salvation outside the church' and called the other Christians 'brethren' and accorded to other ecclesial communities the name: 'church' which the Catholic Church claimed so far as its prerogative (*UR* 3). The document accepts the sin of division and affirms that the unity of churches is rooted in the mystery of Christ, which is expressed and experienced in the life of the Trinity; and this unity is the work of the Holy Spirit (*UR 7*). Though UR uses the title 'Sister Churches' for the Easter Churches and calls others as 'Ecclesial Communities' and emphasises 'the Church of Christ' subsists in the 'Catholic Church' it still calls 'for a spiritual ecumenism rooted in prayer and a dialogue among the churches to overcome the obstacles to perfect ecclesial communion gathered in a common celebration of Eucharist, into unity of the one and only Church, which Christ bestowed on his church from the beginning'.

*Unitatis Redintegratio*is indeed a watershed in the ecumenical history of the churches. Catholics and Lutherans began seeking theological common ground after the Council, which opened the Roman Catholic Church for better relations with other churches, and have ironed out many of their differences over the decades. The outcome of the initiatives from both the sides encouraged the Roman Catholic Church to become the full-pledged member of the Faith and Order Commission of WCC in 1968 in order to explore the theological understanding for a common understanding on matters of faith and life in the Christian communities. The result of these ecumenical initiatives started bringing positive results. Cardinal Gerhard Ludwig Müller, the Prefect of the Congregation for the Doctrine of the Faith from 2012 to 2015, underlines one of the main outcomes of the ecumenical dialogue in view of 500 Years of Reformation:

> The Catholic image of Luther has now been corrected after centuries of polemics. We need only think of the 1983 statement of the Roman Catholic/Lutheran Joint Commission entitled "Martin Luther – Witness to Jesus Christ", marking Luther's 500th birthday, in which Luther was "honored in common as a witness to the gospel, a teacher in the faith and a herald of spiritual renewal (in *Perspectives 2017*).

"That They May be One"

The encyclical of Pope John Paul II, *Ut Unum Sint* (*UUS*), *issued in* 1995 using the prayer of Jesus in the Gospel of *John* 17, 21 is another important landmark in the ecumenical process. He underlined that to believe in Christ means:

- to desire unity
- to desire unity means to desire the Church
- to desire the Church means to desire the communion of grace which corresponds to the Father's plan from all eternity.

Hence, unity among Christians is understood as the hallmark of Christian witness. Emphasising the teachings of Vatican II the document called for open and genuine dialogue 'to eliminate words, judgements and actions which do not respond to the condition of the other Christians with truth and fairness' (*UUS 29*). Pope John Paul II called on the Christians to work for 'full communion among the believers of the same faith but with legitimate diversity' (*UUS* 57). Bishop Joachim Wanke of Erfurt recognises the merits of Reformation as underlined by the papal document:

Since Luther, Catholicism has become poorer. This may come as a surprise, but I am in good company as this papal quote from the 1995 encyclical *Utunumsint* illustrates: "we are aware, as the Catholic Church, that we have received much from the witness borne by other Churches and Ecclesial Communities to certain common Christian values, from their study of those values, and even from the way in which they have emphasized and experienced them (in *Perspectives 2017*).

The document also explained the nature of ecumenical relation among the Christians and the focus it should have in the future. It should be based on the 'solidarity in the service of humanity for freedom, justice and peace' (*UUS* 43) and spelled out this solidarity in tangible action plan:

a) to defend human dignity
b) to promote peace,
c) to apply gospel to social life,
d) to bring Christian spirit to the world of science/art,
e) to meet the sufferings and needs of our time (hunger, natural disaster, social injustice, etc) (*UUS* 74).

The document *UUS* recognised such 'a mission not merely humanitarian but that which is derived from the Gospel, a joint witness, a form of proclamation' (*UUS* 75). The papal documents appreciated the success of the ecumenical dialogue so far however it calls for further efforts avoiding the double danger of 'irenicism and half-hearted commitment' but with the 'obligation to respect truth is absolute' (*UUS* 79).

Joint Declaration

The representatives of Lutheran World Federation (LWF) and Pontifical Council for Christian Unity (PCCU) had signed the *Joint Declaration on the Doctrine of Justification* (*JDDJ*) on October 31, 1999 in Augsburg, Germany, officially declaring that the mutual condemnations at the time of the Sixteenth Century

Reformation do not apply to their current teaching. *JDDJ* says in No. 13: "A common understanding of justification is therefore fundamental and indispensable to overcoming that division". Now the Common Understanding of Justification:

> In faith we together hold the conviction that justification is the work of the triune God. The Father sent his Son into the world to save sinners. The foundation and presupposition of justification is the incarnation, death, and resurrection of Christ. Justification thus means that Christ himself is our righteousness, in which we share through the Holy Spirit in accord with the will of the Father. ***Together we confess: By grace alone, in faith in Christ's saving work and not because of any merit on our part, we are accepted by God and receive the Holy Spirit, who renews our hearts while equipping and calling us to good works*** (**No.15**).

The document says further that 'we confess together that good works - a Christian life lived in faith, hope and love - follow justification and are its fruits' (No.37). Cardinal Müller acknowledges the value of this document for Christian unity as he says, "Measured against the years of strife, it gives us hope to seehow the atmosphere has changed in such a relatively short period of time and what results have emerged from discussions, with a significance for the ecumenical movement in the coming years that cannot not be overestimated" (*Perspectives 2017).*

However there was a setback in the ecumenical process diminishing the euphoria evoked by the joint document. The Congregation for the Doctrine of Faith issued on 6 August 2000 the declaration, *Dominus Iesus* (*DJ*), emphasising the 'uniqueness of Christian revelation'. It insisted that except the Catholic Church and those who are in communion with her, the rest are not 'churches in proper sense though the baptised in these ecclesial communities are in a certain communion, albeit imperfect, with the Catholic Church' (*DJ* 17). It was unfortunately a death blow for the ecumenical efforts to Christian unity and it took nearly more than a decade thereafter to restore the process of dialogue among the Christian communities.

'Protest is over!'

In 2014 at a Charismatic Evangelical Leadership Conference hosted by Kenneth Copeland and Tony Palmer, an Anglicassn bishop said: "The protest is over!" And he invited the participants to forge unity among the Christians. The audience of many charismatic leaders seemed to embrace this message. The general secretary of the Lutheran World Federation, Rev. Martin Junge, says that relations between the Lutheran and Catholic churches have reached an epoch-making turning point. He was speaking during preparations for the 500th anniversary of the Protestant Reformation in 2017 and hoped that Lutherans and Catholics are expected to cooperate in an act of Christian unity "towards a profound communion that frees us to serve God and the world."

"From Conflict to Communion"

The joint statement, *From Conflict to Communion, Report of the Lutheran-Roman Catholic Commission on Unity* by LWF and PCCU was issued in 2013 proposing the Lutheran-Catholic Common Commemoration of the Reformation in 2017. It revived the relationship among the churches and hoped that in 2017, Lutheran and Catholic Christians would commemorate together the 500th anniversary of the beginning of the Reformation as they have come to acknowledge that there are more things among them that unite than divide them. Pope Francis has also responded positively to the invitation given by LWF and agreed to join the Common Celebration of Reformation (which was already inaugurated in 2016 in Lund, Sweden with his active participation). His encyclical *Evangeli Gaudium* (2013) called for an openness to learn from each other: "How many important things unite us! If we really believe in the abundantly free working of the Holy Spirit, we can learn so much from one another!.... Through an exchange of gifts, the Spirit can lead us ever more fully into truth and goodness" (*EG*).

The Report, *From Conflict to Communion,* stated that 'Luther had no intention of establishing a new church, but he played an increasingly active role, attempting to contribute to a reform of practices and doctrines that seemed relying on human authority alone and contradictory to the Scriptures' (No. 59). During a friendly meeting with an ecumenical delegation from the World Lutheran Federation on 19 January 2016 Pope Francis seemed to have made a positive compliment to the great German reformer saying that 'the intention of Martin Luther five hundred years ago was to renew the Church, not to divide her.' Pope Francis has revealed his commitment for Christian unity by partaking in the inauguration of the 500 Years of Reformation Jubilee on 1st November 2016 in Lund calling on the Catholics for a joint commemoration of Luther's era as a period of *reform and renewal* of Christian witness.

Pope Francis joined with Lutheran leaders on 31 October 2016 in Lund to commemorate two historic events: a) the start of the 500th anniversary of the Reformation inaugurated by Martin Luther, and b) the 50th anniversary of the start of the Catholic-Lutheran ecumenical dialogue. He said that his participation in these events had 'confirmed our desire to advance towards full communion'. The theme of the ecumenical prayer service was *From Conflict to Communion: Together in Hope.* It expressed thanksgiving, repentance, and a commitment to joint witness and service in future. Pope Francis insisted in his short homily that Catholics and Lutherans must "look with love and honesty at our past, recognizing error and seeking forgiveness." The division among Christians, he said, 'goes against Christ's will for his disciples, weakens their ability to serve the world and often makes it difficult for others to believe Christianity is a religion of peace and fraternity'.

'From Counter-Reformation to Co-Reformation'

Pope Francis on receiving the invitation for the joint celebration from the Council of the Evangelical Church in Germany (EKD) underlined how important it is for him that 'we, as churches, walk together on the path of testifying the faith in this world'. He said further that Catholics and Lutherans should 'remember together' the 500th anniversary of the Reformation 'not in the form of a triumphalist celebration, but rather to confess our common faith in the Triune God'. The Counter-Reformation had a totally different objective and approach but the last decades are proving things have drastically changed and Pope Francis is giving a much needed direction for the ecumenical movement. Bishop Gerhard Feige of Magdeburg, Germany points out rightly to these positive developments as he says 'that the Catholic Church has set out from the path of the Counter-Reformation onto that of the Co-Reformation'.

Conclusion

However, it should be also stated that not all are enthusiastic about the joint celebration and pope's participation in it. The headlines in *Catholic News* on 12 July 2015 read: "Catholics have no reason to celebrate the 500th anniversary of the Reformation". Some Catholics voice their opinion that it is wrong to 'celebrate' the wound that Luther opened in the body of Christ. They have their valid reasons. However, there are also sufficient reasons to say why Catholics cannot let it go with their participation in it.

The basic trust in the divine providence and Christian charity demands to accept history as unfolding from the ever guiding hand of God the Father and the present is an opportunity to bury the hatchets and the future is an invitation to explore the life of common witness to the Good News entrusted with all of us. It is true that there are seemingly irresolvable and divisive matters, before we enter into full communion. However those theological and pastoral hurdles need not to be viewed as barriers but as theological fields of endeavor for future pastoral care of all Christians to serve the entire humanity. The occasion of *500 Years of Reformation* is an opportunity for all the believers to explore the possibility of living the *unity in diversity*. 'While preserving unity in essentials, let everyone in the church, according to the office entrusted to him, preserve a proper freedom in the various forms of spiritual life and discipline, in the variety of liturgical rites, and even in the theological elaboration of revealed truth. In all things let charity prevail' (*Ut Unum sint*).

The answer to the question, (*Quanta estnobis via?), How far is our journey for unity?* is in the papal document which says in no. 78 that 'the basic agreement has been reached on 'Baptism, Eucharist, Ministry and Authority'. Of course there are other areas to be explored jointly and also in collaboration with other religions in order to create harmony and peace in the world that is struck by conflicts and violence unfortunately contributed also by religions. What Pope Francis said during a service to mark the end of the Week of Prayer for Christian Unity in 2014 holds good also in the context of the joint remembrance of Reformation:

> We have all been damaged by these divisions. None of us wishes to become a cause of scandal. And so we are all journeying together, fraternally, on the road towards unity, bringing about unity even as we walk; that unity comes from the Holy Spirit and brings us something unique which only the Holy Spirit can do, that is, reconciling our differences. The Lord waits for us all, accompanies us all, and is with us all on this path of unity.

Hence, let the 500th Anniversary of Reformation be the *kairos of new paths for peace and harmony* for the entire universe which is *the common home for all* humans and the entire creation.

"Our God is not the author of division, but of peace; and the Son of God, who came to destroy the works of the devil, is not the minister of sin" (John Calvin 1536).

Suggested Readings:

Scott H. Hendrix, 1981. *Lutherand the Papacy: Stages in a Reformation Conflict* (New York: Fortress Press)

Vatican II Document, 1968. *Unitatis Redintegratio (UR)*

Pope John Paul II, 1995.*Ut Unum Sint* (Vatican: Acta Apostolicae Sedis)

LWF & PUUC, 2013. *From Conflict to Communion* (Leipzig: E. Verlaganstalt)

Nickolas Schneider, 2013. *Perspectives 2017. Writings on the Reformation.* (Hannover: EKD)

17

Re-look at Reformation and Theological Challenges of Martin Luther towards Transforming Reformation

Songram Basumatary

Before venturing to re-look at the theological challenges and significance of reformation towards Transforming Reformation, let me make a conscious initial remark that we are at the junction of both the theological openness as well as ecclesiological closed mindedness. Evidently, there is reciprocal trust deficit and even enmity between theo-academia and *ekklesia* or between theologians and the Churchians. The mutual intellectual and moral arrogance between theo-intelligentsia and *ecclesial* leadership often hinders theological reflections from making impact on the life and ministry of the Church.

With this note, let me set an assertive hypothesis for this paper that "The Church of our times needs more radical reformation than the Church of Luther's time in all aspects; and after 500 years of reformation, we have no choice, but listen to the reformation cry and the prophetic reformation praxis for transforming the Church into a true *ekklesia* of God." In fact, reforming the so called reformed Churches or rather fragmented Church of our times is not that easy than what Luther attempted to reform just a single Catholic Church. Nonetheless, it is not a mere challenge, but an inescapable theological necessity. For that matter, even bridging the gap between a mere "theo-intellectualism" devoid of proper reality check and the 'kyriarchic ecclesio-moral arrogance' devoid of true theological test appears inevitable task. For Church of our times certainly needs transforming vision of reformation in order to be a true *ekklesia*, the Assembly of God.

Keeping these challenges in mind, this paper intends to re-look at the theological challenges and significance of reformation by locating some of the key reformation theologies into the contexts.

In order to meet the set hypothesis and objectives, the paper is structured into three sections. First is setting significance of reformation into its original context. Second is the exploration of Luther's theological challenges. The third section is a summary and a re-look at the theological significances of reformation for present day Church.

I

Reformation in its Context[1]

In order to understand the significance of reformation in its original context, let me first highlight some of the general factors as well specific ecclesiological context that favoured and necessitated the reformation during Sixteenth Century. For it was in the fullness of time,[2] perhaps, the reformation movement exploded. The confluence of political, economic, social and cultural developments in medieval European society greatly helped reformation to set off.[3]

First, ***the political developments*** by the close of the Fifteenth Century shattered the medieval vision of a universal ecclesiastical-political order where Church and state were one entity. The largely self-sufficient nation-states of North Western Europe led by powerful rulers became independent of the Church. They maintained their own military and civil service and thus opposed the intervention of Rome. Papal interference in local affairs such as Church ownership of land, Church appointment of ecclesiastical officials, control of education, taxation, tithes, the sale of offices and indulgences, clerical appeal to Rome, etc. were strongly resented.

Secondly, *the economic* factors paved the way for reformation. Since the economic structure of society was predominantly agriculture and as there were revival of city life, growth in discovery of economic resources, development of commerce, opening of new trade markets and a monetised economy, the middle class merchants strongly resented the confiscation of their profits by the Church and replaced the medieval feudal lord as the leader in society.

Thirdly and most importantly, the *Renaissance* and *Humanism* and the resultant intellectual developments effectively ushered the reformation. For Renaissance as Italian cultural movement, by the late fifteenth and early sixteenth centuries, had spread to the cities, academies, and princely courts of almost entire Northern Europe and strongly influenced for emergence of a new wave of renaissance which unlike Italian renaissance that emphasized 'civic humanism', was concerned with 'Christian humanism' with strong emphasis

1 Most of the contents in this section is taken from a paper – "Theological Significance and Challenges of Reformation" presented by the author at the National Colloquium on "Such a time as this": A Re-imagining of Reformation" organized by Research Division of the Senate of Serampore College (University) at Tamil Nadu Theological Seminary, Madurai from 8th to 11th August, 2017.

2 The Renaissance and Humanism, rise of German nationalism, unpopularity of Rome among most Germans, long-term economic hardships in some parts of Europe, depressed condition of German peasants, university environment, in which Luther worked, invention of the printing presses etc. have made easy passage to reformation.

3 Most of the narratives of historical events in this section is taken from Philip Schaff, *History of the Christian Church, Volume VII. Modern Christianity: The German Reformation* (Grand Rapids, MI: Christian Classics Ethereal Library, 2002).

on religious texts and issues. Humanism as an intellectual movement sought to study, understand and translate the original scriptural texts so as to recover uncorrupted interpretations. By questioning the accuracy of the Scriptures, the Humanists challenged the issues within the Church particularly the interpretations of key catholic doctrines such as penance, purgatory, indulgences etc., and the morality of clergies. These Humanists were interested not merely in the revival of classicism but even more profoundly in the revival of a purified and biblical form of Christianity.[4] They often emphasized the importance of Scripture and treated Early Christian communities as a classical model to be emulated and restored. Erasmus was instrumental in producing one of the first critical editions of the Greek New Testament in which he applied humanist philological methods to religious texts. This had become basis for many latter translations of the Bible by Protestants. Even it is said that "Erasmus laid the egg that Luther hatched."

The renaissance also impacted to emerge various other developments. The *cultural achievements* nurtured a sense of self-worth, dignity, etc. which is not tied to or dependent on the Church. It has created a spirit and an increased sense of individuality and a focus on personal uniqueness and self-determination. People celebrated the centrality, beauty, power and potential of human beings. This in fact led *anthropocentrism* grow as over against the *ecclesiocentrism* of the medieval period where the focus of intellectual and cultural efforts was on human and this world rather than God and the heavenly world. This period also experienced a surge of activity in painting, music, poetry, other forms of literary production, sculpture, architecture, philosophy, law, ethics, etc.[5] The entire socio-cultural landscape of Europe was dramatically altered with the development of movable type printing press which Luther described as "God's highest and most extreme act of grace, whereby the business of the Gospel is driven forward."

These are some of the key non-theological factors that collectively created the spirit and atmosphere conducive for reformation movement undertaken by the reformers. Particularly, these factors in general, and the growing Anti-clericalism spirit in peculiar German environment have greatly helped Luther to explode the bombshell of reformation on 31st October 1517 by nailing the *95 Theses* at the door of Castle Church, Wittenberg. Nevertheless, the reformation without any doubt was necessitated more by wrongs within the Church itself than any external

4 For instance, the Humanists like John Colet, Jacques Lefèvre d'Étaples, and 'Prince of Humanists' Erasmus of Rotterdam highlighted the importance of living a moral life over understanding theological subtleties or carrying out complicated religious rituals. Bard Thomson, *Humanists and Reformers: A History of the Renaissance and Reformation* (Grand Rapids, Michigan: Wm. B. Eerdmans Publishing Company, 1996), 347.

5 Schaff, *History of the Christian Church*..., 5.

forces mentioned above.[6] Perhaps, the essential condition of the Reformation's success was aggrieved hearts and minds of common people.[7] Therefore, people in no time responded so favourably to Luther's revolutionary movement.

For Papacy became extremely secularized and transformed into a selfish tyranny during late Fifteenth Century and early Sixteenth Century. As a result, the Church became worse than ever. For example, it is said that the Pope Alexander VI (1431-1503) was a monster of iniquity[8] who gained the papacy through bribery. Pope Julius II elected to the papacy in 1503 was a politician and warrior rather than a chief shepherd of souls. He has been termed "the saviour of the papacy" for his attempts to restore dignity and culture to Rome. Pope Leo X who succeeded Pope Julius in 1513 continued the construction of St. Peter's Basilica for the glory of Rome and Papacy. He was considered as a political and military barbarian[9] whose primary passion was warfare! Also he took far more interest in the revival of heathen literature and art than in religion, and is said to have even doubted the truth of the gospel history.

The *Religious Culture* of the Medieval Church on the eve of the Reformation was almost completely saturated with theological indifferences and monetary as well as non-monetary corruptions. Corruption undoubtedly existed at the top of the Church hierarchy. Corruption and abuses of position and power had been part and parcel of clerical life. Following the example of the popes, many cardinals and priests indulged in scandalous activities and weakened the respect of the laity for the clergy. The bishoprics were monopolized by the youngest sons of princes and nobles without regard to qualification. The power mongering and holding multiple offices were common trend.[10] *Discipline* and *piety* were nearly ruined. It is said that the whole monastic establishments and orders had become nurseries of ignorance and superstition, idleness and dissipation. Even the religious life of the laity was dominated by superstition, magic, perfunctory ritual such as the worship of saints, relics, the Mass etc. *Piety* which should proceed from a living union of the soul with Christ and a consecration of character, was turned outward and

6 It is perhaps true that the Latin Church elevated Europe to a higher plane of intellectual, moral and spiritual culture than it had ever attained before as whole Europe had been Christianized and civilized, and united into a family of nations under the spiritual government of the Pope and the secular government of the Emperor, with one creed, one ritual, one discipline, and one sacred language. See Schaff, *History of the Christian Church...*, 4.

7 Steven Ozment, *The Age of Reform, 1250-1550: An Intellectual and Religious History of Late Medieval and Reformation Europe* (Yale University Press, 1980), 204.

8 He is generally regarded as the most notorious pope in all of history.

9 Upon his installation as pope he is reported to have said: "Now that God has given us the papacy, let us enjoy it!" And evidently, he did.

10 For example, the Archbishop Albrecht of Mainz was at the same time archbishop of Magdeburg and bishop of Halberstadt. Similarly, Cardinal Wolsey was archbishop of York while chancellor of England who received stipends from the kings of France and Spain and the doge of Venice, and had a train of five hundred servants. Schaff, *History of the Christian Church...*, 7.

reduced to a round of mechanical performances such as the recital of *Paternosters* (Lord's Prayer) and *Ave Maria* (Hail Mary), fasting, alms-giving, confession to the priest, pilgrimage to a holy shrine etc.

All these, perhaps, were because of the *theological mess*. Instead of the Word of God and gospel of grace being foundation of theology, it was filled with Speculative scholastic subtleties and philosophical dialectics. It was perhaps due to the lack of Bible available among the common people and the neglect of preaching by the priests.[11] To prove the fact, Carlstadt, the older colleague of Luther confessed that he had been doctor of divinity before he had seen a complete copy of the Bible. Since the education in general and Theological education in particular was confined only to the nobles and priests, the common people could neither read nor write, and had no access to the word of God except the Scripture lessons from the pulpit that too without exposition. For priest's chief duty was to perform and offer the sacrifice of the mass mechanically for the living and the dead.

One of the most erroneous theological fallacies was the doctrine of Penance – Remission of sin and purgatorial salvation. Perhaps, the reformers, particularly Luther was provoked most by the Sacrament of *Penance* than any other sacraments. For this Sacrament not only enslaved the laity, but captivated the entire Church. With the treat of eternal damnation and hope of salvation, the Church set forth the *treasury of merits* – the *indulgences*.[12] Forgiveness and salvation could be bought with money. When religiously earnest people sought forgiveness for immoral behaviour, they encountered a very demanding penitential system, one that provided only temporary relief, and even that with conditions attached and the threat of purgatorial suffering for unrepented sins.[13] It was taught that though forgiveness is secured from the eternal guilt of sin through confession and absolution, there is still the temporal guilt for which one has to undergo punishment and suffering in purgatory. A person secures his/her place in heaven not by the suffering of Christ Jesus, but one's own suffering. Even it is not the Lord Jesus, who makes 'satisfaction', but the sinner himself or herself.[14]

---

11 Instead of preaching the word of God, the references were mostly, to indulgences, alms, pilgrimages and processions. The churches were overloaded with good and bad pictures, with real and fictitious relics. Saint-worship and image-worship, superstitious rites and ceremonies obstructed the direct worship of God in spirit and in truth. See Keith Thomas, *Religion and the Decline of Magic* (New York: Charles Scribner's Sons, 1971), 25-166.

12 The Papal Bull *Unigenitus* of 1343 proposed that "the Catholic Church holds as a treasure the infinitely copious merits of Christ and of all the saints – merits far in excess of any that they themselves may have needed – and that the church may dispense these merits in the inexhaustible treasury to remit *poena*, that is, the recompense owed by living Christians" Thomson, *Humanists and Reformers…*, 395.

13 Steven Ozment, *The Age of Reform…*, 216.

14 See, Thomas Tentler, *Sin and Confession on the Eve of the Reformation* (Princeton: Princeton Univ. Press, 1977), 14. ; Thomson, *Humanists and Reformers…*, 318.

In *sum*, the Church was on the brink of utter ruin – as a result of the doctrinal abuses and corruption. The Church could no longer provide for the spiritual needs of the people. Such reality of Church is not only pinpointed by the Protestants alone, but even the honest Roman Catholic scholars admit in strong terms, the decay of discipline and the necessity of a moral reform in the Sixteenth Century.[15] The best proof of it is furnished by a Pope of exceptional integrity, Adrian VI who made an extraordinary confession of the papal and clerical corruption to the Diet of Nürnberg in 1522 and tried earnestly, though in vain, to reform his court. The Council of Trent was called not only for the extirpation of heresy, but in part also "for the reformation of the clergy and Christian people." The Pope Pius IV in the Bull of Confirmation likewise declared that one of the objects of the Council was "the correction of morals and the restoration of ecclesiastical discipline."[16]

Looking at such contexts and historical facts, let us now see what did the reformers, particularly, Martin Luther do against such odds?

II

Luther and Reformation

The Sixteenth Century reformation carried out by Martin Luther was basically a challenge for ordering the theologically disordered ecclesiology. For, Church, the "Body of Christ" was erected to a pyramidic and hierarchic ecclesiastical orders that underprivileged the common believers from the free gift of salvation. Luther stood hard against the distorted and disordered theological notions that were used to maintain the hierarchic ecclesiastical supremacy. Being a restless agonising monk at the first hand, and the enlightened Biblical scholar saint on the other hand, Luther could not tolerate the doctrinal and sacramental disorders created by ecclesiastically justified theology based on false Scriptural hermeneutics. He was angry enough that the divine election was converted into divine privilege of few, and the divine economy of salvation was literally translated into market economy by introducing theologically justified salvation currencies. Salvation as free gift of God was made "Salvation on sale!" It was so that the helpless people sought for gracious God who would help in times of need, but the Church offered them an angry and dreadful God. Loved deprived people looked for loving and forgiving God, but the Church presented them a wrathful and punishing God.

15 For examples, Möhler in his *Kirchengesch comments,* "We do not believe that the period before the Reformation was a flourishing period of church history, for we hear from it a thousand voices for a reformation in the head and members." Möhler, *Kirchengesch*. III. 99.; Likewise, Joh Janssen, the eulogist of mediaeval Germany, also considerably writes about some of the crying evils of those times. He devotes the concluding section of the first volume of his *Geschichte des Deutschen Volkes* (594-613) on this. See, Schaff, *History of the Christian Church*..., 8.

16 See Schaff, *History of the Christian Church*..., 8.

Lifeless people cried out for life to the God of life, but the Church shut their mouth with suffocating divine demands.

Such doctrinal and theological disorders paved the way for the sacramental and ritual disorders and finally ecclesiological disorder. A clear expression of division, disunity, disparity among the believers could be seen in the sacramental doctrine and rites. The sharp distinction was maintained between the clergy and the laity. Therefore, considering the failure of the late medieval Church to provide a theology and spirituality that could satisfy and discipline religious hearts and minds, the reformers, particularly, Luther not only attacked the papal authority vehemently but attacked theology and doctrines of the Church. Unlike other previous reformers who attacked the life of the Church, Luther confronted the theological root of the problem – the Church's theology and doctrine of grace and redemption. He was concerned more on the theological sickness of the Church than any other things. Expressing his disappointment with the whole scholastic scheme of redemption, Luther countered strongly against the manipulation of anthropology and soteriology through the doctrine of penance and indulgence – the treasury of merit. Being a pastor and an enlightened professor at the University of Wittenberg, he could not see the entanglement of God's free gift of grace in an expensive and exploitative sacrament of penance.

Luther challenged the doctrine of Penance first through the *95 Theses* strongly questioning the authority of the pope, the very nature of penance and the usefulness of indulgences. He particularly challenged three key issues – the financial abuses, doctrinal abuses and religious or ecclesiological abuses. He attacked the indulgence system, insisting that the pope had no authority over purgatory and that the doctrine of the merits of the saints had no foundation in the gospel. Here lies the key to Luther's concerns for the ethical and theological reform of the Church: *Scripture alone* is authoritative (*Sola Scriptura*) and justification is by *Faith alone* (*Sola fide*) in the *Grace alone* (*Sola gratia*), not by works.

In the article 27 of *95 Theses*, Luther challenged the false doctrine that "They preach only human doctrines who say that as soon as the money clinks into the money chest, the soul flies out of purgatory." Further he argued that "They who teach that contrition is not necessary on the part of those who intend to buy souls out of purgatory or to buy confessional privileges preach unchristian doctrine." In *Christian Nobility of the German Nation* Luther brought out some of the great manifestos of Reformation where he called upon the ruling class in Germany, including the emperor, in whom Luther had not yet lost confidence, to reform the Church externally by returning it to apostolic poverty and simplicity. Luther countered the clericalism and sacerdotalism[17] with the doctrine of the *Priesthood of all Believers*. In *Babylonian Captivity of the Church*, Luther strongly attacked the

17 A religious belief that emphasizes the powers of priests as essential mediators between God and humankind.

doctrine of sacraments.[18] In particular, he challenged against the divine injustice done to the laity in the Sacrament of Lord's Supper by withholding the cup from them. For by withholding the cup, the liberty Christ has given to the sinners is completely taken away. Citing Paul's words, "The bread which we break, is it not a participation in the body of Christ?" [I Cor. 10:16], he argued that "the sacrament is participation in the Body of Christ." For Paul does not say, "In the bread there is," but "the bread itself is the participation in the body of Christ." And while instituting the Lord's Supper Christ's emphasis was not on wine but on cup. It is not "this wine", but "this cup." "This cup is the new testament in my blood" [Luke 22:20; I Cor. 11:25]. Luther affirmed that his blood is in the cup and his body is in the bread. There is no mass for the dead by a priest alone without communicants, so the cup should be given to the laity along with the bread. For Eucharist involves communion not only with Christ but also fellowship among the believers.

In order to understand such theological challenges of Luther and his theologically justified transforming vision of reformation, we need to explore a bit on his idea of *Communion of Saints* (*Communio Sanctorum*). Perhaps, this is one of the most challenging theological aspects of reformation movement that has rich contextual relevance to the present day Church.

In Luther's conscience and theological convictions, the *Communion of Saints* is what "the Body of Christ" – "the holy Christian Church" is all about. Though the term *communio* translated in English as 'communion' it actually means number of things. In Luther's exploration, it has two sets of meaning. First, 'a congregation' or 'a group' or 'community' or 'gathering and assembly'; Secondly, it refers to 'participation' (*Gemeinschaft*). *Communio* as the ideas of participation and *communicare* as contribution were closely associated in Luther's thinking. He occasionally equated the *communio* even with Latin *congregatio* and at other times used it to describe the act of mutual sharing – *communicare*. Yet, he did not merely use *communio* in the sense of understanding or trusting one another as it is in the modern usage of *Gemeinschaft* which means 'to being bound together with' or 'participating together with someone' or 'an act of common participation' or 'having common right to something.'[19] More than this inclusive gathering, he also used it to speak about the unity. He wrote, "There is on earth a

18 In his introduction to the "The Babylonian Captivity of the Church: Lord's Supper (1520)" Luther wrote: "*To begin with, I must deny that there are seven sacraments, and for the present maintain that there are but three: baptism, penance, and the bread. All three have been subjected to a miserable captivity by the Roman curia, and the church has been robbed of all her liberty.*"

19 *Dr. Martin Luthers Werke, Kritische Gesamtausgabe*, 30[I] (Weimar: Böhlau, 1883-1993), 189. Hereafter *WA – Weimar Ausgabe*. [All the references of WA in this paper are taken from Paul Althaus, *The Theology of Martin Luther*, translated by Robert C. Schultz (Philadelphia: Fortress Press, 1966) and Bernhard Lohse, *Martin Luther's Theology: Its Historical and Systematic Development*, translated and edited by Roy A. Harrisville (Minneapolis: Fortress Press, 2011)]. See also T. G. Tappert, ed. *The Book of Concord* (Philadelphia: Fortress Press, 1959), 417.

little holy flock or community of pure saints under one head, Christ. It possesses a variety of gifts, yet is united in love without sect or schism.... I am also a part and member of this community [*Gemeine*], a participant and co-partner in all the blessings it possesses."[20] He interpreted *communio* as sharing of goods among the believers, the giving and receiving of the members to and from each other, the becoming one with all others, and working for one another.[21] Sharing of goods and suffering in common, therefore, is the key in Luther's interpretation of *communio*.

In line with such understanding of *communio*, Luther defined the term – Saint (*Sanctorum*) in new light. Over against the traditional medieval understanding of the saints,[22] Luther expressed that the saints in NT especially in Pauline letters are not a particular group in the community but its believing members in Christ are all saints.[23] The *Sanctorum* – 'holy people' or 'holy things' means 'a community of the holy' or 'a community only of holy people' or 'a holy community of a holy people.'[24] It includes all believers who are made righteous through the righteousness of God in Christ and bound together into one body. The lives of the saints are a treasury not because of the merit they produce but because Christians live, suffer, and do everything for each other as members of one body. He replaced merit of saints by serving one another. Since the Church is a community of saints in which each one works for the other, as members one of another, merits of the saints cannot act as treasury for believers.[25] In fact, "saints are not to be found," according to Luther, "only in heaven but here on earth in the community of people." Therefore, one cannot distinguish between saints and ordinary Christians. The distinction is only between the saints who have died and those who are still alive and believers are obligated to serve not those who are dead but those who are alive. It is right here on earth for the lowliest brothers and sisters of Christ that they are to serve. In this regard, look at the strong words of Luther:

> Whatever it is that you want to do for the saints, turn your attention away from the dead toward the living. The living saints are your neighbours, the naked, the hungry, the thirsty, the poor people who have wives and children and suffer shame. Direct your help toward

20 *WA* 30^{I}, 190.

21 Althaus, *The Theology of Martin Luther*, 296.

22 It had two dimensions. First, *Communio Sanctorum* described and believed as participation in the benefits of salvation and in the merit of Christ through the sacraments and participating in the saints as a holy people through their merits. Second, the good works done by saints through the power of love benefits the other members of the church.

23 *WA* 56, 469; 17^{II} 50.

24 *WA* 50, 624 ff.

25 *Luther's Works*, vol. 31 (Saint Louis/Philadelphia: Concordia and Fortress, 1955-1986), 215 f. [hereafter *LW*]; cf. *WA* 1, 607.

> them, begin your work here, use your tongue in order to protect them, your coat in order to cover them and to give them honour.[26]

This shows a sharp distinction on the concept of community between Luther and the medieval understanding. In the medieval Church, there was no room for community concern as it was dominated by the moralistic principle that everyone must first take care of himself or herself. It followed the principle that "love begins at home" or "charity begins at home", and even where love acts for and in the life of another, its final goal is to secure one's own salvation.[27] What happened in this moralistic principle was that since moralism is selfish in its very essence, it destroyed community life by creating righteous or priestly class and ordinary people. On this Luther also argued that

> Those who trust in their own work of righteousness had to establish divisions and differences among Christians. The priest wanted to be better than the laity, and the monks wanted the better than the parish priests, the virgins wanted to be better than married people, and those who prayed and fasted often wanted to be better than those who worked, while those who lived austere lives wanted to be more than those who simply lived normal lives.[28]

Such moralism and pious selfishness distorted the concept of Church as one body and love as the law by which the Church must live. Over against this trend, Luther challenged that it is only the Gospel of justification by free grace through faith can really create genuine community. It is the Word of God, which creates faith; and faith makes people come together as the community of believers. Paul Althaus beautifully summarizes this as follow:

> Exclusive and materialized intercession is replaced by inclusive and personal.... In Roman doctrine, men [*sic*] are thought of as a society in which measurable values can be transferred. In the Lutheran doctrine they are involved in the community of men [*sic*] really living together with one another.[29]

Luther claimed that "Indeed this gift is given to me that it may become the common property of the others.... I shall have enough of the food of salvation and everything in my life and possessions are to be used for the benefit of others."[30] For every person has been created and born for the sake of the other.[31] This

26 *WA* 10^{III}, 407 f. cf. *WA* 17^{II}, 50.

27 Duns Scotus and Gabriel Biel asserted this very strongly. *WA* 56, 390, 3.

28 *WA* 17^{II}, 33.

29 Althaus, *The Theology of Martin Luther*, 302.

30 *WA* 15, 607.

31 *WA* 21, 346.

for Luther is the prime significance of Law of Love, bearing the weakness and burden of the others. For him, the great work of love is to make ones' possessions servants of someone else and the greatest of all is giving up one's righteousness and allowing to serve neighbour's need.[32] He further challenged, "You have heard that we should trust in God and love men (*sic*) with our external possessions; this is the least we can do. Beyond this we can allow our righteousness to serve a sinner and this is the greatest thing of all, just as poor as the greatest sinner."[33]

In short, the real essence of community in Luther's theological exploration is its pastoral care to individuals and the real responsibility of a believing individual is his/her sacrificial love and service for the other individuals of the community. This is clearly expressed in the sacramental theology of Lord's Supper that when we partake the sacrament, we must in turn share the misfortune of the community. Our heart must go out in love and learn that this is a sacrament of love. We must render love and support to Christ and his needy ones.[34] Perhaps, what we get out of it, is not important but what goes out of it, is important while we partake in Lord's Supper. But unfortunately, as Luther laments, "What a terrible blasphemy against God that we all take the sacrament and want to be good Christians, but none of us is willing to stoop down and serve our neighbour."[35]

Such strong emphasis of Luther on the "*Priesthood of all Believers*" and "Communion of Saints" is perhaps rooted in his *Theology of Cross*. All of Luther's theologies, in fact, hang around this theology. This is the theology which provides inner logic and coherence in his entire theological arguments. For example, the very primary doctrine of justification is all about God declaring the unrighteous as righteous, not by virtue, work or merits of a believer, but on the basis of an alien righteousness – the righteousness of God in Christ. God's righteousness which is completely opposite to human righteousness declares a sinner who is really unrighteous, deeply mired in sin and who deserves only damnation; a pure and righteous person, the lord and the priest.

Luther's *Theology of Cross* stems out from the Heidelberg Disputation on the subject of indulgences that took place in the meeting of Augustinian Order in April 1518. At the meeting, Luther put forward a *Theology of the Cross* as opposed to a *Theology of glory*. Luther strongly argued that the *Theology of Cross* is the essence of true theology. Therefore, true theology and knowledge of God are to be found only in the crucified Christ. The Cross of Christ is the only instruction in the Word of God, there is purest of theology.[36] Even Luther was of the opinion that, "That person does not deserved to be called a theologian who looks upon the invisible things of God as if it were clearly perceptible in those things which

32 *WA* 10^{III}, 217.

33 *WA* 10^{III}, 238.

34 *LW* 35, 54.

35 *WA* 12, 470.

36 *WA* 5, 217: 2-3, on Ps. 6:11.

have actually happened. He deserves to be called a theologian, however, who comprehends the visible and manifest things of God seen through suffering and the cross."[37]

The crux of Luther's exploration on the *Theology of Cross* can be understood from the following statement:

> ... men (*sic*) misused the knowledge of God through works, God wished again to be recognised in suffering, and to condemn wisdom concerning invisible things by means of wisdom concerning visible things, so that those who did not honour God as manifested in his word should honour him as he is hidden in his suffering.... Now it is not sufficient for anyone, and it does him no good to recognise God in his glory and majesty, unless he recognises him in the humility and shame of the Cross.[38]

This statement express clearly the heart of Luther's theology that human beings cannot speculate about who God is or how God acts through what they think and see God reveals to them. For God has revealed himself exactly opposite of what human reasonably think and anticipates. Luther was convinced of the fact from the Scripture that God reveals himself not in power and glory, but in the weakness and shame of the cross at Calvary. Luther sometimes called "Christ crucified" as "God's backside". It is like Moses trying to see the face of God or the glory of God in the burning bush, but contrary God showed him his back; or like Moses wanted to see a mighty God, but God told him to go to Egypt and find him among the suffering Israelites. Similarly, disciples wanted to see the glory of Jesus, but instead, Jesus showed them the Cross, the site of utter shame. Therefore, Luther argumentatively expressed that the 'theologians of glory' are those who build their theology in the light of what they expect God to be like and they make God to look something like themselves. But the 'theologians of the cross' are those who build their theology in the light of God's own revelation in Christ hanging on the cross.

This perhaps is a revolutionary theology which demands entire Christian faith and theology to recast on the centrality of cross. For cross is not simply the point of God's atonement for sin; it is the site of true revelation of God, in where we know who God is and how God acts toward God's creation. In the in light of cross only, we can understand the divine power which is opposite of what we think and see divine power is to be. In his apparent defeat at the hands of evil powers and corrupt religious and political authorities that Jesus showed his divine power and conquered the death and powers of evil. God had chosen the foolishness of the world to shame the wise. God's wisdom is demonstrated in the

37 Article 19 & 21 of Luther's Theses for Heidelberg Disputation, 1518. See *WA* 1, 261; *LW* 31, 52.

38 *WA* 1, 362; *LW* 31, 52f.

foolishness of the cross. Divine power is revealed in the weakness of the cross. In the ugliness of the world God revealed his glory.

Another important point to be noted here is that Luther does not restrict *Theology of Cross* to an objective revelation of God alone. He also sees it as the key to understanding Christian faith, ethics and responsibility. The Cross is the foundation of faith and work. To the eyes of unbelief, the cross is nonsense; it is what it seems to be – the crushing, filthy death of a man cursed by God. But to the eyes opened by faith, the cross is seen as it really is. Faith is the gift of God offered at the feet of cross, not a power inherent in the human mind. It is not an acquired faith of an intellect or heart of a person that boast of himself or herself, but a true faith that allows a believer to understand how he/she is to behave and act as faith response to the grace of God at the Cross.

Through this faith, a believer too, like Christ, is both a king and a priest. This kingship and priesthood, however, is not for lording over others, but for the service of others through suffering and self-sacrifice. A believer is lord of everything by being a servant of everyone; and a believer is completely free by being subject to all. As Christ demonstrated his kingship and power by death on the cross, the believers are 'little Christs' to neighbours in their service. Therefore, one should bear the cross not to save oneself but so that one's neighbour might benefit by seeing it and be encouraged to bear his/her cross.[39]

Such understanding of Cross is perhaps explosive against the question of authority in the Church. It gives a whole new understanding of authority. The Elders, Leaders, Pastors, Bishops, for example, are not to be powerful tyrants who with their position, wealth and credentials enforce opinions and rule others. They are to be the crucified ones like Christ who devote their whole life to the uncomfortable, painful and humiliating service of others. This is the true power, the authority of God supremely revealed in the Cross of Christ.

III

Theological Significance of Reformation for Church Today

In order to understand the theological significance of reformation beyond its original context, we need to acknowledge first what changes reformation really brought. There is no doubt that the Church was divided into two because of reformation – the Catholic and the Protestant Church on the ground of theological issue, particularly, the doctrine of justification. However, notwithstanding the various weaknesses, the reformation certainly brought transformation in the Church and society. In fact, the Reformation of the Sixteenth Century was considered as the greatest event in history of Christianity. It is next to the introduction of Christianity itself. It marked the end of the middle Ages and the beginning of modern times. Starting from religion, it gave, directly or indirectly,

39 *WA* 10^{III}, 119.

a mighty impulse to every forward movement, and made Protestantism the chief propelling force in the history of modern civilization.[40]

The reformation perhaps was a providential work of God and Luther was a prophet in bringing the Church back to the basics of Christian faith. Theologically, the reformation brought various reversal order. For instance, the authority of Scripture over human authority, Word of God over sacraments, Grace of God over the merit of human, Faith over the works, *Priesthood of all Believers* over the clericalism, *Theology of Cross* over theology of glory, self-sacrifice and suffering over power and glory etc.

Through such theological challenges, the reformation movement in general and Luther in particular have brought number of transformation in the life of the Church. Practically, reformation opened the eyes of common believers to see the reality of the Church by revealing and discovering the true doctrine of salvation based on the Scripture. In fact, the translation of Bible into people's language and the emphasis and preaching on the Word of God greatly changed people's understanding and outlook on Christian faith and traditions. It has made connection between the Gospel and the experiential world of ordinary believers. The true identity, dignity and role of common people were discovered thereby the gap between the clergy and laity was bridged to a great extent. In general, common believers were brought closer to God through the theology of the *Priesthood of all Believers*. In general, reformation restored the integrity and the public image of the Church. It also brought home the importance of Christian education and teaching the Word of God. It also advanced the idea of justice and equality by making clear that there is no spiritual distinction between the laity and clergy. The *priesthood of believers* and the *Communion of Saints* brought spiritual equality of all believers that all are equal under the grace of God; all are forgiven sinners.

In sum, the reformation movement in general, and Martin Luther's theologies in particular have certainly made turning point in the life of the Church and showed forward movement. Theology and ecclesiology were clearly refined and defined. The doctrine of Salvation, Church, Sacraments, ministry and theological themes such as Scripture, Grace, Faith, Work, Law and Gospel etc. were clearly defined. Reformation to a great extent had renewed the theology and reformed the ecclesiology and gave a vision and direction for transformation. It was indeed a transforming reformation.

What challenges do the reformation and Luther pose to the present day Church of our times? As already stated above, we must accept the fact that the Churches of our times are no better than the Catholic Church of Luther's time. In many aspects, the present Church also is full of corruption such as politics over priestly ministry, fights over position, power, privilege and property. Often the Church authorities are above the authority of the Word of God. Instead of

40 Schaff, *History of the Christian Church...*, 3.

governed by the Gospel and the Word of God, the Church is governed by the wish and words of the human authorities. The self-righteousness overshadows the God's righteousness. Many a times, unjust and corrupt leaders are enthroned, but the faithful and just are dethroned from the leadership of the Church. The Churches are mostly busy with management of Economy rather than Testimony of Christ.

In such reality of the Church, Luther's theological challenge perhaps come a fresh that the Word of God be the authority over the life of the Church and the Church be governed by the authority of the Word of God alone. Secondly, in order to make the Church inclusive and participatory in carrying out the mission of God, the Church need to understand and emphasise strongly the Luther's theologies, especially the *Priesthood of all Believers*, *Communion of Saints* and the *Theology of Cross*. The Church must constantly be aware of the fact that there is no division, distinction and hierarchy in the Body of Christ. All are equal under the grace of God. For "All Christians are free Lords over all things and subject to nobody", in terms of his or her identity in Christ. At the same time, "All Christians are dutiful servants of all and subject to everybody", in terms of his or her responsibility for the world in Christ. In other words, under the grace of God in Christ, all are free, but in responsivity as followers of Christ, all are servants and all serves one another. Such kind of inclusive and participatory Church where all believers are part and parcel of the Body of Christ, where all are equal in identity, dignity and responsibility, can surely help our Church to be the witnessing community in the world of chaos and confusion.

Conclusion

While relooking at the theological challenges and significance of reformation and derive relevance for Church in our times, it is not too much to say that "there is hardly an issue confronting Church and society in our times today where reformation in general and Luther's theological insights in particular have no relevance." For the issues facing the Church and society in our times are not different from context of reformation times. There is certainly an undeniable significance of reformation both theologically and ecclesiologically. Notwithstanding some of the reformation lacunas and some of Luther's vicious and deplorable sentiment, and ambiguous theological expressions, one can convincingly conclude that there is enormous theological significance for the transformation of present day Church and society. Contextually, what makes reformation more significant in our times is its very vibrant context oriented 'people centric theology' and its vision of gospel oriented 'community centric ecclesiology.' To conclude with, perhaps with a bit of rhetoric, the challenge ahead of Church in our times is:

Transforming Reformation…. the need of the hour…!

The Church needs no hyper-critical theologian who walks above the ground, but a prophetic reformer who walks on the ground and toil on the soil…!

The Church needs no clergies who hang cross on their neck, but the ones who hang themselves on the cross…!

Can the 500 years old transforming reformation reform the Church of India Today?

Contemporary 95 Theses

The historical account tells that on October 31, 1517, the priest Martin Luther defiantly nailed ***95 Theses*** on the door of the Castle Church in Wittenberg, Germany as protest against the erroneous and abusive teachings of the Catholic Church on the nature of *Penance*, the *Authority of the Pope* and the usefulness of *Indulgences* for salvation.

500 years after, the Church of our time appears no differencefrom the Catholic Church of Luther's time in all aspects. In fact, as body of Christ is broken into pieces, Pope and indulgences got multiplied into thousands. Considering this challenge Gurukul Lutheran Theological College & Research Institute nails the following *Contemporary 95 Theses* as a mark of Reformation Day Celebration 2016:

1. Christ alone is the Head of the Church, not the church authority.
2. God alone is authority over believers' life, not the church authority.
3. God alone can give grace and salvation, not traditions and human authority.
4. God alone can forgive sins, not the court nor the priest.
5. God alone is to be feared and obeyed, not human persons or authority.
6. All glory belong to God alone, not to the church authority and leaders.
7. Christ alone is the Head of the Church, not the church authority.
8. Word of God alone is the supreme authority, not human words or rules, or court orders.
9. Word of God alone is the ultimate authority on all matters of faith and conduct of a believer, not church traditions, rules and regulations.
10. The word of God for life is preached less than that of tithes and offerings.
11. Too much grace has created too many nominal Christians.
12. Church has lost the fear of God due to over emphasis on grace of God.
13. The world is shaping the "church" more than the "church" shaping the world.
14. Church has too many leaders and organizers, but very few agonizers for her.
15. The Lordship of Jesus Christ is replaced with lordship of the leaders in the Church.
16. Church at large has forgotten that the chief end of a believer is to glorify God, not human persons.
17. Churches are filled with cross, there is cross everywhere, but no real Cross anywhere
18. Church is full of seekers of self-righteousness rather than God's righteousness.
19. The greatest treasure of the church is the Gospels and the grace of God, but the church leaders have more faith in wealth than in God.
20. Churches are more into money making enterprises rather than disciple making mission.
21. Church must repent of its idolization of personality, and of business principles

22. Church at all cost must stop glorifying leaders, let God alone be glorified.
23. Church must count the cost of discipleship, not the money.
24. Church must teach that money is not the blessing of God, but piety and love of the cross and service to others.
25. Church leaders wish to spend more budget on their own mission than in God's mission.
26. Church treasure must be used more on mission and service than on management.
27. Church must inculcate a strong spirituality that corruption, misuse of church treasure and funds meant for the poor and needy is completely against the gospel and the justice of God.
28. Churches are very particular about following the traditions, rather than following the gospel call.
29. Church at all cost must condemn any kind of discrimination based on race, class, caste, gender etc. as sin.
30. Church must re-vision the beauty of the early believers' *Ekklesia*.
31. Church need to recover the discipleship of equals of the early church.
32. Church must be inclusive community rather than exclusive and divisive community.
33. Church needs to exist for its non-members as well, rather than only for those who are members.
34. Church must be democratic assembly of believers rather than autocratic and hierarchical institution.
35. Church and the church institutions need to have democratic and collaborative model of functioning the ministries and programmes rather than authoritarian model.
36. Church must be community-centric rather than leader-centric.
37. Church must be open to the new realities and new avenues of ministry.
38. Church must repent from the sin of silence against injustice
39. Church needs gospel of resistance rather than Gospel of compromise.
40. Church needs prophetic voice rather than complacency.
41. Church must demythologise any elements that are superficial and too other-worldly.
42. Church is an *Ekklesia* bound by love of Christ, rather than fellowships bound by doctrines and traditions.
43. Church must stand high on gospel values for justice and equality and fight against discrimination and corruption, rather than a mere Sunday community
44. Church must condemn the authoritarian power used to formulate, alter and change the constitution of the church according to leaders' interest as unforgivable sin.
45. Church at all cost must stop the traditions, rules and regulations that subordinate the weaker sections of people.
46. Church must be delivered from the curse of apathy and complacency.

47. Church at all cost must raise prophetic voice against the silencing of the voice of the voiceless.
48. Church at all cost must declare the practice of bribery within church as abomination against God and unpardonable sin.
49. Priesthood and priestly blessing cannot be bought with money.
50. Priest cannot buy power to bless nor can the believers buy blessing.
51. Priesthood and greed cannot go hand in hand
52. Priesthood is neither power nor a status, but a service
53. Priests are not to be served, but to serve the community of believers
54. Pastors hardly pray more than they do in the worship services on Sundays.
55. Pastors must be servants, not professionals
56. Pastors and leaders must trust in the Spirit, not statistics.
57. Priests and pastors ought to understand that witnessing Christ in their lives matters more than mere preaching of Christ to their congregation
58. Church ministers' conscience must be captive of the Word of God, rather than on their wisdom and crafty desires.
59. Every Christians want to draw near to the cross, but never want to bear the cross.
60. Believers must not be overburdened with excessive payments for spiritual services.
61. All believers are right with God, not with who is on their left and right.
62. Christians must follow Christ at all cost, but not at the cost of Christ.
63. Priesthood of all believers must be acknowledged and affirmed in all the Churches.
64. A Christian who passes by a beggar but buys luxury goods next door is not a follower of Christ
65. Theologically qualified trans-genders and other stigmatised people should be considered for ordination and equal opportunities must be provided to serve in the church.
66. Reservation should be made to the economically poor and marginalised members in the Church to take part in the church administration.
67. Church should be dis-abled friendly and incorporative of their life and talents.
68. Theologically trained differently-abled people should be considered for the ordained ministry.
69. Gender justice should be the prerequisite for all the ministries of the church.
70. Traditional misinterpretation of the Bible about the subjugation of women should be challenged reinterpreted without any prejudice.
71. Women must be treated with equal dignity and respect rather than objects of use and abuse.
72. Church must recognise the potentials and ability of women and their commitment for ministry.
73. Church must give heed to the cries of the people at the margins, rather than only hearing the voice from the centre and making decision unfavourable to them.

74. Church and church institutions need to engage competent and appropriate personnel suitable to handle the program or problem, rather than mere filling the post.
75. Church election must be on the basis of gospel call and democratic values, rather than undemocratic and corrupt means.
76. Church leaders and minsters must repent and return to the servant leadership model of Christ, rather than lordship model
77. Church leaders and ministers must demonstrate humility, integrity and simplicity in their life rather than pride, dishonesty and arrogance.
78. Most importantly, the Protestant Church and its leaders must repent from the sin of breaking the body of Christ into pieces on account leadership, authority and money.
79. Tithes and offerings must be exclusively used for the service of the poor and needy, rather than using for luxury in the church.
80. Stewardship, Accountability and Transparency are not mere slogans, nor an option, but must be heart cry of church for good governance.
81. A Christian buying luxury goods beyond what is needed is no better than a person buying an indulgence.
82. Repentance and forgiveness is a forgotten treasure in the Church today.
83. Repentance is believed as one-time act rather than continual act
84. Everybody preach gospel of repentance, but nobody to repent.
85. All acts like Prophet Nathans, none is king David in the Church.
86. People love more to preach their words rather than God's word.
87. Forgiveness without repentance and discipleship without obedience has become the Christian way of living.
88. Everybody wants to live in heaven, but nobody lives heaven on earth.
89. Sacraments are more adored than the Christ which is no better that adoring relics.
90. The powers and authority given to or assumed by heads of the church should be decentralized because the excessive powers make them to feel and act like God.
91. No politics, no favoritism in matter of recruiting ministerial personnel, but on the basis of who can stand witness for Christ in the society.
92. Wealthy and corrupt person cannot buy salvation through offerings while a poor person who is a friend of God, cannot do so.
93. Church leaders are called to be faithful servants, not to be popular and powerful masters.
94. One cannot thank God for money if money is not shared with the needy
95. Church should be an eco-friendly and stand as advocate of preserving ecosystem.

Contributors

Dr. Walotemjen is Associate Professor and Head of the Department of History of Christianity, Gurukul Lutheran Theological College & Research Institute, Chennai.

Mr. Thomas Manoj Samuel is Assistant Professor in the Department of Communication, Gurukul Lutheran Theological College & Research Institute, Chennai.

Rev. Dr. K. Balakrishnan is Assistant Professor and Head of the Department of New Testament, Gurukul Lutheran Theological College & Research Institute, Chennai.

Rev. Nagaiyasamy N.S. Samuel is an ordained minister of TELC (Tranquebar Mission). At present he is serving Gurukul Lutheran Theological College & Research Institute as Assistant Professor in the Department of Old Testament as well as pursuing Doctoral Studies at Pondicherry University.

Rev. Dr. K. David Udayakumar is Professor and Head of the Department of Missiology as well as the Principal of Gurukul Lutheran Theological College & Research Institute, Chennai.

Ms. Rebecca Azariah is Assistant Professor in the Department of Missiology, Gurukul Lutheran Theological College & Research Institute, Chennai.

Rev. Livingstone Arputharaj is Assistant Professor in the Department of Christian Ministry, Gurukul Lutheran Theological College & Research Institute, Chennai.

Rev. Samuel Logan Ratnaraj is an ordained pastor of Arcot Lutheran Church. Currently he is pursuing his Master of Theology (Final Year) in Christian Theology at Gurukul Lutheran Theological College and Research Institute, Chennai.

Rev. Jeevaraj Anthony is Assistant Professor in the Department of Religion, Gurukul Lutheran Theological College & Research Institute, Chennai.

Rev. J.M.P. Thomas Birla is Assistant Professor in the Department of Religion, Gurukul Lutheran Theological College & Research Institute, Chennai.

Rev. Dr. S. Thomas Kennedy is pastor of Tamil Evangelical Lutheran Church, Trichy and a visiting faculty in the Department of New Testament, Gurukul Lutheran Theological College and Research Institute, Chennai.

Rev. Dr. J. G. Jacob Sundarsingh is pastor of Tamil Evangelical Lutheran Church and he is a faculty in the Department of History of Christianity in Gurukul Lutheran Theological College & Research Institute, Chennai.

Dr. Fr. George Varughese is a priest of Syrian Orthodox Church in India and currently serves as HoD of Christian Ministry Department, Gurukul Lutheran Theological College & Research Institute, Chennai.

Rev. N. Manova Santhosham is Presbyter of CSI Wesley Church, Perambur, Diocese of Madras and former Director of Board for Lay Training and Lay Preachers' Fellowship, Diocese of Madras.

Dr. Florina Xavier is the Program Advisor for Tabish Social Health Education Organization.

Dr. Gladston Xavier is the Head of Department of Social Work, Loyola College, Chennai.

Rev. Dr. habil. Roy Lazar A. is a Teaching Faculty in the Department of Christian Studies, University of Madras, Chennai and the Professor for Pastoral Theology and Counselling, Sacred Heart Seminary, Poonamallee, Chennai. He also currently serves as Secretary of Indian Theological Association (ITA) and Thamizh Iraiyil Mantram (TIM).

Rev. Dr. Songram Basumatary is Professor and Head of the Department of the Department of Theology and Ethics as well Dean of the Post Graduate Studies, Gurukul Lutheran Theological College & Research Institute, Chennai.